Royal Mysteries:
The Medieval Period

Royal Mysteries:
The Medieval Period

Timothy Venning

PEN & SWORD
HISTORY

First published in Great Britain in 2021 by
Pen & Sword History
An imprint of
Pen & Sword Books Ltd
Yorkshire – Philadelphia

Typeset by Mac Style
Printed and bound by CPI Group (UK) Ltd, Croydon, CR0 4YY

Pen & Sword Books Limited incorporates the imprints of Atlas,
Archaeology, Aviation, Discovery, Family History, Fiction, History,
Maritime, Military, Military Classics, Politics, Select, Transport, True
Crime, Air World, Frontline Publishing, Leo Cooper, Remember
When, Seaforth Publishing, The Praetorian Press, Wharncliffe Local
History, Wharncliffe Transport, Wharncliffe True Crime and White
Owl.

For a complete list of Pen & Sword titles please contact

PEN & SWORD BOOKS LIMITED
47 Church Street, Barnsley, South Yorkshire, S70 2AS, England
E-mail: enquiries@pen-and-sword.co.uk
Website: www.pen-and-sword.co.uk

Or

PEN AND SWORD BOOKS
1950 Lawrence Rd, Havertown, PA 19083, USA
E-mail: Uspen-and-sword@casematepublishers.com
Website: www.penandswordbooks.com

Contents

Introduction

This book will give an account of some of the more famous and less well-known mysteries involving medieval English royalty from 1066 to 1485. This era presents less problems concerning basic data and its probable meaning than the era covered in the first book of the series, on the Anglo-Saxon and early Welsh and Scots kingdoms, but accuracy and a lack of bias are still not to be taken for granted. Medieval kings and their advisers and established institutions such as the Church were as conscious as modern ones of the need for 'spin' – making your side of a contentious story was the one accepted as 'fact'. Innuendo, suppressing inconvenient details, and creating 'fake news' were all used as calculated literary weaponry, and a ruler who crossed the Church (as did the oppressive and irreligious William II 'Rufus' and the notorious King John) or was overthrown for incompetence and/or tyranny (such as the controversial Edward II) would be liable to have their reputations 'trashed'. If they lost their thrones their replacements would be keen to have them presented in the worst possible light to justify the revolt, though modern enthusiasm for clearing the names of some of those so treated may have its own problems by letting them off too leniently for genuine crimes. Not all kings went as far as Henry IV did in calling in all the current monastic chronicles for checking after he overthrew his allegedly tyrannical cousin Richard II in 1399, but even if he had favourable references to Richard edited out it does not avoid the fact that the latter was widely deserted by his elite as Henry, a potential heir and rival exiled on dubious grounds, invaded and took his throne.

These problems of interpreting a long-dead ruler's character and motives lies at the heart of several of these 'Royal Mysteries', such as those of the brothers William II and Henry I. Was the first murdered for his throne by the latter in a 'hunting accident' in 1100, or was it just a lucky coincidence that he was shot by a 'stray' arrow while his chosen heir, his elder brother Robert of Normandy, was away on Crusade and unable to stop Henry taking the throne? In the case of the presumed murder of the deposed Edward II, a highly controversial and unpopular ruler overthrown by his wife whose successive male 'favourites' were claimed to be his lovers, he was long assumed to have been killed by agents of either his wife or the latter's lover Roger Mortimer in September 1327 – according to the wilder rumours in luridly violent circumstances. But members of the inner elite including his half-brother still thought him alive two years later (were they conned and if so by whom?), and centuries later a letter surfaced written to his son Edward III a decade later concerning a mysterious hermit living in Italy who claimed to be Edward II – and who the new king seems to have met and not punished. So was Edward II ever killed at all? In the case of his equally controversial, favourite-prone and resented, great-grandson Richard II, also deposed, he too died in suspicious circumstances within months, in February 1400. He was more certainly dead – but was it murder or suicide, and what of the well-supported pretenders who claimed to be him? In the still-famous disappearance of the 'Princes in the Tower', the sons of Edward IV, arguments still rage about whether the late king's brother Richard III had them murdered or not, and if not what happened to them. Passionate legions of 'Ricardians', with their own modern society set up to defend Richard's reputation, still insist that the hitherto honourable and upright strongman of his brother's reign would never have committed the sin of killing his nephews (or other murders alleged to be his responsibility) and he was the victim of unscrupulous 'smears' by his replacement Henry VII.

Thanks to a prolonged campaign of vilification by the 'Tudor spin machine' and the brilliant portrayal of Richard on stage by William Shakespeare over a century later, Richard was unfairly portrayed as a serial killer driven by lust for power, as twisted in character as in his body – and the continuing interest in Richard had a new focus when in 2014 his missing remains were discovered under a car-park in Leicester, with a twisted spine from scoliosis which showed that part of the legend was based on fact. In a struggle worthy of a medieval saint, rival cathedrals then fought over where to bury him and the only English king to be denied a State funeral received one over 500 years late. Other royal mysteries included in this book are also connected to the period of the so-called 'Wars of the Roses' and have a bearing on Richard's seemingly unlikely claim to the throne, namely the question of whether his brother

Edward IV was a bigamist and his marriage to the Princes' mother illegal – meaning that Richard did have a good claim on the throne. Was Edward IV himself a bastard, or was this just a 'smear' by his enemies? Politics was as full of distortions in the 1480s as in modern times, ruling medieval England was a risky business with kings and ministers alike surrounded by predatory enemies, and what the surviving sources say may be flawed and contain hidden agendas.

As Winston Churchill reminds us with regard to the Second World War, history is written by the winners and can be targeted (or falsified) to be kind to their records and to undermine their rivals. Blatant lies can be successful if the defeated party has no means of getting their own story across. Were the 'Princes in the Tower' really murdered at all or if they were who did it, and was there a chance that some Tudor era pretenders could have been genuine or at least of (illegitimate?) royal blood? Some mysteries have only re-emerged in recent years following the discovery of new or 'highlighting' of long-discarded evidence, such as the presumed death by violence of Edward II at Berkeley Castle in 1327 where some still deny that there is any mystery. Others are still ambiguous because the scanty evidence can be interpreted as either a series of coincidences or as a cover-up of a murky plot, as with the death in a 'hunting accident' of William II in the New Forest in August 1100. Some are reliant on the interpretation of later 'explanations' of what happened by interested parties whose reliability cannot be guaranteed and who had a clear interest in muddying the waters, as with Richard III and his rival Henry VII in the assorted mysteries involving the murder of the Princes and the alleged secret marriage (or legally binding engagement ceremony) of Edward IV and Eleanor Talbot/ Butler. The worst could be believed of 'celebrities' even in the medieval era – and even today there are assorted obscure theories floating around regarding a modern sensational royal event, the death of the late Princess of Wales in a midnight car-crash in Paris in August 1997. Conspiracies, coincidences, or 'cock-ups', this is and always has been a hall of mirrors with distorted reflections.

Chapter 1

Murdered or Not?
The Death of William II – An Accident?

When William 'the Conqueror' was dying in September 1087 he appears to have intended his own patrimony, Normandy, for his eldest son Robert 'Curthose' (born c. 1053) and England for his next surviving son, William 'Rufus' (born 1056/60). Having been fatally injured by his stumbling horse throwing his stomach against the pommel of his horse's saddle while sacking the rebel town of Mantes in the Seine valley, he was taken unawares by the need to resolve the succession. Robert, who he seems to have enjoyed mocking for his weight-problem and lack of height, was currently in rebellion (for the second time) and had left his domains, and the young men's mother Queen Matilda (who had interceded for Robert before) had died in 1083. Robert was thus at risk of dispossession even if William had intended England for him earlier. Instead, the king apparently gifted England 'to God' as he had received it from Him but gave its crown to William 'Rufus' and told him to go and claim the kingdom.[1] An intervening son, Richard, had been killed 'accidentally' in the New Forest – perhaps by an overhanging branch knocking him off his horse – around 1070/4.[2] Robert seems to have been less capable and ruthless a ruler than William II, given the chaos into which Normandy descended under his rule in 1087–96 and 1100–06 with more rebellions seen then than since the early 1050s, and his father may have already worked this out. Recent attempts have been made to rehabilitate him and to point out that his local enemies could always call on either his feudal overlord the King of France, Philip I, or one of his brothers to help them and even his fearsome father had faced rebellion at the time of his greatest power.[3] Robert's good military record on the First Crusade and ability to attract and keep followers shows that he was seen as a 'winner' not an incompetent by hard-headed ambitious men. But his youngest brother Henry I (born 1068/9) was to hold down Normandy more ruthlessly and successfully after 1106,even when Robert's son William 'Clito', his potential challenger, was adult and so could lead a revolt, and the likelihood is that Robert was seen as easier to defy than were his father or brother.

In addition the impatient and treacherous Robert had raised revolt against William I in Normandy in 1077 after some sort of dispute with his siblings William 'Rufus' and Henry, seizing the castle of Gerberoi in alliance with William I's overlord King Philip of France and even defeating him in a skirmish. Queen Matilda had arranged a settlement and Robert had returned to court, but he may still have been distrusted. But the decisive reason for the choice of heirs was probably the French 'feudal' custom of granting a ruler's own main inheritance – his paternal lands, in this case Normandy – to the first son and any maternal inheritance or personal acquisitions to younger sons. (There is some uncertainty if this custom applied yet, and no comparable French duchy or county in this era faced the problem of apportioning conquered territory as well as inherited lands.) Robert challenged his brother's succession by joining in an English revolt masterminded by his uncle Bishop Odo in 1088, but was defeated and forced to be content with the rule of Normandy. After some complex manoeuvres the two brothers – both unmarried – came to an arrangement that each would be the other's heir in 1091, and excluded their younger brother Henry (born 1068/9). The question of whether the subsequent breach between them only months later, and William's intrigues with Robert's disloyal feudatories (including Henry) in 1092–6, affected this grant of the English succession remains unanswered.[4] But a grant of the succession – or even forcing the principal barons to swear to uphold one candidate – was one thing, enforcing it in the event another – as the overturning of Henry's plans to have his daughter Matilda succeed him in 1135 was to prove.

More significantly, William remained unwed despite possible interest in Edith/Matilda, the elder daughter of Malcolm III of Scotland, who was being educated at Wilton nunnery and was probably born around 1076–80. Her mother (St) Margaret (c. 1047 – 1093) was the sister and heiress of Edgar 'Atheling', the unmarried (as far as is known) great-nephew and nearest genealogical heir to Edward 'the Confessor' who had been the focus of Anglo-Saxon revolts in the late 1060s. Her formidable mother, an enthusiastic 'moderniser' and educator who according to her chaplain and biographer Turgot brought the outdated Church in Scotland up to date with new Continental practices, education, monasteries, and charitable works, had sent her south to be schooled in England where she herself had grown up, along with her sister Mary (who later married the Count of Boulogne and gave birth to King Stephen's wife, the second Queen Matilda). Marrying Edith thus would give her husband a claim on the loyalty of disaffected Saxons who regarded the Normans as usurpers – and as soon as Henry became king in 1100 after the sudden death of his elder brother William II in a hunting-accident in the New Forest he was to hasten to marry her.[5] There was however a legal problem in that she had been forced to wear a nun's habit by her aunt and guardian Christina, a nun at Romsey Abbey when Edith was being educated there, either at Romsey or at the more luxurious nunnery at Wilton (which included what amounted to a school for well-born girls) when she and her younger sister Mary were there shortly before her father King Malcolm III's visit to Wilton in 1093. This was apparently unwelcome to and resisted by her, and indeed the current Archbishop Anselm (who would now have to approve her being able to marry) had written to local Bishop Osmund of Salisbury at the time condemning Edith for taking her habit off and telling him to ensure that she wore it. Anselm had also declared Edith's classmate Gunnhilde (King Harold II's illegitimate daughter)'s running away to marry Count Alan of Richmond as illegal as she had also worn a veil. Edith's arguably taking monastic orders by wearing a nun's veil, would not have put the irreligious William II off seeking her as a wife, as he habitually mocked and outraged the Church, but a new king Henry had to be more careful of annoying the Church. But it was successfully argued by Henry and his backers in this matter (apparently including Edith herself) in 1100 that Edith had not consented to wearing a nun's veil and had been under the legal age to give consent at the time.[6] Arguably making unwed heiresses being educated in convents wear a veil as if they were trainee nuns was partly a measure taken to protect them from rash young Norman lords who hoped to carry them off, marry them by force, and take their lands – as well as devious churchmen hoping to pressurise the girls to become nuns once they were older and thus give their lands to the Church. Edith wearing a veil would have served to keep would-be suitors at a distance, and assist her father King Malcolm III and her devout mother (St) Margaret in keeping her unwed until they had found a suitable husband for her. This lapse in William II marrying has led to speculation that his refusal to marry was due to his homosexuality, with the proliferation of effete young nobles at Court (with long hair and foppish cloaks) which the monastic chroniclers deplored cited as evidence. Carelessness is more likely, as William did not bother about fierce criticism on other important matters such as his blatant keeping church benefices vacant for far longer than was normal in order to live off the revenues. He was only around 40 in 1100 – though he had already been reminded of his mortality by a severe illness in 1093, when his life was despaired of and he had hastily repented of his anti-religious actions.[7] By 1100 the stern and impressively educated Archbishop Anselm, a respected Italian theologian from the abbey of Bec in Normandy who he had appointed belatedly after a four-year vacancy in the archbishopric of Canterbury in 1093, had quarrelled with him and gone into exile. Arguably this gave a possible impetus to regicide by Henry in 1100, as he would need Anselm to crown him if he took the throne and Robert had been named in legal documents as William's heir in 1091. In Robert's absence on Crusade the strictly moralist Anselm, had he been in England, was unlikely to back anyone else for the throne as Robert had been William's legal heir in the early 1090s and the king had never openly changed this plan.

But even if William was at odds with his 'heir' in the mid-1090s, when Robert left Normandy on Crusade in 1096 William took over its government as effective regent. He promised to return it when Robert came back from the Middle East. Robert did not turn to Henry as his 'stand-in' in Normandy instead though he was already living in Normandy, had shown his capability as a vigorous ruler of his lands, and was more readily available to supervise the barons than the distant king in England. Deprived of his small county of the Cotentin peninsula in Normandy (granted by Robert in 1087/8) by his brothers in 1091 after an earlier stint in prison for alleged plotting with William, Henry had since rebuilt a minor landed fief centred on Domfront on his own and had an uneasy relationship with his siblings. When William took over Normandy in 1096–1100 while Robert was on Crusade he was less tolerant of private feuds and land-grabbing among the nobles than Robert had been, and Henry's frequent residence at his court in England then may have been due to William's orders to keep him under surveillance.

Henry I – his motives for murder?

Character

Henry usurped the throne from the absent Robert Curthose on the sudden death of William II, rather than acquiescing in William's own promise to Robert that the latter could succeed him and ruling as regent while waiting for Robert to return from the First Crusade and claim his inheritance. The fact that Robert, newly married to Sybil of Conversano in Italy so possibly soon with a son to succeed him, would be back in Normandy (and able to succeed to England) a few months after William II's murder has led to claims that the timing of the death was not an accident. If Henry did not act before Robert returned, his chances of seizing the throne when William died would be much smaller. Henry was a ruthless character as capable of violence as most contemporary great lords, as shown by his chequered career until 1100 – though the negative aspects of thee element in his character have been criticised more by modern historians than they were by contemporaries. At the time, his ability to enforce peace by overawing his turbulent nobles – like William I and II and in contrast to Robert – was seen as more important. Importantly, in 1087–1100 he had been used to living on his wits and seizing opportunities. But is this an indication that he was capable of gambling for the English throne too – and was August 1100 an optimum time to do it? Probably left out of the allotment of lands in his father's will (apart from possibly his mother Matilda's English estates, which William II then refused to give him),[8] he had been dependent on the goodwill of his elder brothers. He had been given short shrift when attempting to claim his mother's lands from the new King William in 1088, and had chosen to reside with his eldest brother Robert and make his fortunes out of Normandy. He was soon imprisoned for some months on suspicion of plotting with William to stage a Norman revolt after he had visited England. The accuser appears to have been the brothers' meddling uncle Odo, Bishop of Bayeux and Earl of Kent, a highly secular ecclesiastic seen wielding his mace (so as not to incur the sin of spilling blood) at the battle of Hastings in the Bayeux Tapestry. Arrested by his brother William I for alleged plotting in 1083 and deprived of his earldom, he had been restored by William II and had ungratefully attempted to overthrow him in league with Robert. Driven out of England again when the revolt failed and forced to depend on Robert's goodwill, he now attempted to have his dynastic rival Henry disgraced and briefly succeeded; Henry's 'treason' to Robert may well have been invented by him.[9] The fact that Henry had been caught returning to Normandy in company with the notorious 'robber baron' Robert de Belleme, a hot-headed young warlord who ruled a semi-independent county on Normandy's southern borders and was implicated in revolt after revolt there and on his lands in the Welsh Marches, could easily be interpreted as showing his hostile intentions to Robert. But de Belleme, son and brother to the first two Earls of Shrewsbury and successor to the latter in 1098, was one of Henry's friends at the time, and as a vigorous young lord with a military following was of use to Henry in constructing his own dominions in south-western Normandy. Henry allying with him was not necessarily aimed – immediately – at Robert, though both men were ruthless opportunists and may well have had eventual revolt in mind, encouraged by their recent host William II. (Eventually, when Henry was king, de Belleme raised revolt against him in turn in the Welsh Marches and was deprived of all his English lands).[10]

Three years later, an end to the initial round of sparring over the succession between Robert and William led to them agreeing that each should be the other's heir, not Henry; the Cotentin was confiscated (presumably to deprive him of the resources to stage a revolt).[11] In the intervening time, Henry had attempted to play them against each other and had shown his mettle for brutality by throwing the leader of a pro-William revolt in Robert's capital of Rouen, a burgess called Conan, out of a window in the castle to his death in autumn 1090. This duly helped loyalist troops to put down the accompanying riots in the city. The event had made a great impression on contemporary writers.[12] But they, unlike modern commentators, regarded it in a favourable light, as a sign of his resolve – firmer than the dithering Robert's – to defeat the Rouen riots. Whatever was made of the sincerity of Henry's alleged justification for the defenestration – i.e. his loathing of treason to one's lord – he was not accused of excessive brutality, and the same was true of his penchant for mutilating rather than killing plotters as king after 1100. By the standards of the time, mutilation was merciful as it allowed the accused time to repent their sins rather than sending them to the next world as unrepentant rebels. As for Conan's fate, there was even an element of 'class snobbery' in the attitude of chroniclers that he had deserved to be killed in this manner. Applauding a generous grant of mercy for rebels did not extend from the knightly class to rebellious townsmen like Conan, who were socially excluded from the benefits of the knightly code. A lord could be forgiven for revolt – particularly on a point of honour or out of friendship – sooner than an ordinary citizen, whose duty was to pay taxes and not interfere in politics. Indeed there were no strictures from writers at Henry's father William I's bloody revenge on rebellious townsmen in Normandy in his turbulent early years as duke, or at the execution of similarly low-class 'traitors' who murdered Duke Robert's son William 'Clito' in Flanders in 1128. As far as contemporaries were concerned, Henry was a strong and just ruler who only used a necessary degree of violence.

Thus it is using false premises to look at Henry's acts of calculated brutality as showing him as being capable of murdering his brother. By contemporary standards, his actions were nothing out of the ordinary; indeed, he was a better lord than his weak brother Robert whose nobles notoriously defied him. Henry himself scoffed after 1100 that Robert could not even keep order in his household, and the latter's south Italian wife Sibyl of Conversano was seen as a stronger character[13] – unfortunately she died young and Robert's duchy continued to decline into private feuds. But the question of Henry's willingness to commit fratricide should not be excluded – although no contemporary writer accused him of it. As King of England for thirty-five years after his surprise accession, and Duke of Normandy from 1106 too, he was the liege lord of chroniclers such as William of Malmesbury and Orderic Vitalis; they were hardly likely to mention any unsavoury rumours about his behaviour. In any case, the scene of his alleged killing of William was a remote area of countryside in the New Forest, with only a small hunting-party present and most of them Henry's allies; it was not at court with hundreds of witnesses. And the fact that Robert, his rival for the throne, was still away on Crusade at the time of William's death provided Henry with a motive to act before Robert returned home. Did he kill William to seize England before Robert returned from Crusade and could oppose his succession?

The timing

In fact, it is unclear if William did regard Robert as his successor as of 1100; the succession-agreement of 1091 may have lapsed by this time. And it would still have been feasible for Henry to take the throne of England while Robert was back in Normandy. In December 1135 his nephew Stephen of Blois was able to take possession in place of the rightful heir Empress Matilda who was further away from London (site of the coronation since 1016?, certainly since 1066) when Henry I died. Stephen was able to reach London and be crowned – probably crossing from his wife's domain of Boulogne – before Matilda could arrive from her husband's distant Anjou.[14] Had William died anywhere in England after Robert's return and Henry been in the country, he would have been nearer at hand and could still have staged a coup. Indeed, even if Henry had been on his lands in Normandy – in the west around Domfront – a swift message to him from William's court could have brought him to England (via the Cotentin) quicker than Robert could arrive from Rouen. He would not have lost his chance of the throne when Robert returned; indeed, the mutual distrust of all three brothers would have had a new element as Robert was married and would soon have a son. Robert might well have wanted his son's potential challenger Henry to be kept out of Normandy after 1102, as he had confiscated his lands before at times of challenge; Henry would thus have been in England and have had the reason to work on William.

Henry could still have seized the English throne by a coup if William had died after Robert's return. Even if William finally married, a very young heir was insecure as a claimant to succeed in England, as shown by the exclusions of Edmund I's young sons in 946 and of Edgar 'Atheling' in January 1066 – though the new post-1066 Norman aristocracy had not managed to exclude an under-age, illegitimate heir (Henry's father) in their own Duchy in 1035. In 1199 the under-age son of Richard I's next brother Geoffrey, Arthur of Brittany, was to be denied the throne as the Norman and English barons both backed his genealogically junior but adult uncle, Geoffrey's younger brother John. In 1216 the barons rebelling against John offered the throne to his sister's daughter Blanche's adult (French) husband, rather than choosing her or her son Louis (later IX). Nor did they kidnap the king's son Henry (aged eight) to act as their puppet – though in this case his parents' marriage was open to legal challenge. A boy as heir stood a greater chance of being accepted in Norman law and practice after 1066 than under English law and practice before then, though the events of 1199 shows that there was no firm legal rule on this matter. Once William II had a son Henry's position would have been weaker. But until that eventuality occurred Henry would still have had a good chance of securing the throne. He would, however, have had to face invasion from the excluded Robert, as William II had done in 1088. This would have been sooner after the date of his coup if Robert was just across the Channel than in August 1100, when Robert was still en route from his marriage in Italy. The prospect of an early invasion might have deterred some crucial barons from backing Henry. The timing of the succession in August 1100 was thus useful for Henry in giving him a few months to consolidate his position before Robert returned; in 1088 the invading challenger for England, Robert, had failed to win enough baronial support to remove the new king (William) so Henry would know that an incumbent had the advantage over an invader.

The accident in the New Forest. The circumstances – and the question of the site

It was easy enough for William to be killed by a 'stray' arrow-shot in the forest without any witnesses except Henry's men – or to blame an innocent party for it. The list of lords attendant on William at the time of the 'accident', as will be examined later, shows that they included men loyal to and later senior advisers of Henry. The question of William's death has been exhaustively analysed by Frank Barlow in his biography *William Rufus* (1983); he concludes that the details are reasonably straightforward and a number of coincidences and possible motives do not add up to the possibility of a plot.[15] Duncan Grinnell-Milne (*The Killing of William Rufus*, 1968) and Hugh Williamson (*The Arrow and the Sword: an Essay in Detection*, 1955) point the blame at Henry and/or a group of nobles eager to do him a service.[16] They believe that the king's violent death at that crucial moment for Henry's fortunes was more than coincidence. Once Robert was back in Normandy Henry would have had two powerful ruling brothers between him and the Conqueror's empire as he had in 1087–96, and he had to strike quickly before Robert resumed control of his domains.

After his midday meal 2 August 1100 William left a royal hunting-lodge in the New Forest for a day's hunting and never returned.[17] The late start to the hunt was noticeable, and some monastic writers later attributed bad dreams of divine wrath which had disturbed the blasphemous king's sleep,[18] but this was *ex post facto* rationalisation. If it was accurately remembered by witnesses that William had had a poor night's sleep or woken up late, this was probably due to being drunk. Myths were bound to grow up around the king's surprise death, and the nature of twelfth-century attitudes towards the supernatural meant that divine intervention was a logical explanation for the event quite apart from William's scornful attitude towards the Church. A mixture of a hangover and the need to transact some of the routine of royal business before setting out are more likely than bad dreams, which the usually unrepentant William was not likely to take much notice of. If the king had referred to bad dreams in talk with his intimates before he set out, one of them or an eavesdropping servant could have mentioned it to a churchman later and the story duly reached the chroniclers. But this can only be guesswork.

William was not a reflective person likely to be impressed by dreams, though he could have mentioned them in passing over his meal. His only notable occasion of taking note of 'Divine warnings' had been at the time of his serious illness in 1093, when he had temporarily repented of using the Church as a 'milch-cow' and belatedly appointed a new Archbishop of Canterbury, Anselm, after four years of keeping the see vacant to use its revenues. It is also unfortunate, though inevitable, that all the contemporary chroniclers were monks – and thus open to modern charges of 'bias' and hostility to William due to his irreligious behaviour. The historian William of Malmesbury, giving the first detailed account of the killing c.1125 and writing at his home-abbey, not that far from the New Forest, indicates that some business was transacted before the king's meal and departure. There is an implication in his unflattering description of William's bilious condition that morning that he had been drunk[19] – as a monastic critic of the king's policies he was likely to reach a disapproving conclusion about his lateness, though his writings in general show relative objectivity.

How far the king ventured from the lodge is also unclear, as the site chosen to put the commemorative 'Rufus Stone' in Canterton Woods in 1745 was miles from the most probable royal residence at Brockenhurst.[20] The largest village remaining after William I's presumed clearances in the New Forest at the time of the 'Domesday' survey in 1085–6, Brockenhurst was the site of the best-known early mediaeval royal hunting-lodge which seems to have been in use throughout the forest's royal patronage. The question of the extent of clearances of previous settlements for royal hunting was probably exaggerated by local legend; few archaeological sites abandoned around 1070 have been found and the ground around Brockenhurst and Lyndhurst is notoriously infertile and boggy and/or open heathland.[21] There were other lodges, including probably the site at Beaulieu ('Beautiful Place' in French) given by King John to the Cistercians in 1204 which was probably another hunting-lodge. No chronicle says exactly where the king was staying in August 1100. The problem is that it is unclear when precisely various sites were brought into use as royal residences, which the sparse written evidence does not make clear; it is no use assuming that all late medieval royal hunting-lodges existed as of 1100. Logically, the first to be brought into use would have been the most convenient to the founder of the forest as an institution dedicated to the hunt, William I. A major village with existing accommodation for the royal entourage, such as Brockenhurst, is most likely; an isolated site without a known pre-1066 village, such as 'Castle Malwood' close to the 'Rufus Stone' site, is less likely. The latter was assumed to be the site of William's stay on the night of 1/2 August by Victorian writers such as Charles Kingsley, due to the 'Stone' being nearby. But there are no early medieval remains at this site, which was an abandoned pre- or post-Roman fortified enclosure.

There was probably a special organised 'drive' used to bring the deer close to the hunters rather than them just seeking out stray deer at random, not least to save time – which the fact that the hunting-party did not set out until after a midday meal makes likely. This manoeuvre (which royal servants could have been setting up for hours before the king set out) was later to be more commonly used within the enclosed 'deer park' fences and ditches near a lodge rather than in the open 'forest'. The main site for such 'drives' by the later thirteenth-century was the 'Old Park' near Lyndhurst, which had special banks set up to corral the deer, but we have no idea of the arrangements in the early days of the Forest. Special areas for the corralling of deer and easy access for the hunters may not have been laid out yet. Indeed, a vigorous and active Royal horseman with only a few companions in attendance may well have preferred to ride out for miles in search of his own prey, by the later thirteenth-century enclosed 'parks' may well have been more desirable for access by a larger and less mobile court. The sovereign at the time that the 'New Park' was created, Edward I, also had his wife Eleanor of Castile and her entourage to accommodate; the naming of Forest sites after her, e.g. 'Queen's Bower' near Brockenhurst, shows her participation in the Royal visits to the Forest. The whole paraphrenalia of royal visits, and the elaboration of life at court, had developed since the time of the early Norman kings. William II, in contrast to later monarchs only had a few recorded colleagues with him on his hunt in August 1100; this may have been the norm for 'holiday' hunts during his reign.

The hunt on 2 August 1100 could have been done in the open forest miles from the lodge, and the royal party ridden over to the site in an hour or so. Anywhere within ten miles or so of a royal hunting-lodge is possible as their destination, which would include the 'Rufus Stone' site as within reach of Brockenhurst or Lyndhurst. But it would equally include another possible site, south of Beaulieu (see below). Darkness was still late in early August, so there would have been hours left for shooting even if the site was an hour or so from the lodge. The king's party included his younger brother Henry, the latter's friends the Beaumont twins (Count Robert of Meulan and Henry, Earl of Warwick); William of Breteuil; possibly Henry's Norman associate Robert FitzHamon (later lord of Glamorgan and the king's chief ally in the southern Welsh Marches), and according to the more inaccurate account of Geoffrey Gaimar also members of the De Clare family, lords of Tonbridge in Kent. Also present was Walter Tyrrell, lord of Poix in Normandy, who had been drawn to the court by the King's generosity according to William of Malmesbury.[22] Poix being near the Norman frontier, he may have been invited along by William as a useful ally among the Norman baronage once Robert returned; was William thinking of using his lands to infiltrate agents to stir up rebellion? According to one source Tyrrell was asking about William's intended route next time he campaigned in northern France, but this is not proof that he was sent to England as a spy – or a murderer? – by the ageing French king's ruthless and devious heir, Prince Louis (later Louis VI) as recently suggested by Emma Mason.[23] Tyrrell was to be blamed for the killing by the others present – but was this 'outsider', with no powerful friends or relatives at court to support him, the 'fall-guy'?

The Forest – and other recent royal hunting-accidents.

Two males of the Conqueror's dynasty had already died in 'accidents' in the forest, namely William's elder brother Richard around 1074 (possibly due to being hit by a low-hanging tree-branch and knocked off his horse) and Robert's illegitimate son Richard earlier in 1100.[24] The possibility that these were not accidents but ambushes by vengeful evicted peasants has been considered, though murder by the locals has never been suggested as likely in William's case. This brings into the question the nature of the 'clearances' of villages and farms for the Forest by William I. The traditional myths certainly have it that the clearances were extensive, with many hapless Saxon villagers evicted by brutal Normans for the king's private pleasures and a whole countryside laid waste. Early modern histories of the forest held this view, often written by people who had no conception of the barren moorland nature of much of the forest soil which made nonsense of the idea of a flourishing countryside. 'Forest', in the legal mediaeval sense, meant the area governed by 'Forest law' not the modern sense where it means woodland; the planting of large acreages of timber in the area was a later phenomenon, and most of the modern plantations would have been open woodland in the mediaeval period. Nor is there evidence of many existing villages being razed by the Normans; the soil could not support the population of thousands which some later writers believed had been evicted and there was no fertile soil for growing corn except in the lower reaches of the main valleys and by the Solent. The number of villages laid waste and agricultural fields seized for royal use in the 'New Forest' as it was laid out by the Conqueror in the 1070s was probably not as great as later legend has it.

This ancient Jutish territory of 'Ytene', noted as separate from the rest of the West Saxon kingdom by Bede in the 730s and still known as distinct from the rest of West Saxon Hampshire in the twelfth-century, was not a rich agricultural area swarming with wealthy peasants who the arrogant Normans evicted in their thousands for their private pleasure.

The number of churches destroyed – thus bringing divine wrath on the guilty parties according to legend – was not that large either. Certain major settlements survived within the forest, such as Brockenhurst and Lyndhurst, along with villages such as Burley; a few isolated villages may have been taken over and demolished, such as the former Roman pottery-site near Linwood to the north. Nor should the sharp reduction in the taxable value of the forest settlements in the 'Domesday' survey be read as implying wholesale pillaging and seizure of their fields by the Normans; it is now clear that the value was reduced to compensate for the inhabitants now being under forest law. The latter – in use over much of England, including far more productive agricultural land – meant that ownership and use of dogs was severely restricted and nobody was allowed to harm the king's deer or impede their freedom to roam and graze, and no doubt the ravenous and rapidly-breeding deer had a deleterious effect on the villagers' crops. But the savage punishments imposed for harming the animals or being caught in suspicious circumstances that implied an intention to poach, may not have been carried out that often. Much used to be made of the Normans routinely mutilating their hapless peasant victims, with the excessively brutal punishments seen as a cause of widespread resentment and the rise of 'freedom-loving' outlaws such as Robin Hood.

Undoubtably there were cases of injustice and oppression by local officials, and the completely unprecedented and extensive nature of 'Forest law' served as a sharp reminder of how legal practices had changed after 1066. But it is quite possible that the harsh code of 'Forest law' was more of a deterrent than something which was routinely enforced, with fines – which had more practical use and helped the royal exchequer – imposed on those who could afford them. Nor was mutilation of offenders that rare in eleventh-century England, though its official introduction into law seems to have been a post-1066 innovation using Continental rather than English law and the idea of imposing it for harming animals was particularly unwelcome. It could be imposed for political reasons, as when Cnut mutilated his East Anglian and Mercian hostages in 1015 as revenge for their relatives defecting from his cause. The most that can be said is that William I used it far more frequently than the English kings before 1066, particularly on rebels – such as the insolent residents in one rebel Norman town who had made public mockery of him as the grandson of a tanner.[25] The sufferers from such strict enforcement of the letter of the law in a forest court would have been the lowest in society, those unable to pay to avoid it. The 'Forest laws' were undoubtedly highly contentious, as shown by successive Kings having to promise to ameliorate them at the time of their accession when they had to listen to the grievances of their more articulate subjects – who thus suffered from these laws as well as the peasants. But the traditional picture of an enraged local Forest populace bent on resistance to the Normans is an unrealistic simplification. Certainly there has never been any suggestion that some evicted villager, or refugee from justice, could have shot the king in 1100.

There may thus have been long-established royal hunting-lodges already in the area of the later New Forest by 1066. What was 'New' was the extension of a rigorous and continental system of special legal status to it, and indeed to many other areas of countryside used for royal hunts. The Conqueror (as he was called by later generations, not by his own contemporaries), who according to the *Anglo-Saxon Chronicle* loved the deer as if he had been their father,[26] was a passionate huntsman who created a whole new administrative system of separating off areas of the country for the preservation of wild animals for hunting, giving them legal priority over the local human inhabitants and punishing anyone who impinged on the royal monopoly on hunting.

The 'accident' and the aftermath

The 'official' version of the killing, which could only have come from Henry and the others in the day's hunting-party, appears in the monastic chronicles of William of Malmesbury (an assiduous researcher able to analyse sources and distinguish obvious fable, as with his remarks on 'King Arthur'), based not that far from Hampshire, around 1125, and the Anglo-French Orderic Vitalis writing in Northern France c.1135. They give more details than the brief statements in other sources like the *Anglo-Saxon Chronicle* that the king was shot with an arrow in the forest in an accident. They say that William was shot in the late afternoon or early evening, as (William of Malmesbury) he was dazzled by looking into the sun as he gazed at a passing deer and did not see his danger. Another huntsman in the party, aiming for a deer standing near him, did not see the king and the arrow missed its target and glanced off either the deer or a tree to hit William in the chest. Orderic states that Walter Tyrrell let fly at a deer near him and accidentally hit the king, without mentioning the sun dazzling him or William; the *Chronicon ex Chronicis* by John of Worcester says that the king was killed by rash shooting by Tyrrell which implies the same version. The king fell dead, and as soon as the rest of the party realised that he was beyond aid Henry galloped off to Winchester to seize the Treasury. Some of the party accompanied him, which would logically have included his personal friends and others who tok their chance to show their loyalty to the potential coup-leader and so gain rewards later; other members headed home to their estates to prepare for possible civil war or revolts.[27] By traditional etiquette the King should have had the first shot and not the other huntsman, but perhaps he had granted his companion that favour as a goodwill gesture. If anyone fired deliberately at the King under cover of his own shot it would probably have been a member of his own party, as they would have had their positions near him and could creep up on him through the undergrowth. If the site of the 'Stone' is accurate, the site of the killing was a mixture of patches of thick woodland and open 'rides', with the deer driven along one of the latter by the attendants – probably Eastwards down from Stoney Plain towards Canterton village.

An attacker would have been able to approach easier from the direction of the setting sun (north of west) so the king and any attendant lord not 'in' on the plot would not have spotted them and wondered what they were doing. The etiquette of royal hunting – if this was already sufficiently formal as of 1100 – would have made it more risky for someone not in the king's party to leave their own 'stands', probably at least a hundred yards or so away, to approach the King unnoticed; there is plenty of open ground around the site of the 'Stone' which they would have had to cross. The thicker woodland, where an assassin could sneak up on the king much easier, was to the east, downhill. If the identification of Tyrrell as the killer was due to his arrow being found in the King's body, this may have been purloined from his quiver earlier to set him up as the 'fall guy'; he claimed he had not been in 'that part of the wood',[28] presumably quoting his own words, and this would seem to imply that the hunting-party were in woodland rather than on an open 'ride'. (This is not definitive as the statement would have been made in his homeland of northern France, where the difference between tree-covered woodland and 'Forest', ie land under formal Forest Law, might not have been realised; Tyrell could have said 'Forest' and had it interpreted as woodland.) He was thus not one of the King's immediate companions, but he was close enough for it to seem logical that he could have fired at the king. If the details in William of Malmesbury's account about the killer accidentally not seeing the king due to the sun in his eyes is correct, William would have been to the West of the latter, standing in the direction of the sun. But Duncan Grinnell-Milne's 1968 'reconstruction' of the killing and reckoning that Tyrrell, who as he was accused of the killing by the other members of the party would have been the next shooter 'along the line' from the king and so 'must' have been around eighty yards away to be 'in cover', is too flawed to rely on. After all, we have no certainty that the 'Rufus Stone' was put up at the correct site or what the local scrub and trees looked like in 1100; some woodland may well have been cleared or burnt down since then.

The King's body was left unattended until eventually someone, either junior attendants to the party or a forester (called Purkiss in later legend), put it in a cart and took it to Winchester for burial at the cathedral. By that time Henry was on his way to London to be crowned.[29]

The clerical reaction to the accident – and alleged 'advance knowledge'

The appropriateness of the publicly anti-clerical, blaspheming king – the man who had kept sees and abbeys vacant for years to embezzle their revenues and had a turbulent relationship with the currently exiled Archbishop Anselm – being killed without time to confess his sins to a priest was exploited by the Church. Anselm's biographer John of Salisbury was particularly able to claim that it was God's punishment on William for treating a saint so badly, and remarked on its similarity to the death by a chance arrow of Emperor Julian 'the Apostate', another military man and 'blasphemer'.[30] Julian, who had similarly turned his back on the Church and mocked clerics, had been shot in a minor skirmish on the banks of the Tigris during an invasion of Persia in June 363; his death had enabled the Church to regain support at the Roman Imperial court after an unexpected and much-resented eclipse under his rule. As with William, there were suspicions that he had been shot by one of his own men, not a Persian cavalryman though it is unclear if John was hinting at this explanation in choosing to refer to Julian's death as being like William's. More probably, he was concerned to point out divine justice on blasphemers and compare Julian's exiled foe St Athanasius of Alexandria, who was able to return to his see once the emperor died, to the exiled Archbishop Anselm.

William could be consigned to hell as an awful warning to other sovereigns that divine vengeance would catch up the most powerful tyrant. Around 1125 William of Malmesbury, writing at that abbey where, no doubt, the king's depredations on the clerical estate had made him loathed, was the first historian to mention in detail the portents and miracles that accompanied the king's death.[31] The *Anglo-Saxon Chronicle* had, however, earlier briefly referred to this. Such miraculous occurrences were supposed to herald or accompany great events in contemporary belief, though stories could easily improve in the telling or their (vague) dates be altered with hindsight to fit in with the timing of a catastrophe. The story in the *Anglo-Saxon Chronicle*[32] of a pool in Berkshire oozing blood in the summer of 1100 was expanded into a whole series of otherworldly apparitions and appearances by the Devil, all aimed at indicating the divine wrath about to fall on the king. The English monk Eadmer provided a particularly impressive list of occurrences to show that the supernatural was indicating a major event and the death of the irreligious tyrant.[33] But the multiplicity of omens – and their list in the *Chronicle* – was a common occurrence at times of political upheaval, as seen by their alleged appearance in 1066. This time there was no comet, but the event which occurred was not a major disaster for the nation but a personal settling of accounts by God with an impious tyrant.

In the fullest version of the event, written by the monk Orderic Vitalis in Northern France c.1135, a monk of Gloucester arrived at the hunting-lodge on the morning of 2 August to warn that he had had a vision of Christ promising a virgin that the king's treatment of the Church was about to be punished by his death. He was sent packing with a scornful joke about monks always seeking money. Fulchred, abbot of Shrewsbury, had said in a sermon at Gloucester on 1 August that a change in great affairs would shortly free England from iniquity and the 'swift arrow' of Divine vengeance was already out of its quiver.[34] This could be coincidence, a reference to the expected return of the (Church-approved) Crusader Duke Robert to Normandy and a hoped-for English baronial revolt in his favour, or a posthumous exaggeration of stories current at the time to fit in with the manner of the king's death which Orderic had picked up. William of Malmesbury reported – after the king's death had shown what the portent meant – a story that a foreign monk had come to Court before William died to report a vision where a crucifix had kicked William for abusing it.

None of this is definitive enough to be regarded as proof that there was a 'clerical conspiracy', or that monastic chroniclers were aware of a secular conspiracy, to murder William. As Frank Barlow has analysed the mass of portents, they may have been collected by their recorders and been multiplied by rumour long after the event. Even if some, such as the dreams, were genuine and occurred before 2 August they could have been a result of the widespread monastic indignation at the way in which William was treating the Church as a 'milch-cow' for his treasury and keeping offices vacant. His alleged contempt for churchmen and 'blasphemous' jests was in contrast to the reverence exhibited by his father and most great magnates of the later eleventh-century (though his disrespectful swearwords were not so uncommon, his devout father having used similar language despite founding abbeys and honouring Archbishop Lanfranc). His whole tone of behaviour, not caring what he said or fearing divine judgement, would have perturbed churchmen and made them wish for proof that the divine was not to be mocked without retribution. The dreams and portents, responding to a mood of anger and disgust at the ceaseless evidence of royal misbehaviour which Anselm's exile had exacerbated, only seemed to have significance after the event.

William, Walter Tyrrell, and the modern theory of a 'pagan sacrifice'

Eadmer's brief statement of the incident says that William went out hunting after his midday meal and was shot in the heart in a wood while his party were shooting at deer according to the most common theory, though others said that the king had stumbled and fallen on an arrow. He did not name the alleged killer. William of Malmesbury had it that the delay until after the meal was caused by William's companion and guest Robert FitzHamon (the first Norman lord of Glamorgan by marriage c. 1093 to the daughter of its Welsh ruler Iestyn ap Gwrgan, and with his own lands probably in Gloucestershire near lands inherited by William II from his mother) earlier receiving a visiting monk who claimed that a vision had warned of danger to the king that morning. Accordingly FitzHamon (probably in charge at the hunting-lodge that morning while William was asleep after a late night drinking?) and/or his companions decided for safety's sake to persuade the king to stay indoors and do business that morning, and the party went out after a meal which would have been around noon. Orderic records that before setting out for the hunt that day William had a bizarre exchange with his killer-to-be Tyrrell, giving him the best of a bunch of six new arrows which had been brought for his use by a local blacksmith as he was the best marksman in the group and telling him to carry out 'justice' on some matter.[35] Who or what William meant is unclear – justice on the deer by killing them? – though Orderic clearly meant his readers to think that it turned out to be a prophetic hint at what was about to happen. Again, if the remark was not invented or misinterpreted to fit in with the afternoon's events it was probably entirely coincidental. It is too far-fetched for a whole theory to be erected on the basis of this exchange, alleging that William the 'Red King' was not only a critic of the Church but a secret adherent of a 'pagan' cult and wanted Tyrrell to kill him in some sort of ritual sacrifice.[36] There is no evidence that the latter cults even existed in eleventh-century England, and the shaky modern theory of survivals of 'paganism' (suppressed in Anglo-Saxon England in the seventh-century) presents the latter in modern terms as a clearly defined 'cult' bearing similarities to its modern derivation 'Wicca'.

In these terms, there was allegedly worship of the old pre-Christian gods, eg the 'Horned One' who was a mixture of man and stag with deer's antlers (the pre-Christian, 'Celtic' god Cernunnos), and this was maintained by a secret group of adherents and was written off as 'devil-worship' by the church. There had indeed been major setbacks for the Christian Church in England as recently as the later ninth-century with the arrival of non-Christian Scandinavians to seize lands and settle in the 'Danelaw' in eastern and north-east England, and these people had only slowly been Christianised following Anglo-Saxon reconquest in the 920s-50s. But they worshipped the Norse gods led by Odin, Thor, and Freya, not any 'Celtic' gods, and they had never settled in the Hampshire region anyway. The pre-Christianised Saxons in southern England had also worshipped the same pantheon, not 'Celtic' gods; the latter's final extant temples in England date from the late Roman period (eg the sanctuary of the god Nodens at Lydney in Gloucestershire). The survivals of pre-Christian mythology in Christian England analysed (and romanticised) by late nineteenth-century writers such as the famous Sir James Frazer (in *The Golden Bough*, a 'cult' book of the period) probably reflect a sporadic influence on 'low-level' culture, eg the legend of 'Herne the Hunter' haunting Windsor Forest (as used by Shakespeare in 'The Merry Wives of Windsor') but no more than that. The same applies to pre-Christian gods and myths in Wales, though in that case more of the mythology survived into literary culture as it did in Ireland. At best, some pre-Christian (Scandinavian not 'Celtic') stories were retold and written down in Anglo-Saxon England into the eighth-century, such as the famous legend of Beowulf (a Swedish dragon-fighting warlord of dubious historicity). The 'Celtic' gods also seem to have produced the popular legends of the 'Green Man', who was celebrated (as a 'good luck' charm?) in church sculptures. Any notion of coherent secret pre-Christian and pre-Anglo-Saxon cults surviving into the eleventh-century is as unlikely as the mercurial and mocking William II taking such beliefs or rituals seriously enough to be an adherent. William's easy-going and cynical attitude towards religion makes it unlikely that he believed devoutly in any religion let alone paganism.

There is no proof that Henry planned the 'accident', however convenient it was to his cause. Henry's biographer C. Warren Hollister argues that the timing of the killing was more inconvenient to Henry than it would seem with hindsight – he did manage to take the throne and fight off Robert's invasion in 1101–2 but it was a large risk to take. The non-co-operation of the royal household officials and attendant barons at either Winchester or London (not to mention of the Church as taking part in the coronation) would have halted Henry's coup abruptly. He did not know on 2 August that the custodians of the royal treasure in Winchester – or the churchmen at Westminster Abbey, now the site of Royal coronations and probably holding the coronation-regalia – would back him when he arrived demanding access rather than telling him to wait for Robert's arrival. In Prince John's attempt to depose the absent Richard I when he was seized by the German Emperor Henry VI during his return from the Third Crusade in 1192, a King's absence did not mean that he lost his throne if his officials stayed loyal. There was no guarantee that leading officials would not refuse to abandon their loyalty to William's designated heir Robert and arrest Henry. He would stand a better chance if William died naturally, designating him his heir (he had had a severe illness in 1093), or if he waited until William quarrelled with the returned Robert and designated Henry as his heir; he could have murdered William with more of a chance of success in claiming the Crown at that point.

The man named as the killer by those in the king's escort at the scene according to William of Malmesbury and Orderic was Walter Tyrrell of Poix, a minor Norman lord who was in the hunting-party. He immediately fled to the coast (supposedly via 'Tyrrell's Ford' on the Avon near Ringwood), took ship to Normandy, and never returned to England. But his hasty departure could have been due to panic rather than guilt, whether or not his arrow had been found in the king's body. He had no reason to stay and argue it out, with the chance that Henry would have him executed as a scapegoat and thus prevent him from resisting the 'official version' of the events. According to Abbot Suger of St Denis near Paris, writing the biography of William's fellow-sovereign Louis VI decades later, Tyrrell was heard many times in later years back in France claiming that he was not even in that part of the wood at the time the king was killed. He insisted it was an accident even when he was dying, according to John of Salisbury (Anselm's biographer).[37] This would logically suggest that he was not part of any conspiracy, which he had no reason to deny at this late date. If there was a plot, was his arrow stolen to be fired at the king and 'frame' him?

Is the 'Rufus Stone' at the right site?

Attempts have been made to 'reconstruct' the killing and work out if it was more likely to be an accident or a plot, but the basic evidence of how it could have been carried out is lacking. With regard to Grinnell-Williams' reconstruction of the scene, it should be noted that there is not even definite proof of the site as being at the place chosen to put the commemorative 'Rufus Stone' in 1745. This choice of site, near Canterton in the extreme north-east of the forest, was based on a local identification that Charles II and his courtiers had been given on a royal visit to the forest, probably in 1670.[38] (That monarch was the last to visit the Forest on numerous occasions for the hunting, staying at New Park, Lyndhurst, and even rebuilt a palace at Winchester in the early 1680s.) But at least one assumption that developed with regard to the site – its closeness to the royal lodge at Castle Malwood – was inaccurate as that site was not in use that early. The main royal hunting-lodge was at Lyndhurst, with its 'Old Park', by the thirteenth-century but in the late eleventh-century was probably at Brockenhurst. It is not clear who gave Charles II the identification, but a note of caution should be raised in any mention of 'tradition' as recounted by local Romanies (which was also cited in the twentieth-century). These travelling people, originally from the Indian sub-continent and marked off as 'alien' to the fearful locals by their language and choice of habitation, did not enter England until the early sixteenth-century. There were none in the Forest in 1100, though they could have picked up local stories about the killing from foresters and transmitted them to the royal visitors in 1670.

There was also probably a lodge at the site of Beaulieu, which was set aside for a new abbey (called after a French version of its nickname, 'Beautiful Place') by king John in 1204. Assuming that the king's entourage had journeyed to the forest from Winchester, Beaulieu would have been easier for the Royal party to reach quickly – down the River Itchen and by sea from the embryonic port at Southampton – than inland Brockenhurst or Lyndhurst. Other early royal hunting-lodges presumably include the now abandoned site at Churchplace at the north end of Denny Wood Enclosure, near Matley Bridge several miles East of Lyndhurst – and did this have a church as in the story in 'Florence' of Worcester's chronicle of a demolished church at the site of the killing? But this question of distance may all be irrelevant, given the mobility of William who was an expert rider who was known for covering large distances quickly. After the killing Henry rode straight to Winchester, though this does not mean that the site must have been in the centre-north of the Forest not near the south coast like Beaulieu. The latter was closer to an alternative choice of site for the killing which was suggested in the 1960s, based on etymology. The clerical chroniclers of the 1120s heard that the king had been killed at 'Througham', evidently the site of a pre-1066 settlement destroyed by the Normans as they created the forest (or falling into disuse in later centuries) as the name did not survive into the modern era. William of Malmesbury (c. 1125) said that there was subsequently a chapel built at the site, and 'Florence' (probably John) of Worcester (thirteenth-century) said that a chapel had stood there until it was demolished at the creation of the Forest – making the killing of the anti-clerical King there seem appropriate proof of Divine wrath.[39]

This is an important clue as to the site. There is no evidence that any chapel was constructed near the 'Rufus Stone' site, or that there was a local village which it would logically have been built to serve. This is barren heathland and thick woods, not near a road or stream; the nearest settlement is downhill at Canterton. On the other hand, there was a chapel at another site in the forest that was known as 'Throwgham' according to a document of 1606 and said there to have been at 'Beaulieu Park' – nowhere near the site chosen for the 'Rufus Stone'. This sounds like the 'Thoroughham' where John Leland said William had been killed, writing in the 1530s after an intensive tour of the country where he would have picked up current traditions. The 'Stoney Cross Plain must be the site of the killing' theory was backed up by the identification of the 'Throwgham/ Truham' location as Fritham, the nearest village to the site of the Rufus Stone, by amateur historian (and creator of the artistic cult of the 'Picturesque') local vicar the Revd William Gilpin of Boldre, in 1791. But the name was also used of the isolated Park Farm south-west of Beaulieu, miles away from Malwood to the south-east.[40] This lowland site by the shores of the Solent, a short distance from the mouth of the Beaulieu River and near the later Beaulieu Abbey 'grange' (farm) of St Leonards, is totally different in nature to the woodland glade at Canterton near Fritham. But it was within easy reach of the royal lodge at Beaulieu – which was only called by that French name after the Abbey was founded in 1204 – and arguably of Brockenhurst too, and had been a settlement with a church before 1066. It has continued as a farm within the Forest limits to this day. A magnificent monastic barn still stands nearby, the remains of the monastic grange of St Leonard's. Accordingly a suggestion was made that it was the real site of the killing.

Does the outcome suggest that killing William was an unlikely risk for Henry to have taken in Robert's absence? Who else could have done it?

The story put about that an arrow glanced off a tree and hit William when the later afternoon sun obscured the huntsmen's vision is perfectly logical. Even if it was not true that Tyrrell fired it and he was 'set up', it may have been to protect one of Henry's friends who had actually fired the shot. If someone like one of the Beaumonts had done it, who would believe that it was not a deliberate shot done at Henry's request? This was a logical conclusion for Henry to reach, and Tyrrell had no powerful friends at court to look after his interests or to complain at his being named. There is no more than circumstantial evidence to indicate a deliberate killing, either by Henry's friends (e.g. the Beaumont brothers, present at the scene, or the De Clare family) or by a baron hired by Emma Mason's proposed candidate – the heir to France, Prince Louis. These have been suggested as people who might be glad to see William out of the way; Henry in order to succeed himself and Louis to prevent William renewing his offensives in northern France and/or to start an English civil war. Louis, born in 1081, was already taking over war-leadership from his ageing father (who died in 1108) to bring the feuding barons of the French royal domain – the 'Isle de France' around Paris – under control by a series of aggressive campaigns. At this stage, the military resources that the monarchy could use against their local rivals were limited but Louis was prepared to spend years fighting or besieging castle after castle. This was to continue on his accession. Despite his weight-problem (a symptom of his aggressive pursuit of pleasure as well as war?) he had boundless energy and determination, and started the revival of French royal power which his son Louis VII was to continue. Unlike his son, he was not noticeably pious or scrupulous; the religious aura which was to surround the monarchy only emerged with Louis VII's alliance in the 1140s with abbot Suger of St Denis, the Capetian royal mausoleum and the 'national' shrine.

The French monarchy was under something of a cloud in its reputation as of 1100, with Philip having been excommunicated by Pope Urban II at the Council of Clermont (which launched the First Crusade) in 1095 for abandoning his wife Bertha of Holland, Louis' mother, for Bertrada of Montfort. The pope, as opposed to bishops within the 'Isle de France' who were more accomodating, refused to recognise Philip's divorce. The fact that Philip had lured Bertrada from the ruler of the rival 'power' to his south-west, Count Fulk of Anjou, added to his problems in providing Fulk with a grudge. Ultimately the monarchs sought to restore the power of the monarchy beyond the borders of the 'Isle de France', returning it to its powers under the Carolingians when the king had been more than a 'primus inter pares' and his territorial neighbours had not openly defied or ignored him. The French monarchy had immense potential and prestige as the lineal heirs of the great Charlemagne, who had ruled most of continental Europe and been the grantee of the Imperial title (now lost to Germany), although this potential was dormant as of 1100. (It was Louis VI's son Louis VII who was to reassert monarchical prestige in alliance with the Church under Abbot Suger of St Denis.)

The Carolingians to 987 had had direct or indirect control of their feudal vassals in Northern and Southern France alike, and the early Capetians – Hugh and Robert II – had still had some influence over lay rulers and church appointees beyond the Seine basin, backed by the landed patrimony of their ancestors around Paris. This had declined since Robert's death in 1031 – and William's expanding role as the most powerful and aggressive lord in northern France was a barrier to the kings reasserting their power. Normandy, the semi-independent new Duchy (originally County) set up by Viking adventurers on the north-western borders of the 'Isle' by William II's ancestors in 911, was a particular threat to the French kings – particularly after 1066. The two neighbouring powers were in constant conflict over their border, particularly the crucial lordship of the 'Vexin' on the Seine between Rouen and Paris which was the geographical gateway to invasion aimed at each power's capital. Towns and minor lordships in this region changed hands constantly between Normandy and the monarchy throughout the later eleventh- and twelfth-century – and indeed William I met his fatal injury in late summer 1087 when his horse stumbled while he was sacking the rebel Vexin town of Mantes. Unlike the equally large and powerful southern duchies such as Aquitaine, Normandy adjoined the 'Isle de France' and could assist its rebels. It was geographically part of the lands of Neustria, of which dynastic founder Hugh 'Capet's great-uncle Odo (King of the French from 888 to 898 and heroic defender of Paris from the Vikings) had been ruler. The County/Duchy had been granted as a fief to the Viking leader Hrolf/ Rollo 'the Walker' in 911, with the Norman rulers doing homage to the king, and the kings were always keen to see that every new Norman ruler did homage and recognised him as his superior. If rebellious, a vassal could legally be deposed – a powerful weapon for the king against the Dukes of Normandy which they were not going to give up, and which legitimised their backing of disobedient 'pretenders' to the Duchy of Normandy. But as of the later eleventh-century the Dukes of Normandy were neglecting to do this homage, as no records of any such ceremonies exist unlike for the second half of the twelfth-century – and this ultimately implied their potential to break away from being the king's legal vassals. Their defiance was undoubtedly boosted, and probably inspired, by their acquisition of England in 1066. Henry I (d. 1060), Philip's father, had been William the Conqueror's protector and ally as a young and insecure Duke of Normandy facing rebellion from 1035, and had aided him against his rebels at the crucial battle of Val-es-Dunes in 1047; he had also been uncle to William's wife. Matilda of Flanders. (Ironically, Henry I of England, born in 1068/9, was probably called after him.) The acquisition of England by William in 1066 made the dukes 'Kings' in their own right and gave them more military and financial resources than the Kings of France, exacerbating the problem. Philip had turned against William, and the two had clashed over the disputed succession to Flanders – William's wife's homeland – in 1070–1. Philip was technically overlord of Flanders as of Normandy as it was within the legal boundaries of France, and his ability to install his own candidate Robert as the new Count was a major success for the French monarchy. It provided a potential template for doing the same in Normandy itself should the opportunity arise – or at least of threatening this to undermine William. Accordingly Philip backed William's rebel son Robert against him in 1077–9, and Louis was to back Henry I's rival, Robert's son William 'Clito', against him in the late 1110s and 1120s.

But we should be wary of assuming that there was a fixed 'policy' by the French monarchy of breaking up the Norman-English realm, given what did not happen during the Norman dynasty's internal feuds in 1087 – 1106 – surely a time for constant French meddling had such been Philip's and Louis' fixed intentions. The division of England and Normandy into two separate dominions after 1087 must have relieved Philip, but he had not done much to support Robert (useful as a weaker and less hostile neighbour?) against William II in the 1090s. William II's stewardship of Normandy after Robert left for the Crusade in 1096 reunited the two states – temporarily – and was seen as a threat by Philip, as was William's rumoured plans in 1099–1100 to meddle with affairs in Aquitaine once Robert returned and he had to hand Normandy back. William was also more able than Robert to deal swiftly with French-backed rebellions in Normandy, as shown in 1099 when he was caught away in England by a revolt but rode straight to the English coast and crossed the Channel with a few followers rather than waiting prudently to gather his army. Laughing at his followers' worries about an impending storm as he set sail, he said that he had never heard of a king of England being drowned yet – and he duly reached Normandy safely, rallied his local troops, and caught the rebels unawares.[41] With or without possession of Normandy, the bold and restless William was a formidable and ambitious foe to the Capetians and was the main obstacle to their reasserting their influence over northern France. Robert, by contrast, had never shown interest in the affairs of his northern French neighbours as Duke of Normandy in 1087–96, and Henry was an unknown quantity who if William died would be insecure on his new throne due to Robert's claim on it. If William died, Henry and Robert could be guaranteed to fight each other over England and Normandy – giving the Capetians time to build up their own power undisturbed. So might Prince Louis have decided to remove William and cause civil war in England and Normandy? Walter Tyrell, moreover, had lands on the border between Normandy and the Capetian domains – so was he more amenable than most Norman barons to helping out Louis, who could protect him militarily if needed?

The case against Louis is based on guesswork rather than evidence, though he benefited from William's sudden removal as much as (more than?) Henry did. There is no indication that Tyrell ever received a reward of more lands from Louis for ridding him of William, as would have been likely had he been a cold-blooded assassin. The argument that the French monarchs' ally Abbot Suger – by definition, a foe of Normandy? – cannot be believed in any assertion of Tyrell's innocence is ingenious but unlikely. Henry had more motive than Louis to dispose of William, and had more obvious connections to the other personnel present on the hunt on 2 August 1100. He was a ruthless man, denied his lands in the Cotentin thanks to his brothers uniting against him and probably aware that Robert was now married and could soon have a heir. He himself was around eight years William's junior, but he had no guarantee that the king would quarrel with Robert again and make him his heir to England – or that William might eventually marry to provide his own heir. He made the most of his chance when it occurred by hurrying to Winchester to seize the crown and treasury rather than nobly proclaiming Robert as the new King. Moreover, within weeks he had secured the hand of the one Royally-bred woman available in England in whom William had shown an interest – Edith (Matilda), niece of Edgar 'the Atheling' the rightful Saxon heir. As in 1088, Robert challenged his exclusion from England as soon as he could and staged an invasion with local assistance, his army ironically including Edgar 'Atheling' who had been on friendly terms with him since the 1070s and had been on Crusade with him. But he was faced with a powerful enough resistance to make him avoid a risky battle and accept peace at Alton,[42] though arguably he was too timid and might have won an open battle. Possibly his leading supporter Bishop Ranulf Flambard of Durham, William's acquisitive treasurer who had been arrested on Henry's accession and fled abroad to Robert, deviously 'pushed' him into accepting peace as Henry had offered him his lands and goods back if he did so – he was duly allowed back to England. Robert went home to Normandy and proved once again unable to control his bickering and robbery-prone vassals, and ultimately Henry was able to retaliate with an invasion of Normandy and secure the Conqueror's whole dominions in 1106. The question of whether the ruthless Henry had rid himself of William to cheat Robert of the throne remains unanswered and the evidence is too scant to solve it – but in practical politics he proved a better ruler.

Chapter 2

Edward II – Murder or Escape?

The background

Edward II was a unique sovereign in many ways, and has a certain appeal to the modern reader for his brazenly unconventional ways that puzzled and annoyed his ferocious father Edward I and horrified his elite. He was the first king since the Conquest to be deposed, by means of a forced 'voluntary' abdication at Kenilworth in January 1327 following his wife Isabella's invasion of the country in his elder son Edward's name. Despite his unquestioned legitimacy as sovereign unlike many predecessors, his excessive grants of lands and honours to a small and widely disliked group of 'favourites' had sparked off violent political opposition throughout his reign and led to attempts by leading nobles to force him to remove the offenders and govern according to their 'guidance' instead. Hatred was shown by the leading Earls towards the 'low-born' royal favourite Piers Gaveston, a young Gascon knight who Edward's father had originally enrolled as his son's 'squire' and companion but had soon banished as a bad influence on his son. This is supposed to have been the occasion when the angry king attacked his son and pulled his hair out, but this typically violent reaction from the ageing warlord may have been due to the insolence of the prince asking for the earldom of Cornwall (usually restricted to Royals) for his ambitious friend rather than outrage at their alleged homosexual relations.[1] Not learning his lesson about what the elite would tolerate, once he was king Edward II blatantly loaded patronage (including the earldom) on to Gaveston and married him to his own niece, co-heiress to the major Welsh Marcher dynasty of De Clare (Earls of Gloucester).

Edward's lack of interest in his overbearing father's warlike pursuits was shown by his failure to pursue the royal campaign against Robert Bruce on which Edward I had died in July 1307, which arguably annoyed the late king's warlike aristocratic associates at the very start of his reign.

Edward I died in his tent at Burgh-by-Sands near Carlisle on his way to Galloway to try to put down a rising there by Bruce, a local landowner as earl of Carrick (via his mother) and heir to centuries of De Brus/ Bruce lords of Annandale, who had been chased out of mainland Scotland after his coronation in 1306 but had now returned. The new king abandoned the attempt to put down the rising, though Bruce was a master of guerrilla warfare and would probably have eluded him or his father by hiding in the hills had they continued the war, and as Edward II headed back to London his over-stretched armies in Scotland proved unable to stop Bruce regaining control of Galloway and then heading north to Argyll. The local MacDougalls, lords of Argyll and Lorne who were Scandinvian-Gaels warlord allies of Edward I and had driven Bruce out of the region in 1306, were left to face the insurgents alone and were duly destroyed by a combination of Bruce and their own Hebridean kin, the MacDonalds. By the time that Edward II bothered to invade Scotland again at his nobles' insistence in 1310–11, the Bruce army had also driven their Comyn foes out of Buchan in NE Scotland and most of the country North of the Firth of Forth and Clyde had recognised 'Robert I' as King – for which Edward was duly blamed by his senior nobles. Indeed, his first choice of army commander to take on Bruce when the power-usurping English noble junta of the 'Lords Ordainers' (see below) demanded it was his friend Gaveston, despite the latter's complete lack of military experience or skill – loyalty mattered more than ability.

Edward's own preference for spending his leisure lay in 'unseemly' manual crafts which the nobility regarded as only suitable for the lower classes. He was as keen on horses as many young nobles, possessing a notable stud-farm at Ditchling in Sussex, and his arrogance, spendthrift nature, and violent antipathy to his critics as a prince were not particularly unusual or regarded as reprehensible. (Edward I had been guilty of lawless assaults on passers-by as a young man when he and his knightly companions rampaged through the countryside.) But his sporting pursuits centred not on tournaments or combat but on activities such as rowing; he also enjoyed digging and building walls, regarded as fit pursuits only for labourers. The change of 'tone' at court at Edward's accession, with a manly warrior-king who had been a Crusader hero replaced with an unmilitary young man who preferred boating to tournaments, was always going to alienate a number of important peers but might have been without drastic political implication but for the new king's open showering of power and presents on his objectionable close friend. Gaveston was married to Edward's niece, given the Earldom of Cornwall and governorship of Ireland, and played an important part in the coronation in 1308, carrying the Crown to the fury of the great nobles who usually had this honour. Unfortunately his ambitions and ability to collect titles, land and money were not equalled by his competence, and the ceremony was full of a series of mistakes, missed cues, and minor disasters and ended with a poorly-cooked banquet in Westminster Hall which arrived late – for all of which Gaveston was blamed by fulminating noble guests. In fact there had been no coronation for thirty-three years for people to use as a precedent and the Royal Household had been laxly supervised for a decade with Edward I mostly away campaigning in Scotland, with scandals including an audacious 'heist' of the poorly-guarded royal jewels, so it was not all his fault. Gaveston openly flaunted his monopoly of royal patronage and made no effort to conciliate other nobles who had made the most of their relationships with and the right to give advice to the king under Edward's father and were now ignored.

The displays of affection between Edward and Gaveston gave rise to suspicions of an unhealthy and possibly homosexual relationship, which was exacerbated by Edward's lack of interest in or granting of traditional funds and a separate household to his admittedly under-age teenage bride Isabella of France, who he married in 1308. Worse, the French noble escort who accompanied her to London were unsettled by the lack of concern that Edward at first showed her and his unseemly failure to grant her the usual residences, lands, gifts, and large household – as with Gaveston (who they blamed for this), the King did not care to act with politic propriety. Within contemporary cultural 'mores', however, Edward himself may have thought of the relationship as a perfectly respectable 'brotherly' bond, as between David and Jonathan in the Old Testament or between Achilles and Patroclus in the Ancient Greek epic 'Iliad'. Contemporary chroniclers agreed that Edward had an unusual and passionate bond with Gaveston, who the usually scrupulous Ranulf Higden says he loved above all others with intensity, showered with gifts, and would not be separated from, and some (eg the *Chronicle of Lanercost* and the overseas *Chronicle of Meaux*) refer to it in terms of sin or explicit sodomy so there were clearly contemporary rumours of that.[2] In political terms, it was disastrous although the unwise showering of land and titles on brash 'outsiders' by an English king was not that unprecedented – Henry III, Edward's grandfather, had similarly infuriated the inner clique of senior nobles by favouring firstly his ex-mentor Hubert de Burgh and later his Poitevin half-brothers in the 1230s-50s. Gaveston showed open contempt for the uncouth and militaristic leading peers at court and used his cutting wit on them with every sign of royal approval, leading to a first 'coup' by his infuriated victims and enforced restraint of the king in 1308.

Gaveston was banished to evident widespread approval among the upper classes, but returned from banishment with royal support in 1312. The king even invited him to stay at the royal palace at Westminster, where his 'secret' visit was bound to leak out through court and household gossip, rather than being more discreet and meeting him at isolated rural royal estates. Firstly he denied that Gaveston was even in England, and when it became impossible to hide this he adopted an air of defiance and alleged that the 'Ordainers' law banishing him had been illegal, had been forced on him, and could be revoked by his sole command. As impractical as ever, he lacked the military support from the elite to see that his wishes were obeyed and was driven to resort to taking Gaveston north to prepare for a campaign against the Scots. This time Gaveston was hunted down across England by a group of his leading aristocratic enemies and their armed retainers with the presence of the king in his company not restraining them, and the king and queen were driven to scuttling around the north-east to keep ahead of a baronial army looking for Gaveston. At one point they had to flee down the Tyne without their luggage, which was abandoned at Tynemouth Priory; indeed, the king even left his wife behind in his haste to make sure that Gaveston was safe from capture. Gaveston was cornered at Scarborough Castle, a formidable coastal stronghold where Edward had sent him from the River Tyne for his safety, and forced to surrender, and was promised a proper trial in an agreement with the king's cousin, Aymer de Valence, the Earl of Pembroke. But his arch-enemy the Earl of Warwick, who he had referred to as the 'Black Dog of Arden', promptly ambushed his escort en route to London, and dragged him out of his lodgings to be packed off, tied up, to Warwick Castle for trial by a 'kangaroo court'. Technically Gaveston had flouted government orders issued by the ruling committee of barons (the

'Lords Ordainers') that had forced the king to cede administrative control of the country to them in 1308 to go into exile on pain of death. The king had declared this law void, but Pembroke's and Warwick's group of barons ignored this and Gaveston was sentenced to death for returning despite the king's frantic written pleas. Warwick then had him taken out of Warwick on to nearby Blacklow Hill and beheaded to prevent the king restoring his power again.[3]

Aristocratic hostility to 'outsiders' monopolizing patronage and royal 'incompetence' and untrustworthiness, and a forcible and violent resolution to the problem, had been used before, against Henry III's partisanship for his stepbrothers and his wife's relatives in 1258–65. The king had been restrained by a self-appointed council of his mistrustful leading nobles in 1258 and on a more legalistic basis in 1264–5, and the acts of the anti-Gaveston faction as the 'Lords Ordainers' in securing Parliamentary backing and requiring the king to let them run his administration and issue laws (nominally through him) was in that tradition though aimed at the recent monopoly of patronage by one individual rather than decades of incompetent decisions and resented grants by the sovereign. The royal distortion of patronage in favour of an 'outsider' instead of the king's 'natural' allies, the great nobility, was more important than any allegation that Gaveston or later the younger Hugh Despenser was the king's homosexual lover, assuming that the charge was more than a piece of – highly plausible – slander dreamed up by the favourites' enemies to destroy their reputations and excuse their murders. Edward's extravagant affection for Gaveston made that charge plausible, and Gaveston had delighted in thinking up spiteful names to ridicule the great nobility and had had a knack of infuriating powerful people since the reign of Edward I. Any allegations made of 'unnatural' sexual practices would undoubtedly add to the anger of aristocratic critics, explaining the reasons for Edward II showering gifts and offices on him and refusing to accept his exile in 1308 in the worst possible way. The king's relationship with the more politically effective and ruthless Marcher baron Hugh le Despenser in the 1320s was less easy to portray in purely sexual terms, as although Edward deferred to his favourite's advice and showered him with offices Despenser was a capable political leader and administrator. (The charge of homosexual relations in this case was first made, hesitantly, by the later fourteenth-century chronicler Froissart).[4] Despenser, unlike the Gascon squire Gaveston, came from the Marcher nobility, albeit a minor family, and his rise to fortune had begun under Edward I who granted him the hand of his De Clare niece Eleanor (not yet co-heiress to Glamorgan as her brother was still alive, but semi-royal). He was politically valuable to a king who was seemingly incapable of governing without relying heavily on one trusted character from outide the traditional circle of royal advisers, though the blatant monopoly of patronage that his family received was a sign of Edward's failure to realise or care about the inevitable reaction.

The locality of Despenser's base of power was also particularly problematic, as it centred on his marriage to the king's niece as heiress to the vast estates of the De Clare family in Glamorgan and Gwent, the south-east region of the semi-independent Marcher lordships on the former Welsh frontier. The previous dominant figure in the southern Marches had been a De Clare, Edward I's son-in-law (but near-contemporary) Gilbert De Clare, Earl of Glamorgan, known from his hair as 'the Red Earl', who had been the most powerful man in England after King Henry III and (Prince) Edward after the fall of Simon de Montfort (in which he had assisted) in 1265. He had died in 1290; his weaker son Gilbert, the last of the direct male line of the De Clares, was killed at Bannockburn in 1314. The Earldom's lands had then been divided among the last earl's sisters, with the eldest, Margaret, being Gaveston's widow (which argues that if Gaveston had still been alive then he would have been given the title and bulk of the lands and been the target of furious condemnation). The king's new favourite Despenser, husband of a younger sister (Eleanor), now received the most important part of the inheritance, the lands of Glamorgan, and later the title; and Edward did nothing to stop him pressuring the husbands of the other De Clare sisters, Hugh Audley and Roger Amory, to surrender the rest. Despenser also secured extra local lands, such as Gower, by a blatantly 'rigged' legal process – and it was clear that the only way to curb his acquisitiveness would be by violence given the king's favouritism. The Marcher lords had been given extensive military and judicial autonomy by the earlier Anglo-Norman kings to defend and push back the border, and were accustomed to acting with minimal Royal supervision; they also had large private armies of tenants accustomed to following their orders. Despenser's aggregation of lands and power in the Marches aroused the antipathy of a body of rival lords who were accustomed to call on their tenants to raise armed revolt and had little respect for the king's power; their recourse to 'direct action' to challenge the government had been seen back in the 1220s when the Marshals, Earls of Pembroke, were defying Henry III. More recently it had been a Marcher conspiracy, involving the young 'Red Earl' Gilbert de Clare of Glamorgan, which had aided Prince Edward (later Edward I) to overthrow Simon de Montfort's reformist regime with Marcher troops in 1265. On that occasion the current Mortimer lord, fighting for the prince, had killed the pro-Montfort Lord Despenser in combat on the battlefield of Evesham – and such blood-feuds mattered to their descendants. Edward II's partisanship to his new Lord Chamberlain Hugh Despenser stirred up another bout of violence, and the latter was to be brought down in 1326 by his arrested rival Roger Mortimer, lord of Wigmore. The Mortimers, established as a senior Marcher dynasty for centuries and desecended in the female line from the dispossessed Welsh rulers of Gwynedd, thought themselves far superior to the 'parvenu' Despensers. Unlike the arrogant Despenser, Roger also seems to have had the knack of attracting support and was able to make the most of his victimization by the Despensers – who he defied in arms in late 1321 with a rampage across their estates with his followers that the king complained had caused damage worth two-thirds of his annual revenue. But Roger was penned in behind the Severn and was unable to link up with other rebels in northern England, and early in 1322 the royal army closed in on him at Bridgnorth. He and his eponymous uncle, the elder Roger Mortimer (lord of Chirk and former chief justice of North Wales) whose reputation was for even more ruthless behaviour than him plus assorted murders, surrendered on the promise of a fair trial before their peers – which was promptly broken by the devious king. The two Rogers ended up in chains in the Tower of London with their lands confiscated and their womenfolk packed off to 'house arrest' with loyal lords minus their looted possessions. But as a resourceful adventurer the younger Roger did not accept his dispossession and imprisonment in the Tower of London, escaped from his cell with the aid of one of the prison officials who brought him a crowbar to dig his way out while his guards were drunk on a feast-day, climbed up a chimney from the palace kitchen onto the ramparts, and shinned down a rope to Tower Wharf. His friends had horses waiting and a boat ready down the Thames, and he fled successfully to the continent.[5]

The evidence of Edward's growing coldness to and mistrust of his wife in the early 1320s could also be explained by a sexual liaison with Despenser, who does not seem to have attempted to follow the prudent course of trying to conciliate the Queen and was clearly loathed by the latter. His arrogance and greed for land and power are evident and he showed no caution in amassing enemies, though the violent competitiveness of the Marcher barons plus their ready resort to violence meant that once an ambitious man had achieved major prominence there (particularly if he had unshakeable royal support so disgrace was unlikely) he had to keep his foes on the 'defensive' and intimidate potential challengers to have any security. The more lands and retainers he possessed, the more difficult it would be for his foes to remove him by military action. The more lurid tales that the exasperated king had threatened to stab his unco-operative wife may be explainable as propaganda on her part, designed to show her French relatives and Pope John XXII why she could not do her wifely duty by returning to him in 1325–6, but Edward appears to have considered divorce and sent an envoy to the Pope. Whether or not the allegations of homosexuality against Edward and Despenser were true, the unusual nature of Despenser's death at his enemies' hands in 1326 – public castration in the marketplace at Hereford, in front of Isabella, Mortimer, and a baying crowd – suggests that the latter was regarded as an appropriate fate for the commonly held nature of his crimes.[6] He was also condemned for arrogance and greed, which was a fair appraisal of his relentless building-up of estates and his 'fixing' grants of office and lands as Chamberlain, and he was accused of tyranny and treason by the presiding judge in his 'summing-up'. This presented him as the scapegoat for his master's policies and served to deflect attention from the ex-king's crimes, though Despenser had deliberately encouraged Edward II to excessive confiscations for his own benefit.

The insecure Edward II was only following the precedent set by Henry III in 1264 and his son Edward in 1265 in seeking to overthrow his enforced tutelage by a clique of baorns, raising a royal army to meet his aristocratic critics on the battlefield in 1322, killing their leaders, and then carrying out heavy punishment of the defeated offenders. His spite towards the female relatives and children of the defeated, who were usually flung into prison and had their property seized and given to his cronies, was no worse than his father's treatment of Robert Bruce's family and in both cases all were technically 'rebels' and their landed and portable assets could be used to pay for future revolts. But the royalist 'reaction' in 1265–7 had been followed by a period of wiser reconciliation in Henry III's last years, with most 'rebels' restored to their lands and no excessive royal grants to new favourites; when Gilbert (I) de Clare, Earl of Gloucester (a former ally of De Montfort probably alienated by his arrogant, land-grabbing sons) joined up with surviving rebels to stage an armed protest at London Edward (later I) had reluctantly negotiated a settlement. Possibly the survival of some senior 'rebel's' plus a groundswell of support from the public for them – including in London – in 1265–7 made a stalemate and negotiation easier than it was after Edward II's complete victory over his cousin Thomas of Lancaster in 1322. Nor did Edward I concentrate his generosity on a few, controversial personnel after his triumph – probably learning from his father Henry III's mistakes. But Edward II's success in reasserting his position against aristocratic intimidation in 1322 led to a repeat of the 'offences' he had committed in lavishing patronage on Gaveston as if he had learnt nothing, combined with blatant 'triumphalism'. This time his grants were in favour of the even more greedy and monopolistic Hugh Despenser 'the Younger', until this point a minor Marcher landowner though unquestioningly loyal unlike many of his neighbours, and his family.[7] The new favourite acquired one of the late earl Gilbert (II) of Gloucester's sisters and co-heiresses as his wife, and the other sisters and their husbands were 'bought out of' (or forced to sell/exchange) their claims so Despenser secured a large bloc of land in south-east Wales. Other actions of the king suggest an unbalanced as well as rash nature, eg his excessive punishment of the Badlesmere family for the 'insult' of their refusing the queen admission to Leeds Castle in Kent for a night's lodging. The king's soon alienated wife who he was rumoured to be planning to divorce, using their eldest son as a figurehead, eventually managed to secure permission to leave the country so that she could accompany the prince – who was to do the homage for control of Gascony as a French 'fief' claimed by her brother King Charles IV of France. The Despensers were wary of letting her leave the country, but she persuaded her husband to let her go to Paris as she could persuade her brother to return strategic places in Gascony which he had seized in the recent Anglo-French war. To be fair to her, as she was being threatened with divorce and had had her possessions in

England confiscated during the Anglo-French war as she was an 'enemy national', making her dependent on the fickle king's charity, her position was becoming untenable.

At first Charles was unwilling to risk a major war by helping her and was amenable to Edward II's (and his ally the Pope's) written complaints that it was unheard of and immoral for a wife to abandon her husband and refuse to return, but Isabella won him round to see that her husband was dangerously unstable and under the control of the belligerent and greedy Despensers. But if she was to overthrow this unsavoury regime and put her thirteen-year-old son on the throne, they would be loyal French allies. She then raised an army to overthrow Edward II with the assistance of her fellow-plotter and presumed lover, Roger Mortimer, who had arrived in Paris to join her. They hired a small military force from Count William of Hainault in the Low Countries in exchange for marrying his daughter Philippa to Prince Edward and sailed to the Orwell estuary in Suffolk to invade England in late 1326, and despite their small numbers virtually nobody among the English landed elite raised a finger to stop them. Edward II, deserted by his leading subjects and with the Londoners in revolt and lynching his ministers, was forced to flee into Wales and was eventually captured hiding with a few followers led by Hugh Despenser the younger near Llantrisant in Glamorgan. The rebels and the enthusiastic populace exacted a gory revenge on Hugh (who was publicly eviscerated like a common felon in the marketplace at Hereford in front of a large audience led by the queen). On previous occasions no king had actually been deposed, though Matilda would have removed King Stephen after her partisans captured him in 1141 had her plans not been foiled and in 1216 a large number of barons withdrew allegiance to King John in favour of his niece's husband Prince Louis of France. This time the triumphant rebels, headed by the queen, could not trust Edward II to keep any promises after what he had done in 1310 and 1322 and removed him permanently. Technically he abdicated voluntarily as a deputation from Isabella's new Parliament arrived at his place of custody, Kenilworth Castle, though this left the possibility that if he escaped from custody he could claim that it had been invalid as done under duress. The Pope could absolve rulers from legal promises – as Innocent III had done for King John over his being forced to accept Magna Carta in 1215.

Isabella and Mortimer took over the government for the fourteen-year-old new king, though their relationship remained prudently 'low-key'. Isabella was the effective regent as holder of the royal seal and Mortimer no more than her unofficial adviser, though he clearly exercised enormous influence as well as securing large grants of land and local office and a degree of hubris soon became apparent. He married off his children to important dynasties to surround himself with a 'bloc' of great magnates who would have a 'stake' in his survival in power, and within a year had acquired an earldom for himself – though this was normal for a rising landed magnate and at least his family were an old and respected one from their home region of northern Herefordshire, older and more prominent than the Despensers had been. The technical head of the Council as the king's guardian, Edward's oldest male blood-relative, Henry, Earl of Lancaster (brother of Earl Thomas who Edward II had killed in 1322), had little political power and patronage matters were decided solely by the acquisitive Isabella. Lancaster was swiftly rebuffed when he raised his tenants in arms, occupied Winchester, and endeavoured to secure real power by taking custody of the new king.[8] It is unclear if Lancaster accused Mortimer and Isabella of killing Edward II, and some private information which Earl Edmund of Kent told him but which he allegedly could not reveal might refer to the ex-king's not being dead after all (or to the identity of the real killer?). Notably he did not accuse the queen of taking Mortimer as her lover, but he and his allies clearly intended to remove the pair from government by force. Arguably, Isabella had overplayed her hand by relying so heavily on Mortimer, but in her uneasy situation as the first female regent of England she was probably right to fear overthrow by the new king's male kin as a French interloper if unwise to acquire so much lands and goods at once. Obviously Isabella owed a debt of gratitude to Mortimer, was anxious for lands and riches after her relative penury in the early 1320s as her huge acquisitions in 1327–8 show, and could not trust Lancaster – or any chief adviser but Mortimer – to keep her in her new position. But no queen had exercised such an important role in government before, the titular and 'de facto' regents of the young King Henry III (who lacked close adult male kin) having been experienced warrior-nobles such as William Marshal and Hubert de Burgh.

Mortimer's leading role, though he was not a senior peer and only a minor Marcher lord until his accession to vast estates in 1326–7, presented dangers to Isabella's regime although it would appear that their sexual liasion was discreet and she was not accused of immorality by her challengers at the time. Indeed, after their stay at the more sexually lax French court in 1325–6 their relationship was not openly acknowledged, though some modern commentators have alleged that they had a child secretly in 1328/9. The very fact of the affair was, however, enough to blacken her reputation in subsequent centuries, adding to the unease felt about her 'unnatural' action in overthrowing her husband. Edward's follies and misrule might justify his removal, but unlike in other medieval English revolts the queen rather than his nobles had taken the lead in removing him and then had a liasion with her principal male associate. The shocking nature of both occurrences was added to by the rumours of her involvement in Edward's murder, and her behaviour was seen as being worthy of total condemnation as an affront to the natural order of things – and thus to God. The literary genius of Christopher Marlowe provided the final touches to her reputation. In his 1592 tragedy on Edward II's reign Isabella was presented as a vengeful and over-sexed harridan who had unnaturally betrayed, deposed, and murdered her husband in association with her lover, and this picture was not seriously challenged for centuries. In 1757 the poet Thomas Gray transferred to Isabella the epithet 'She-Wolf of France', used by Shakespeare for that other 'unatural' Queen Margaret of Anjou (who had also led armies).

The supposition that her long residence away from court at Castle Rising in her son's reign was not voluntary but just punishment – imprisonment for murdering her husband – followed. Lurid legends grew up that she had gone insane through remorse, an appropriate fate for an adulteress and husband-murderer. The subsequent interpretations of the events of 1327 owed much to this unusual and sensational aspect of the rebellion. As played up in literary myth from the 1350s, sexual licence and wifely betrayal by a brazen – foreign – queen had combined with the subsequent violent death of her husband. Before this, the only female to raise a revolt against the current king had been Stephen's cousin Empress Matilda back in 1137–53, a time when Stephen's own wife (Matilda, Countess of Boulogne) had also led armies. This was too far distant to be well-known to the fourteenth-century, and the cases were not parallel as Empress Matilda had claimed the throne for herself and had had a better genealogical claim to it than Stephen as daughter and intended heiress of the previous king. The deposition and convenient death of an incompetent and much-disliked king was to be repeated in 1399, and three more kings died violently (one definitely murdered in the Tower, one probably murdered there, one killed in battle) in fourteen years in 1471–85. All were to be turned into compelling drama by Shakespeare. But the events of 1327 would continue to attract a special sense of horror, which can be explained by Isabella's unusual role and the powers acquired by her lover. Conversely, that was to revive sympathy for her as a feminist heroine denounced by 'sexist' medieval male chauvinist nobles in the late twentieth-century.

Edward II was removed from his initial prison at Lancaster's Kenilworth Castle on 3 April by Mortimer's trusted agents headed by Thomas, Lord Berkeley. He was transferred around the country in disguise in great secrecy by a 'posse' of Mortimer's close allies in evident fear of a rescue.[9] Presumably the massive fortifications of Kenilworth, former stronghold of Simon De Montfort's sons as they defied Henry III in 1265–6, were not thought adequate to protect Edward from rescue as Isabella and Mortimer did not trust Lancaster's loyalties. Also, the greedy Isabella had used her triumph to secure a large grant of £20,000 to pay her overseas debts incurred during her exile (in fact these had been paid already) plus an extra £11,843 and all Despenser's property and seems to have been intent on lavish overspending, which had apparently annoyed Lancaster. His complaints had been ignored, so was he capable of plotting to overthrow her and even to free the ex-king? Already in March the pro-Despenser friar Stephen Dunheved, Edward's ex-confessor and a former royal diplomat used on secret missions for Despenser's benefit, and some others had been accused of plotting to rescue Edward, and Lancaster might well have had inadequate security-measures in place with his officials at Kenilworth not as alert or 'action-ready' as Mortimer's even if he was not certain to let Edward escape. Removing Edward under the control of Mortimer's loyal men was as logical for the hard-headed Mortimer and the nervous queen as it was for Richard III to put his own 'trusties' in charge of the Princes in the Tower after a July 1483 plot to rescue them (see next but one section), and was only ominous in retrospect. 1350s chronicler Geoffrey Le Baker accused

Bishop Orleton of persuading Isabella to move Edward, but his source for this was unclear and as he made up various unlikely stories about the bishop this 'sensationalist' writer was presumably trying to implicate him in the subsequent murder. Berkeley's brother-in-law Lord Maltravers, a companion of Mortimer's from his time in command of Ireland in the mid-1310s and a fellow-exile in 1325–6, was Edward's official custodian and in charge of his escort. They proceeded in unobtrusive secrecy around the south-west Midlands and probably central south-west England too.

Edward's whereabouts are unclear after his initial move in early April (leaving Kenilworth Castle on the 3rd) to isolated Llanthony Priory in the south-eastern Welsh Marches, with stories linking him to Corfe Castle in Dorset near Maltravers' estates. This was probably the safest stronghold in southern England, as it was isolated from easy approach in the 'Isle of' Purbeck so that visitors could be watched more easily than at Kenilworth along the single road from the river-crossing at Wareham (which had a royal castle too). Its huge keep and surrounding towers on a 'motte' in a gap in the Purbeck Hills had been used as a prison for dangerous political enemies by King John, who had placed his niece Eleanor of Brittany and possibly the captive De Braoses there. A Mortimer henchman interviewed by Geoffrey le Baker in the 1350s, William Bishop, claimed Edward had been taken to the port of Bristol where there was a plot to free him, though no other trace of this has been found. The likelihood is that the distance from Llanthony to Corfe would rule this out as the king's initial destination and that he was taken around the south-eastern Marches and then into Gloucestershire; the Corfe story arose due to later events in 1329. It is more likely, but not known for certain, that he was held at one point in the royal castle at Bristol, the main seaport serving the south-west Midlands.

Bishop wrote that the ex-king was humiliated en route to Berkeley Castle, being crowned with straw, dressed poorly – though if this was true it would have been as a disguise – and forced to shave with ditchwater. The 'fake crowning' insult had also been carried out on Mortimer's arch-foe Despenser, so it was a genuine contemporary means of humiliation in 1327 not just a later glorification of Edward as suffering like Christ. When Edward was on his journey Bishop said he was only allowed thin clothes to wear (in the hope that he would get pneumonia?) by his jeering guards, and he was given poisoned food in the hope that he would die and solve the problem of what to do with him.[10] He ended up at Lord Berkeley's eponymous castle near Gloucester, an isolated and near-impregnable fortress, though this was probably as much due to the security threat after the alleged plot at Bristol as a planned prelude to an already-decided murder. Alison Weir in *Isabella: She-Wolf of France, Queen of England* (2005) believes from the Berkeley family documents that he was probably taken to Berkeley via Llanthony in April and that any sojourn elsewhere occurred later, possibly in July after the Dunheved gang's attack on the castle when it would have had to be checked and its personnel added to for improved security.[11] The evidence of the contemporary chronicler Adam Murrimuth and the stories collected by Froissart later in the century indicate that Lord Berkeley treated Edward well although Maltravers did not. The ex-king's traditional chamber in the castle, at least as shown to tourists thereafter, was not the noxious dungeon, open to foul smells that the gaolers hoped would poison their captive, of Baker's story. It was a reasonably-sized room on an upper storey, in residential quarters. The supposed pit full of rotting bodies which was intended to spread noxious vapours was certainly not adjacent to the king's chamber as the legend would have it. The lurid stories reported decades later of passers-by hearing sobbing and screams from Edward's apartment may well have been invented to generate sympathy for the 'martyr' ex-king, at a time several decades later when the reasons for his overthrow – his favouritism and incompetence – had faded from the public memory. Alternatively, if the writers had heard rather than invented the stories it would have been from local witnesses – staff at the castle, tenants on the Berkeley estates, or passing travellers on the Gloucester-Bristol road. Any screams heard from Edward's chambers could have been due to a nervous breakdown; the emotional Edward had had fits of depression then furious rage before, notably on Gaveston's murder.[12]

Edward was a constant threat to the regime from devoted loyalists trying to free him, however willing the 'political nation' had been to be rid of him earlier that year. On 1 July a warrant was issued for the arrest of the outlawed Edwardian partisan Thomas Dunheved, along with members of his gang, for what a letter by Berkeley on 27 July makes clear was a successful infiltration by raiders into Berkeley Castle.[13] Berkeley and Maltravers were both away at the time and a clerk called John Walwayn was in charge, logically supervising the current building work and clearly not expecting an attack. Thomas' brother Stephen, a Dominican friar of dubious reputation, had been the ex-king's envoy to the Pope a few years before – apparently concerning a divorce from Isabella – so he was a natural choice for a plot to free his old employer and had reason to fear Isabella's rule.[14] The guards were overpowered by the gang and the ex-king was carried off, probably aided by the current building work at the castle which could have enabled the raiders to disguise themselves as labourers and smuggle weapons into the buildings. The letter does not mention Edward's recapture, which therefore must remain uncertain, but the next plot to free him by Rhys Gruffydd in early September indicates that the latter's South Wales conspirators believed Edward to be back in custody then.[15] One theory has been raised that the Dunheved raid was the occasion of Edward's permanent escape from custody, as is argued by Ian Mortimer in *The Greatest Traitor: the Life of Roger Mortimer, Ruler of England 1327–1330*. But that ignores the information that the Rhys Gruffydd plotters heard that he was back in custody after the Dunheved attack, and others prefer a later date for any escape.[16] Dunheved eluded capture (and letters referring to the hunt for his gang only mention them as being at large, not the ex-king), but his brother Thomas was taken prisoner and flung in Newgate Prison in London where he died; another of the accused, William Aylmer, was arrested but released on bail by Isabella's orders then acquitted in October so he may have turned informer.

Edward's 'death' at Berkeley Castle on Monday 21 September 1321, the feast of St Matthew the Apostle, was duly announced at the royal court at Lincoln, the news being delivered to the court late on Wednesday the 23rd by one of his guardians (Thomas Gurney). On the 24th Edward III wrote to his cousin, the Earl of Hereford, saying that he had heard the news the previous night.[17] It was then publicly announced on the 28th, the last day of Parliament's meeting – a convenient date as it was too late for suspicious MPs or peers to make much comment on what might have been the cause. The date of death announced to the public is confirmed as being the 21st by contemporary chroniclers; and Berkeley and Maltravers duly claimed back expenses of £5 a day for looking after the live king until the 21st (and for looking after his body until the monks of St Peter's Abbey, Gloucester took over that duty on 21 October.) A grief-related illness was blamed, as was to be the case for the equally sudden and convenient death of the deposed Henry VI within days of his son and heir's killing in battle in 1471. His body was kept for several months under guard by Mortimer's underlings at Berkeley Castle and then by the monks of Gloucester until the tomb ordered at the Abbey was ready – suspiciously, the royal sergeant-at-arms in charge, Willliam Beaucaire, arrived there on the day of his death, not after it had been reported to the court, as if it was anticipated.[18] In December it was escorted to Gloucester for a 'low-key' funeral at the Abbey, which the court attended; the delay was not unusually long by mediaeval standards as the pageantry of the ceremony had to be arranged in detail and preparations such as the embalming made.[19] But the circumstances were dubious, both because he was only forty-two and in good health and because there was no public viewing of the body as was usual. Only one Mortimer partisan had been in charge of the body for several months, and no courtiers or great nobles had come to check that it was the real king. A local woman, not the royal physician, did the embalming. Only one party of visiting clerics was allowed to view Edward, and then standing at a distance and only viewing his uncovered head.[20] Claims were duly made that he had escaped or been freed in disguise.

The secrecy surrounding his captivity was such that an escape was plausible. Two years later his half-brother Edmund, Earl of Kent, could believe stories that he had really been kept alive at remote Corfe Castle under the care of its custodian (from 1329) Lord Maltravers, who had earlier been his captor at Berkeley. He accepted a statement from a Dominican friar that Edward II was alive, though the 'official' version of his confession when he was arrested said that the latter had 'raised a devil' to inform him (presumably to cover up the real source of the story). According to later accounts a couple of friars had seen a man resembling the ex-king dining in the castle's hall at Corfe, and apparently the castle's custodian in 1328–9, Sir John Pecche, also backed up the claim.[21] Ian Mortimer points out that the terminology of the subsequent treason charge accused Kent of trying to free a live Edward II, not a known 'fake' – did this slip let out the fact that Kent's accuser Roger Mortimer knew the Corfe resident to be genuine? Besides, was it treason to free a 'fake' king rather than a real one? If the charge was to be proved as treason (ie to Edward III by trying to overthrow him), the 'ex-king' who Edmund wanted to free surely had to be genuine – although Edmund could have been accused of treason by setting up or assisting a 'fake King' and this was not done. Was Mortimer careless in his terminology? Kent has usually been assumed to have been fooled by an insubstantial rumour, and so desperate to overthrow Roger Mortimer that he would believe anything. But it should be said that other important people believed the rumours too, notably Archbishop Melton of York who wrote in 1330 that he had heard definite news from a messenger that the ex-king was still alive. Accordingly he was prepared to write to Lord Mayor Simon Swainland of London on 14 January 1330 asking him for a loan of £200 to pay for supplying the ex-king (who was 'in a safe place at his own wish') with suitable clothes and six pairs of stout boots.[22] The archbishop said when questioned by Mortimer's investigators that the messenger who had informed him of the ex-king's whereabouts was a 'William Kingsclere', who was and is untraceable. Could Kent's unsupported claim, apparently based on what he had been told of Edward being seen at Corfe by certain friars, have been the sole source for all these beliefs?

Kent mounted a plot to free and reinstate Edward, which swiftly leaked out to the government resulting in his arrest and execution. Edward III pleaded with Mortimer to spare his uncle's life and was ignored, which may well have been a major factor in his brave decision to tackle the arrogant 'co-regent' himself – which he did with a band of armed retainers at Nottingham Castle that October. (Edward was so angry with Mortimer that after the arrest he was reported to have proposed to execute him without trial.) The stories of Edward II living at Corfe are usually presumed to have been invented or used by Mortimer, as a means of luring his enemy Edmund to his doom to provide an excuse for executing him.[23] It remains uncertain if the friars were in Mortimer's pay and were told to lure Kent into a plot, or if they were genuine partisans of the ex-king – linked to friar Stephen Dunheved? – whose indiscretions enabled Mortimer to discover Edmund's intentions. They may have genuinely heard gossip on a visit to Corfe that an unknown guest, who they saw dining in the hall but only at a distance, was the ex-king. Alternatively, Mortimer or Maltravers may have told their men at the castle to spread this story to encourage any spies who Edmund sent there to report back to him favourably. Pecche's role remains uncertain: was he acting to help Mortimer, or assisting Edmund and the ex-king? By early 1330 he was believed to be allied to Kent.

The murder and its elaborations

When Mortimer was speedily put on trial after his arrest in October 1330 it was claimed that he had had Edward II killed, and Gurney and another henchman sent to join the guard-party at Berkeley, William Ockley or Ockle/Ogle, were also indicted for it in their absence.[24] Gurney had a price of £100 put on his head and Ockley was priced at £40, so the latter was seen as the lesser criminal; Ockley was never heard of again but Gurney was captured by royal henchman De Thweng at Naples in 1335 and died at Bayonne in Gascony en route home. There was no mention of Lord Maltravers, who had formal charge of the ex-king, which suggests that either Edward III accepted that he was innocent or he still had powerful friends at court. It is apparent from a 1331 court case that Mortimer – then at Abergavenny – sent Ockley to Berkeley around 14 September, with orders to its custodians to take appropriate action to forestall a plot to rescue Edward which he had just been warned of in a letter from Anglesey by his official William de Shalford, lieutenant of North Wales.[25] This was presumably the Rhys ap Gruffydd plot – the timing of Dunheved's arrest warrant at 1 July indicates that his raid had occurred some time in late June. The geographically nearest of the contemporary church chroniclers, Adam Murrimuth, resident in the south-west in June-Deecmber 1327 as administrator of the vacant bishopric of Exeter, reported in his text in the mid-1330s that it was commonly said then that Gurney and Maltravers suffocated Edward with Mortimer's connivance.[26] He was the only local chronicler, and is thus the most crucial witness – at least as to what was rumoured at the time.

The subsequent despatch of Beaucaire from court to take charge of Edward's body before he was known to be dead would indicate that Mortimer knew what was to happen and when. The chronicle of St.Paul's Cathedral ('Annales Paulini') and the shorter of the two versions of an ongoing chronicle of contemporary events known as the Brut give little detail on Edward's death and just say he fell ill. The longer version – a little earlier than Murrimuth, and written by a sympathiser of the anti-Mortimer Earl of Lancaster – says unequivocally that he was 'falsely and traitorously murdered' by his 'false guardians'. It also presents the famous story that Gurney and Maltravers murdered him with a red-hot poker. It is confused about the site, naming it as Corfe at first and as

Berkeley when dealing with the subsequent enquiry in 1330, and also calls Lord Berkeley 'Maurice' not Thomas.[27] It also initially calls Gurney 'Tiourney', but gives him his correct name in its account of the 1330 regicide trial – which reflects the official proceedings in its account so presumably the entry relating to the murder was written before this event which publicised the co-murderer's correct name. The reference to Corfe may be due to confused memories of the later Kent plot which centred on Edward II being at that castle, or reflect real stories that Edward had been at Corfe not Berkeley in 1327. Ranulph Higden's *Polychronichon*, written at Chester by 1340 at the latest, agrees with this version, but he gives the means of death as a 'burning rod' thrust up Edward's bottom (ie to leave no marks) not a 'spit', presumably a kitchen one, inserted through a 'horn' as in the *Brut*.[28] Other chroniclers (e.g. the prior of Bridlington, who refers to 'common stories' which he scrupled to describe) seem to have been aware of the rumour, which has been suggested as being mixed-up with the contemporary story of how King Cnut's agents disposed of his rival Edmund 'Ironside' (by having him stabbed in the rear while on the lavatory) in 1016.

After c.1340 accounts that mention the poker, such as the Northern *Historia Aurea*, can be taken as using the earlier version. Some invented or had heard of new details – eg Geoffrey le Baker, c.1356.[29] Le Baker's account was full of mistakes, eg having the murderers being encouraged to commit regicide by a letter from Mortimer's ally Bishop Adam Orleton (who was in fact on the continent at the time on a mission to Rome). He seems to have been determined to present Edward as a 'martyr', ignoring his incompetent and often spiteful governance that had led to a well-supported rebellion when his elite abandoned him. Accordingly he piled on the details of his Christ-like humiliation on his journey to Berkeley, such as his having to walk and being 'crowned' with hay, and added details of his being tortured while at Bristol and attempts to poison him at Berkeley. The ex-king was then held down on his bed in an attempt to suffocate him by the murderers while they used the poker, but Le Baker does not name his source for this crucial scene. None of his extra details is corroborated by any other account, and he writes about presumably confidential details such as Lord Berkeley being banned from seeing Edward shortly before the murder by his co-plotters (presumably as they feared that he would refuse to help the killing and warn or help the victim) but does not include such significant real-life incidents as Beaucaire's arrival. This elaboration of the supposed details probably reflects the growth of myth about the event plus gossip 'going the rounds', not least as the new King Edward III seems to have tried to downplay and forget the embarrassing and sordid details of his accession and what had happened to his father in the years after 1330. Some modern writers, led by Ian Mortimer, have pointed out that all the chroniclers who report the details of the 'poker story' are northerners, further from the location of events than Murrimuth or the writers of the shorter 'London' version of the *Brut* who are unaware of it. It only appears in southern writings as late as 1346. Hence they could have been using a story put about by Roger's numerous noble enemies in the north, particularly the Earl of Lancaster. The use of the poker was anyway symbolically appropriate as a coarse reference to an appropriate end for a homosexual, and may have been devised as such by those who believed in that interpretation of Edward's extravagant devotion to his favourites.[30]

The inconsistencies concerning details of the 'rescue' or ' escape'

Alleged sightings of Edward in Europe followed in the 1330s; he was possibly the 'William de Waleys' (an appropriate pseudonym for a former 'Prince of Wales'?) who Edward III apparently had tracked down and met at Cologne in 1338. It has also been suggested that Mortimer's unexplained long visit to Abergavenny in September 1327, when he should have been preoccupied at court, was connected to Edward's escape and suspicion that he had fled to the loyal south Welsh borderlands.[31] Mortimer left court at Lincoln on 4 September after a Council request for him to go there in his role as the regional 'Justiciar' and investigate conspiracies – but this was before the revelation of the Rhys ap Gruffydd plot (see below) though he may have heard rumours of it earlier. Another – Scots – old friend of Edward II, the Earl of Mar, had been sent to the region by King Robert Bruce in June/ July to investigate the possibilities of rescuing him while Bruce was fighting the regency's army in County Durham, but he had probably left for home by this time. Was Mortimer trying to find out where Edward was hiding and who might be making use of him? Was he still looking for Stephen Dunheved and his friar-led network? Or had he recaptured Edward but decided that Berkeley Castle was too unsafe to hold him and so was planning to send him elsewhere in secret? Believers in Edward's escape have made the most of a letter written by Edward's custodian Thomas, Lord Berkeley, to Chancellor Hotham on 27 July which makes it clear that Edward had been rescued during a recent raid on his prison at Berkeley by would-be rescuers led by Thomas Dunheved.[32] What if he was not recaptured? He was more likely recaptured on this occasion, as there are no stories in the Berkeley family traditions of the rescue ending the ex-king's captivity, the payments to his captors in court documents continue unaltered, and the Rhys ap Gruffydd plot in early September indicates that his partisans believed he was still at Berkeley.[33] The famous 'Fieschi Letter' (see below), which clearly had some private information on the ex-king's circumstances, does not refer to him being rescued by a gang but escaping on his own – probably with a captor's (Berkeley or Maltravers?) connivance.[34]

It would seem unlikely that a 'genuine' Edward II, as the man who recounted the 'escape' story to Fieschi or his source, would need to hide the fact that he was rescued – the motive for lying would have been to safeguard the rescuers but the man who would have punished them, Mortimer, had already been executed. Mortimer's long sojourn at Abergavenny in September suggested to Ian Mortimer that he was carrying out an intense hunt for the ex-king which he needed to command in person, more important to him than matters at court.If he had recaptured Edward already by this date, why the long delay in returning to Court?[35] He might have been tracking down the rescuers after recapturing Edward – the documentation relating to the search for the Dunheved gang refers to a hunt for them but not for Edward. Logically, if Edward was being sought as well he would have been mentioned in the documentation albeit, as he was supposed to be safe in Berkeley Castle, in the guise of a pretender resembling the ex-king. If the ex-king was back at Berkeley, it was equally important for Mortimer to send someone reliable there to check that Edward's prison was secure this time.

It is possible that Edward was not recaptured quickly, and Mortimer had to organise a prolonged search. But if the warrant for Dunheved's arrest of 1 July means that his raid had already taken place by that date,[36] Mortimer would have been conducting the hunt for Edward during July not in September. He was with the court in July, so there was no desperate search for an escaped ex-king to superintend then. The Dunheved warrant may only mean that Mortimer had heard of the plot and its leader then, and that Dunheved actually attacked the castle after 1 July – when the warrant was already issued. But surely his attack would not have occurred much later? There is no indication that the September plot, by Rhys ap Gruffydd, had a similar success in rescuing Edward.

It has also been suggested that Edward, tracked down somewhere in the Welsh Marches after being freed by the Dunheveds (in July or August?), was killed in combat with Mortimer's men. Thus the latter had to provide a plausible excuse for having the ex-king's body in their charge, and Mortimer was forced to provide an 'official' death for the ex-king. This would explain the long delay between the announcement of Edward's death and the funeral – evidence of violence had to be concealed by Mortimer's hirelings before the body could be shown to anyone. In this case, it is significant that – as with the murdered Henry VI in 1471 – the whole body of the late King was not exposed to public view. When Ockley was sent back to Berkeley from Abergavenny on 14 September, was he escorting (or preparing the way for the return of) the recaptured body of Edward, found dead or killed in hiding in Wales? Or was he sent to tell his comrades that Mortimer had failed to find Edward and they had better arrange for a substitute to be killed so that the ex-king's death could be announced publicly? That way, if the real Edward reappeared anywhere he could be denounced as an impostor. But it would seem unlikely that if the Dunheved raid occurred before 1 July – or before the letter by Berkeley on the 27th, which is definitely the case – the ex-king could have been at large in the Marches and Maltravers and his henchmen guarding an empty cell without some rumour of either leaking out. Installing a substitute on Edward's cell would surely have taken some time to arrange.

The manuscript of Manuele Fieschi – a genuine story or a scam?

The truth of what happened during and after the Dunheved attack on Berkeley Castle – or another plot to free Edward later – largely depends on the veracity of one written statement apparently made to Edward III by a member of the Genoese trading dynasty of Fieschi around 1340.[37] This bizarre story, which a French archivist called Alexandre Germain found in the episcopal records at Montpellier and had privately printed in

1878, was examined by and mystified earlier English historians – Bishop Stubbs in his edition of the chronicles of Edward I and II's reigns (*Rolls Series*, 1882–3) and Thomas Tout in '*The Captivity and Death of Edward of Carnarvon*' in 1921.[38] It was taken more seriously by an Italian scholar, Anna Benedetti, who claimed to have identified the north Italian sites involved in 'Edward II's hiding – Cecima and Milazzo – in 1924, though her research was shown to have been flawed. The tomb at Cecima alleged to be Edward's, with its sculptures supposedly referring to his marital affairs, was thirteenth-century. Other, literary inconsistencies in the accounts of Edward's captivity and death and facts that might seem to support Fieschi were investigated by G.P. Cuttino and T. Lynam in 1978 ('Where is Edward II?', *Speculum* vol. liii, 3) and by R. Haines in 1996.[39]

Manuele Fieschi's letter to the ex-king's son gave a garbled account from 'Edward II' himself, now living in an isolated hermitage at Cecima in Lombardy, of how he escaped from heavily-guarded Berkeley Castle by changing clothes with a 'look-alike' attendant who had warned him that 'Lord' Gurney had arrived from Mortimer to kill him. He killed one porter, and wandered around England and then Ireland with a 'keeper', probably the attendant who had helped him escape, who was apparently keeping an eye on him for his protector – a mysterious 'Lord Thomas'. He was at Corfe Castle for eighteen months, which would take in the period 1328–9 and thus make it seem that he was at Corfe at the time that the friars hired by Edmund of Kent reported seeing him dining in the castle hall; then he sailed to Dublin. From Dublin he travelled back to England, sailed across the Channel from Sandwich to Brabant disguised as a friar, and called on the Pope at Avignon in 1331. He then pursued his devotion to the cult of the 'Three Kings' with a pilgrimage to Cologne – which is where Edward III sought out a man pretending to be him a few years later. After two years at Melasci/Milazzo in Northern Italy he moved to Cecima, where Fieschi found out about him.[40] The move was apparently connected to local warfare, which can be verified, making his first residence dangerous. Critics have pointed to its inconsistencies, particularly the difficulty of the tall and well-known Edward getting out of Berkeley Castle (which had a moat) even in disguise. Gurney was not a lord, and did the escape-story imply that some senior official at the castle – Maltravers? – had connived at Edward escaping or that the friendly 'keeper' had acted on his own? If the latter was true, presumably the 'keeper' had contacted 'Lord Thomas' for help after he had got Edward out of the castle.If Berkeley was 'Lord Thomas', he was not at his castle on 21–3 September so there would have been no time for him to hear of Gurney's arrival and its import and order the 'keeper' to save Edward from the murderers. He would thus have had to be informed of the rescue afterwards, and arrange for Edward to remain in hiding without letting Mortimer – who must have sent Gurney and thus wanted Edward dead – know what had happened.

Why would Edward be based at Corfe Castle for over a year, given that he would have been likely to be recognised there too? Was he sent there by his 'controller', ie Berkeley with the connivance of locally-based Maltravers, knowing that the garrison could be trusted to keep their mouths shut? (If so, the 'leak' by the visiting friars to Kent showed that this risk was miscalculated.) Corfe Castle, a major royal fortress and garrison since the time of Richard I, was swarming with men loyal to his ex-captors – Maltravers was a local landowner and in 1329 took over the castellanship of the castle from Sir John Pecche. The village attached to the castle was too small for Edward to stay there long without being noticed, so he must have been lodged within the castle. He might have been able to remain inconspicuous among a large and busy household in the castle for some months, with all visitors being 'screened' for reliability. But eighteen months was a long period, and if he had been staying in the castle with local connivance there was no guarantee that Maltravers would not come to inspect it and hear rumours of his presence (if he did not know already). Pecche was later to inform Kent that Edward had been at the castle, suggesting that the ex-king was there while he was its castellan in 1328–9. But the fact that Edward was not swiftly moved when Pecche left – if he had left when Pecche did, he would not have been there when the friars arrived – indicates that his 'guardians' regarded his staying on under Maltravers' guard as safe. The implication of this is that not only Maltravers but Mortimer knew he was there. If Edward had been there without the effective regent's knowledge in 1329–30, we could have expected to see a thorough (but secret?) investigation and arrests (less easy to conceal) during the period between the discovery of the Kent plot early in 1330 and Mortimer's own fall that October. This did not occur.

If Edward was the man who Kent's emissaries saw dining in the hall and heard was the ex-king, this implies that his identity was rumoured among the residents and that he was not being particularly careful about his presence. This was dangerous; surely he and 'Lord Thomas' would need to see that Mortimer did not hear of his whereabouts. Pecche, assuming him to be loyal to Kent and not a Mortimer agent, could be trusted; Maltravers surely could not. If Edward, or 'Lord Thomas' supervising him, had no reason to conceal his presence from Mortimer's agents it would suggest that Mortimer knew he was there. But this cannot be used as an argument that Mortimer did not seek to kill Edward in 1327. Gurney's mission to Berkeley in September 1327 was clearly believed to be with regicidal intent when the incident was investigated in 1330; and who but his patron Mortimer would have issued such orders to him? The answer may lie with the failure of historians to distinguish between the intentions of Mortimer and of Isabella in September 1327. Isabella has long been assumed to be as villainous and cold-blooded as her paramour, intent on killing her husband to preserve her regime. The 'She-Wolf of France' was popularly believed to have been imprisoned for life in her Norfolk residence, Castle Rising, by her disgusted son when he discovered the truth – and possibly to have been insane too (due to remorse?). But the latest studies of her role in 1330–58 show that this was not so and that she was treated with honour and allowed to visit court. There is no proof of her insanity, though stories of mental problems and a probable nervous breakdown in the aftermath of her fall in 1330 may be correct.[41] She was certainly held in confinement at Windsor Castle for a couple of years (with the king's personal doctor often in attendance), though that may have been to prevent her fleeing abroad and to show the public that she was paying for her crimes – which undoubtably included embezzling a large sum of money and acquiring much property, most of which was confiscated. But once the scandal of her usurpation and association with Mortimer faded she was slowly rehabilitated at court, and her recorded piety should not be written off as hypocrisy or belated repentance for murdering her husband. What if she had not been involved in the apparent orders to Gurney to kill Edward in September 1327, and it had been Mortimer's idea? And if the murder attempt failed and 'Lord Thomas' (Berkeley?) assumed custody of the escaped Edward in hiding, Isabella could have been approached to secure her help in looking after him and stopping Mortimer from hunting him down. Assuming Gurney to have been sent to kill Edward by Mortimer back in September 1327, someone – Isabella on Lord Berkeley's behalf? – must have persuaded Mortimer to accept the ex-king's survival under guard at Corfe in 1328–9. Does this account for the fact that Isabella was evidently not in disgrace for the rest of her life after 1330?

Spending time in Ireland and Flanders seem a little illogical for an escaped Edward – would not his former principality, Wales, have more loyalists likely to hide him? The answer may have been that Edward was not in control of his own destiny at this point; the role of his 'escort' in determining his route is unclear but 'Lord Thomas'/ Berkeley – loyal to Mortimer, but not to the point of regicide – may well not have wanted to risk Edward mixing with potential rebels. It may also be significant that Mortimer had extensive lands in Ireland, as heir to the De Lacey lands around Trim Castle, and had served there as Edward's lieutenant in the mid-1310s, before his disgrace by Despenser – could he rely on a local network of his servants and tenants there to keep an eye on Edward? Edward seems to have been a bemused pawn in his captors' hands during the months after his deposition in January 1327, with or without stories of his weeping and the screams heard at Berkeley – which may have been exaggerated by the non-contemporary Le Baker to win sympathy. Thus it is possible that he had no clear plan of where to go, quite apart from fearing recapture by Mortimer. Berkeley could thus have 'directed' his route, sending him away from potential sympathisers to keep out of the way in Ireland.

Fieschi said that Edward went to the papal court at Avignon to see Pope John XXII. This could be checked with the papal bureaucracy, in which Fieschi himself served from 1336 after arriving some time earlier to serve his cousin Cardinal Luca Fieschi, so he may have checked this himself though this is not stated; it would be risky to invent this detail which if untrue could be denied. Fieschi certainly had possible financial motives in approaching Edward III with information on his 'father', or a desire for preferment as a reward for keeping quiet. But we shall see that the priority of these motives is not borne out by events.

'Edward's supposed 'protector', 'Lord Thomas', was probably his former captor Lord Berkeley, owner of the eponymous castle, and Fieschi may not have given his surname as his informant (Edward?) was trying to protect this man. But this raises an important point – would Berkeley really risk being arrested and executed by the furious Mortimer, a man known for his ruthlessness and violence pre-1327 as a Marcher lord operating not too far from Berkeley's own estates, if the latter found out that he was harbouring Edward II? Does this mean that Mortimer 'must' have known what was going on and Berkeley had his approval? Or was Berkeley initially looking after Edward for Isabella, who ensured that he did not face Mortimer's wrath for disobeying orders and who only told Mortimer that her ex-husband was alive later (eg during the Kent trial)? Had Mortimer tried to have Edward killed in September 1327, but when his victim escaped accepted the Queen-Mother's orders not to repeat the attempt? Alternatively, was Berkeley now looking after Edward on Mortimer's orders? As long as Edward did not reappear everybody would think him to be dead so Mortimer could go along with it. (This is Ian Mortimer's theory). Berkeley may have acted alone in September 1327 in saving Edward, subsequently telling Isabella who made Mortimer accept it – though as his personal chaplain later wrote a chronicle in the 1380s featuring Edward II's murder he clearly did not tell some of his staff what wsa really going on. As with Richard III and his possible secret exile rather than murder of the 'Princes in the Tower', we have to rely on the characters of the accused as seen by their other actions. Mortimer was a ruthless man preferring to kill possible threats such as the Earl of Kent in 'pre-emptive' strikes, and after the Dunheved and Rhys ap Gruffydd plots there were serious risks in letting Edward go free with only one guardian to ensure he did not link up with plotters. He shamelessly forced Edward III to agree to execute his uncle Kent on a charge of trying to free Edward II, which was legally risky as the allegedly alive ex-king was supposed to be dead by this point so it was not a crime to try to rescue him. It is more likely that this unscrupulous Marcher warlord made at least one attempt to kill Edward (possibly without telling Isabella) than that he meekly agreed to stage a fake killing in order to avoid the sin of regicide.

The story contains much precise information that can be verified about the king's capture and captivity in 1327, details not then available in chronicles that an Italian writing some time between 1335 and 1338 (with no apparent contacts in Edward II's entourage) would have found out for himself. How did he include little-known details of events in

1327 without interviewing one of a limited number of the king's captors who knew them – or the king? The details of how Edward sailed from Chepstow along the South Wales coast and was captured in Glamorgan in 1326 were not generally known, nor was the arrival of Gurney at Berkeley in September 1327. It is highly unlikely that one of the few Mortimer loyalists to be at Berkeley at the time, or to have been at court and privy to Mortimer's secret mission, would turn up at Avignon and gossip about the detail of events to a low-ranking papal bureaucrat. The only logical candidate for this role is Mortimer's ambassador William Walwyn, who announced Edward II's death to the Pope; but this was years before Fieschi arrived in Avignon. (In that case, did Walwyn talk to Cardinal Luca?) The alternative is that Fieschi deliberately collated all the accounts he had heard of sightings of 'Edward II' across England, Ireland, and Europe between 1328 and 1336 – the Corfe details could be worked out from the fact that in 1329 Earl Edmund of Kent had heard that his half-brother was at the castle. In this case Fieschi had heard that the ex-king had been seen in Dublin and Flanders, and had called on the Pope. As a Papal official, he could find the latter out from gossip at the Papal court – but probably not the Irish story. Thus his story could be backed up by all those reports that had emerged of the 'sightings', and make Edward III think that they all referred to the same man – the hermit of Cecima, who had now told his story to Fieschi.[42] But in this case, the logical outcome for Fieschi's letter to Edward III would have been the latter demanding proof. And Fieschi must have been able to lay his hands on a plausible 'Edward II' – i.e. the hermit of Cecima – and confident that he could carry off his 'imposture' in front of Edward III or his representatives. Otherwise there was no point in staging an elaborate 'scam' on the king.

Fieschi's supporters have argued that one of his kinsmen, Niccolinus de Fieschi, was on a Genoese embassy to Edward III in 1336, receiving the large sum of 8,000 marks from the king. Shortly afterwards Lord Berkeley was acquitted of all charges related to the regicide and Queen Isabella had her expenses dramatically increased as a mark of favour. Could this imply that the embassy had brought news of Edward II being alive in Lombardy and made arrangements for the Fieschi family to guard him in alliance with his son?[43] Even if the supposed 'hermit' that Fieschi interviewed was a fake – why would the escaped king have troubled to reveal his story and put himself in danger of murder? – Fieschi may have picked up genuine rumours of what had happened and constructed a story around them to secure money and ecclesiastical advancement. The inclusion in the Fieschi story of events like 'Edward's appearance in Cologne would suggest that he had heard of the latter incident, where a 'pretender' was arrested some time before Edward III arrived. In September 1338 Edward, already in the Low Countries to win financial and military backing from anti-French factions in Flanders, made a journey to Cologne during a visit to his north German allies and had an interview a few miles away outside Koblenz with a man called 'William le Waleys' – probably Fieschi's 'client' from Lombardy.[44]

In this case, Fieschi could have incorporated the story he had heard about 'le Waleys' to add verisimilitude to a partly concocted story. Notably, the English Royal household accounts for 1338–40 make two references to 'William Galeys', arrested in Cologne, who claimed to be Edward III's father.[45] The story of a 'pretender' turning up in Cologne in 1338 does not depend on Fieschi's letter alone. Nor is it mere coincidence that Edward III himself, on the continent seeking funds to attack France at the time, made a point of visiting Cologne during his German tour. Edward was an adventurous and impulsive person who was to enjoy fighting in person in small-scale combats (as in a French incursion at Calais in 1350) when he need not have risked his life, and he clearly wished to investigate the 'Waleys' affair personally. This argues that he had reason to deal personally with the pretender, rather than loftily dismissing the imposture – and as his regime was unchallenged in England the only threat that a pretended 'Edward II' could pose was if the French King Philip VI invited the latter to Paris as his puppet. Unlike with the 'Princes in the Tower' or Richard II, there were no widespread rumours of uncertainty as to the ex-king's fate in England or on the continent. The case of Edmund, Earl of Kent, 's belief in the real Edward II being hidden at Corfe Castle in 1329–30 had been portrayed by Edward's post-October 1330 government as a cunning 'sham' arranged by Mortimer to trap Kent, and the contemporary chronicles have no evidence of men whispering to each other that Edward II was still alive in the 1330s (as they did about Richard II and the Prince's years after their disappearance). More to the point, Edward II had been so widely detested among the governing class in the mid-1320s that there were no major plots to restore the ex-king, as there were to be on Richard II (or his Mortimer heirs), Henry VI, Edward V, and Richard of York's behalf.

Arguably Kent had been intending to free, not restore, his half-brother in 1329–30, and no 'cult' of the murdered king arose at Edward II's tomb as was to be the case with the equally incompetent and controversial (but more saintly) Henry VI. The depositions of Richard II and Edward V led to swift revolts by their adherents within months, which rumours of their deaths (and the production of Richard's body) did not stop. Nor were their successors' regimes secure from plots for years; Edward V's usurping successor was deposed within two years. But despite this endemic tendency to fission within the English governing class there was no move to reinstate Edward II – even though Mortimer and Isabella were controversial and their relationship a potential scandal. Clearly, Edward II's misrule had made that option out of the question for those nobles and gentry who disliked the new regime. Once the regency was overthrown in October 1330, this potential cause for revolt was diminished. This is not, however, to deny that an insecure Edward III could have feared for his regime's security as the cost of his new French wars grew in the mid-1330s – particularly if a pretender was to turn up in France. His personal intervention in Cologne was in character, whether or not he feared that the pretender might be genuine. But it is significant that he does not seem to have ceased his previous trust of the Fieschi family in his private continental business dealings, as he would surely have done had he believed one of them to be trying to blackmail him.

One theory is that the 'Fieschi letter' was written after 'le Waleys' appeared at Cologne, and that this incident encouraged him to write it; but Ian Mortimer argues that it preceded the pretender's visit and indeed led to it, the claimant 'le Waleys' being Fieschi's client. In this argument, the legal role of 'le Waleys' escort should be considered carefully. He was a north Italian royal sergeant-at-arms called Francisco Forcetti/Forzetti – endowed with powers to enforce royal warrants. But such writs had no legal powers on the continent, except in Edward's Gascon dominions. Forzetti therefore could not have 'arrested' the pretender, although he could have received custody of him from a sympathetic local official whose masters had ordered the arrest at Edward's request. So had Forzetti, as a 'local' who knew Lombardy, gone to Cecima to collect the pretender from the Fieschi family, or joined them en route to Cologne to take him before the king? If the pretender had no Italian connection and had only been wandering about the Rhineland claiming to be 'Edward II', why use an Italian to take custody of him?

Fieschi's supporters, such as Ian Mortimer, thus point out that the mysterious 'William de Waleys' who Edward III met near Cologne in 1338 was escorted there by a north Italian. Also Fieschi's kinsman, Niccolinus Fieschi, had arrived in England from Italy in April 1336, as ambassador from Genoa and was trusted by Edward III with important diplomatic negotiations in London in the following years. Logically, the earlier letter which the 'Fieschi letter' says that Manuele had written to Edward III with the news of his father's survival could have been delivered by Niccolinus on that occasion. The fact that Edward III had now been alerted to his father's survival (or the possible threat of a plausible impostor at large in Europe) would explain why he was so keen to go to Cologne in person in 1338 to meet the 'pretender', rather than just sending an envoy to interview and arrest him. Indeed, the way in which Edward III felt able to use Niccolinus as a diplomat would indicate that he trusted the man who had brought news of his father's survival, rather than regarding him and his cousin Manuele as blackmailers. It is possible that the castle of 'Milasci', where the Fieschi letter says that 'Edward II' had lived before he moved to Cecima, is not the 'Melazzo' which Anna Benedetti identified in her 1920s investigation but 'Mulazzo', which is close to family estates owned by Fieschi relatives. Ian Mortimer thinks that if this is the case the Fieschi family were already in charge of Edward by 1334, and that it is significant that Cardinal Luca Fieschi's nephew Niccolo Malaspina had estates near both Mulazzo and Cecima. Malaspina may also have had connections to Forzetti, the pretender's 'escort' to Edward III in 1338.[46]

The visitor to Cologne, who was with an Italian, was logically the 'hermit' from Cecima who the Fieschi were safeguarding, brought to the king to confirm Manuele's story. As former Prince of Wales, 'the Welshman' was an apt name for Edward II to use. The contemporary usage was for men to adopt the name of their birthplace, as with the Earl of Kent (Edmund of Woodstock) or later John of Gaunt (Ghent) and Henry IV (Henry of Bolingbroke). Edward II had been born in Caernarfon, as his father was building the new castle there to control North Wales in April 1284. In any case, if the hermit was soon shown to be a fake, why did Edward III keep him at his court in Cologne for weeks[47] instead of throwing him in the nearest prison or having him sent back to England in chains? In any event, Fieschi only had his current English posts – including the archdeaconry of Nottingham – confirmed by Edward III and gained no further grants of English benefices (though one Italian see did come his way, Vercelli in 1343). So if his story was an attempt at blackmail for a senior post it did not get far. It is noticeable that the Fieschi story gives Isabella a more damning role than is usually agreed in accounts of the ex-king's imprisonment, suggesting that Fieschi might have been threatening to publicise facts to her detriment.

It is noticeable however that Edward III made little effort to publicise or lament his (disgraced) father's presumed murder even once he was secure as ruler and could have blamed it all on his mother's executed paramour Mortimer and exonerated her. Both the owner of Berkeley Castle and thus Edward II's gaoler, Lord Berkeley (who blandly claimed he had not heard Edward II was dead until 1330), and the widely-rumoured murderer Lord Maltravers, in personal charge of the ex-king, escaped conviction once Edward III was given the chance to act and avenge his father by Mortimer's arrest. Berkeley's unlikely excuses of innocence were accepted by Parliament in November 1330 – he claimed he had been away from home at the time of the supposed killing, had no knowledge of it, and was not even aware Edward II was dead.[48] No attempt was made to challenge this story, showing that despite the weakness of his case he was not selected as an appropriate scapegoat for the alleged regicide. Was this politically necessary so that he or his friends did not start spreading stories that Edward II was really alive – or out of gratitude for him saving the ex-king from Mortimer's henchman Gurney?

Maltravers was more certainly guilty, as having personal custody of the ex-king and thus receiving any orders from Mortimer to murder him. He had been at Berkeley at the time, and if Gurney had tried to kill Edward II on Mortimer's orders Maltravers had allowed him to do it rather than ordering him to wait while he checked with Isabella. But he was allowed to flee abroad. A warrant was belatedly issued for his arrest, but only regarding his part in the entrapment of the Earl of Kent on Mortimer's behalf. In 1334 he informed Edward III that he had information of great value to him, which he delivered to Edward's emissary William Montagu, and by 1339 he was acting for the king in Flanders. Submitting to Edward on a royal visit there in 1345, he was allowed to return home quietly in

1352 and was acquitted by Parliament of his part in Kent's execution.[49] Throughout the case, it was Kent's entrapment and execution which was relentlessly pursued, not Edward II's murder.

The information which Maltravers passed on to Edward might have concerned his father's survival – or else just have been an attempt to blackmail or excuse his way into a royal pardon. As custodian of Corfe in 1329–30, he could say if Edward II had really been there – and if Isabella and/or Mortimer had known about it. The other principal accused, Mortimer's agent Thomas Gurney who had had personal charge of the ex-king in his travels as a captive in 1327 and had been at Berkeley at the time of the alleged killing, was of a lower social class than the noblemen Berkeley and Maltravers and was thus a more likely scapegoat. For one thing, there was no legal requirement to try him before a body of his peers who might want to acquit him as forced to carry out any illegal acts by Mortimer. Gurney was pursued and was eventually caught in Naples but died under arrest in 1338 while being escorted home, and no more was heard of Gurney's fellow-henchman William Ockley. One suggestion has been made that Ockley, or another one of Mortimer's thuggish 'henchmen' at Berkeley who were directly involved in any killing, was 'William de Waleys'.[50] But why then was he not brought back to England for trial, or quietly executed in Cologne as an impostor? Even if 'Waleys' was not Edward II, he seems to have impressed the new King and been released after a few weeks in his company – suggesting that he was innocent of any part in the murder.

It is less likely that the 'hermit' who Fieschi allegedly talked to in Italy was a figment of his imagination. He would have known that Edward III would demand that he or his emissaries met the man to check his pretensions, and unless they were satisfied Fieschi could not expect any reward (or blackmail money, if that was the reason for him approaching the King). The man who appeared in Cologne to meet Edward III, claiming to be his father as seen from the Wardrobe accounts, was escorted there by a 'Lombard' (probably Florentine) Royal sergeant-at-arms, Francsico Forzetti – a man seemingly employed by Edward III exclusively on Italian business, and apparently linked to the Fieschi dynasty.[51] Logically he was the 'hermit' from Cecima. But it is not certain that the story the hermit told Manuele Fieschi was accurate, and that the escape in Septmber 1327 was faithfully recounted.It is possible that Thomas Dunheved's raiders, who penetrated Berkeley Castle in July 1327 and overpowered some of the garrison, did free the ex-king and that both Mortimer and Edward III were aware of that. Alternatively, if Edward II was recaptured later he was rescued at a later date before – or on – 21 September 1327. Significantly, a written statement about the Dunheved raid made by Mortimer's agent William Walwayn at the time claimed that Edward was kidnapped by the attackers and says nothing about his recapture. Walwayn was later sent to Pope John XXII to explain the ex-king's death, possibly being chosen to convey the 'official story' to make up for his earlier burst of honesty.[52]

The argument that Mortimer and/or Maltravers knew that the ex-king had escaped but not what had happened to him bears more weight if it refers to events in September. If Gurney's arrival at Berkeley or another plot had led to Edward's escape, whether or not with the connivance of one of his captors, Mortimer would then have been arranging for the captive's death to be announced quickly to make any 'Edward' who appeared in loyal Wales seem a pretender. Only if Berkeley had told Isabella or Mortimer where Edward was hiding could Mortimer have relaxed in the knowledge that he would not reappear at the head of a revolt. Thus Maltravers could also have been able to reassure Edward III in 1330 that his father had not been murdered, if not to say what had happened to him. The ex-king may have died in hiding in Wales, or escaped to the continent and was 'spotted' there some time after 1330 – which enabled pretenders such as 'William de Waleys' to emerge claiming to be him. A hermitage would be a logical place for an ex-king to take refuge, possibly after seeking a papal blessing for his action – and Fieschi could have heard about that at the Papal court, where he was resident by 1336 as an aide to his cousin Cardinal Luca Fieschi. He could then have decided to enact a 'scam' on Edward III using the hermit of Cecima – or, more likely given that Edward trusted his family with important diplomatic work after 1336, have told him the truth. Indeed, the hermit may have been Edward II in person – though it seems risky that he would have run the risk of having his peaceful existence ended by English royal agents seeking his extradition as a possible threat (or even killing him as a fake?). It is possible that either the genuine Edward II, or a man claiming to be him, turned up at the papal court around 1331 and that it was this story which gave the Papal bureaucrat Fieschi the idea of constructing his story.

If Edward II was genuinely the hermit of Cecima, his journey as far as Cologne to see his 'son' may indicate that he knew he could take that risk as he could prove his identity. His non-arrest there shows that Edward III believed him. The new king logically ordered Fieschi to have the claimant sent to him to be investigated and then released the 'hermit' as he was no political threat. Quite plausibly Fieschi was not seeking money or an extra benefice at all by his letter, but wanted to let Edward III know of his father's whereabouts – at the latter's request? – and arrange a secret meeting. This may sound like the plot of a modern mystery 'thriller' rather than a genuine event in fourteenth-century international politics, and has duly been scorned by 'mainstream' historians as unlikely. But it would explain Edward's apparent need to interview and generous treatment of the 'pretender' William le Waleys, and the pardon of not only Lord Berkeley but the more obviously guilty Maltravers.

Indeed, the reason for Mortimer being gagged at his public trial could have been to stop him spitefully revealing the escape to present the new king with political problems, and Berkeley was released and Maltravers not pursued vigorously because Edward III was convinced that they were not regicides after all. Notably, Edward II's body was not examined by a doctor, nor embalmed by the usual officials but by an anonymous 'wise-woman' (who was then placed in custody), and was not paraded in public to show that he was safely dead. Henry IV did this with Richard II in 1400, though Mortimer was as keen as Henry to make it plain that any claimant to be the deposed king was a usurper unworthy of support. And why did Isabella summon the 'wise-woman' to her court later that year – because she had doubts over whose the body had been? Edward III might have been expected to disassociate himself from the widespread belief that Edward II's death was the result of murder, to benefit him with a conspicuous display of filial piety, once he had executed the presumed murderer Mortimer in 1330. To claim that the late king had been unjustly murdered and organise a lavish memorial ceremony would for a start show that he was dead, which his half-brother Kent had not believed in 1329. But Isabella did not found her chantry at Bablake in Coventry to pray for Edward II's soul until 1342 despite the political advantages of doing so earlier, and Ian Mortimer has unearthed the interesting fact that Archbsihop Melton's ordinances for the church of Sibthorpe in Yorkshire – served at the time by a priest who had been abroad in the service of the

Fieschi dynasty in Lombardy in the mid-1330s and may have been 'lent' to them by Melton – were revised by the archbishop to definitely include Edward II amng the dead patrons to be prayed for in 1343. Edward III certainly did not visit Edward II's tomb in Gloucester until 1343 too[53] – so it is possible that the ex-king may have died abroad as late as that date and been secretly buried then.

Chapter 3

Richard II, 1400 – More Certainly Dead. But Was it Murder or Suicide? And Why All the Pretenders?

In September 1399 a second controversial king who had ruled in an autocratic manner, alienating his elites, and given widespread power to a narrow group of resented 'favourites', was overthrown – Richard II, grandson of Edward III. Like Edward II he had already been forcefully 'reined in' by a tightly-knit group of resentful magnates excluded from power, led by his close relatives – in this case the 'Lords Appellant', headed by his uncle Duke Thomas of Gloucester and his cousin Henry of Bolingbroke, earl of Derby, in 1387–8. His 'favourites', like Edward II's in 1308 and 1312, had been targeted by the victorious 'junta' of sernior nobles, with his chief ally Robert de Vere, earl of Oxford and recently made duke of Ireland, having to flee abroad and his tutor Sir Simon Burley being tried by a rigged tribunal and then executed in defiance of the king's pleas. Like Edward II with the 'Lords Ordainers', the king had resented this humiliation and sought vengeance as soon as practicable, staging a counter-coup to restore royal power and subsequently hunting down and murdering one of the most confrontational leaders of the group that had humiliated him, in this case Duke Thomas – in both cases of royal vengeance, Thomas of Lancaster in 1322 and Thomas of Gloucester in 1397, the victim had been accused of seeking the king's throne too. Like Edward II in 1322–7, Richard in 1397–9 set up a dangerously narrowly-based regime centred on the assertion of untrammelled royal power, regarded subsequently as 'tyranny' and denounced as such (with execution of a group of its leaders, some by lynch-mobs) once it was overthrown. In both cases relatively minor and obsequiously pro-royal figures within the elite took power under a suspicious, vindictive and confrontational sovereign, though in Richard's case there was a reasonably wide group of royal intimates, nicknamed the 'duketti' ('little dukes'), who held national and regional power and shared out the rewards in lands, offices and titles not just a father and son (the Despensers) and their clients as after 1322. In both cases, the sovereign then fell to an invasion masterminded by or in the name of their presumed heirs – in Edward II's case, his elder son was used as a 'frontman' by his alienated wife Isabella and her lover, and in Richard II's case his cousin Henry of Bolingbroke, who should have succeeded his father John of Gaunt as Duke of Lancaster in February 1399 but was already in exile and was denied this addition to his prestige and resources by the suspicious Richard. Isabella invaded to prevent her husband's sporadic attempts to divorce her, and Henry invaded to regain his confiscated ducal inheritance and arguably to assure his right of succession in place of the rival contenders, his under-age cousin Edmund Mortimer (whose family had been treated by Richard as his heirs earlier in the reign but were now not so favoured) and his uncle Duke Edmund of York (plus York's son Edward, one of the royal favourites).

Both Edward II's and Richard II's impressive structure of royal power then came crashing down in weeks as a small invading army was joined by large numbers of the alienated provincial elites amidst a degree of popular enthusiasm, and the deserted kings ended up in flight and under arrest and some of their favourites dead at the hands of lynch-mobs or executed in the grisly manner reserved for traitors after biased trials In this era, no king had a standing army and the royal regimes rested on the assent of a pyramid of local landowners, from major regional nobles to junior manorial lords of gentry rank and under them farm tenants – who were all called upon when needed to turn out for military service when required. If an unpopular king or his unpopular war was deserted in an effective 'strike', this was politically and sometimes physically fatal to them – as happened to Edward II in 1326 and to Richard II (who was also at the time away campaigning in Ireland) in late summer 1399. There are many parallels between Edward and Richard, both 'isolated' and suspicious autocrats with a high opinion of their roles and a lack of interest in the dominant military 'chivalric' ethos of the aristocratic elite.

Both were the sons of much-respected (and feared) great military leaders and imposing and ruthless 'strongmen', namely the ferocious Edward I and the paragon of fourteenth-century chivalric virtues, Edward III's eldest son Edward of Woodstock (known later as the 'Black Prince'), hero of the misnamed Hundred Years' War and victor of the crushing English triumphs at Poitiers in 1356 and Najera in 1367. Edward I conquered Wales and nearly conquered Scotland, and Edward of Woodstock played a starring role under his father at his first battle, Crecy in October 1346, aged sixteen and then captured the unlucky King John II of France and destroyed his army at Poitiers and destroyed the Castilian army at Najera before succumbing to a debilitating mystery illness and dying aged forty-six, before his father. Both fathers had an overwhelming reputation in their lifetimes and after (though marred to modern eyes by their atrocities on civilians), and both were in sharp contrast to their successors. The latter were not their initial heirs and came to the throne unexpectedly, Edward II replacing his deceased elder brother Alfonso and Richard (born at Bordeaux while his father was governor of Aquitaine) replacing both his father and his deceased elder brother John. In Richard's case he seems to have had a wider base of support, but he had the disadvantage of coming to the throne aged ten under a regency and so spending much of his formative years at the centre of a hierarchical and flattering court, not with a normal upbringing within the courtly elite. He was then at the centre of the major crisis of the 'Peasants' Revolt' in June 1381 as a huge and disparate army of lower-class regional farmers and labourers, mostly from south-east England, marched on London demanding political, judicial, and social reform to ameliorate the socio-economic stresses that were following the 'Black Death'. The targeted regency government, resented for its 'unjust' and poorly-crafted poll tax, fell to pieces as London was subjected to 'mob rule' and foreign merchants and government ministers were hunted down and killed with impunity, and at the crucial confrontation between the main camp of rebels outside the City and the fourteen-year-old king – who the armed and turbulent protesters insisted grant their list of demands – the rebel spokesman Wat Tyler, a loud and confrontational blacksmith from Maidstone, had a row with the king's attendants and ended up stabbed to death in public. Whether or not this was an accidental quarrel that got out of hand or a targeted killing of the rebel leader by government loyalists to decapitate the rebel army, the shock of the killing in front of the uneasy and potentially violent crowds led to the danger of a massacre of the royal escort, and it was Richard who seized control and reportedly rode over to present himself to the rebels (who had always pledged loyalty to him in person while hating his 'evil counsellors') as their leader and take them away from the scene to a new camp.[1] Arguably, the inexperienced and until then politically marginalised King saved the day by his quick thinking.

The regime was duly able to rally its troops, Richard promised to grant the rebels their demands and they went home – and once their armies had dispersed the government duly reneged on most of the demands, staged a show of force, held mass-trials of arrested rebels, and conducted judicial mass killings to restore order. How sincere Richard had ever been in his promises and whether he believed that he had a personal bond to his people (as opposed to the incompetent and divisive elite that had failed him in 1381) is still debated – but his intelligence and capability for ruling were obvious at an early age even though he was worryingly distrustful of his relatives and reliant on a small group of friends even in his teens. His distrust verged on paranoia at times well before the shock of his physical and political restraint by the noble 'junta' of the 'Lords Appellant' in late 1387, and as early as 1385 he was plausibly planning with his friends' support to have his uncle and ex-regent John of Gaunt, Duke of Lancaster, murdered to pre-empt a supposed coup. The annoyed and alarmed John (whose luxurious London residence, the Savoy Palace, had been sacked by rebel peasants in 1381) firstly fled London to Yorkshire to collect his armed retainers, then rode South to surround the king's country residence at Sheen (now Richmond) in Surrey and burst in to demand that Richard explain what he was up to. Richard denied it all and John more or less accepted this, lacking evidence,[2] but rumours of royal plots to murder his ambitious relatives were to resume in the mid-late 1390s and seem to indicate a degree of sporadic paranoia mixed with a lack of political sense. This all had bearings on the question of how Richard died after John's son Henry – who Richard had left unprotected in the Tower with other courtiers to face an angry mob of peasants with murder on their minds in June 1381 – overthrew him.

How then did the capable and charismatic, if mercurial, Richard come to be overthrown in 1399? This also has a bearing on events after the coup, and the number of well-believed rumours that he was still alive and pretenders claiming to be him. A supposedly much-hated tyrant would not have attracted this sort of devotion, and if his replacement Henry of Bolingbroke had been the popular leader of a well-supported revolution he should not have faced such widespread opposition or attempts to restore his predecessor. And why did Henry's principal supporters in September 1399, the Percy dynasty (earls of Northumberland and dominant landowning family in north-east England), then try to restore 'Richard' or his Mortimer heirs in 1403? Any consideration of Richard II's character and its connection to his downfall in 1399 is under a disadvantage from the sources. History is written by the winners, and nobody in the late mediaeval period was more careful in that regard than his replacement Henry of Bolingbroke. The current monastic chronicles were all called in to be examined after his seizure of power in September 1399, which was a clear sign to their writers that any accounts sympathetic to Richard would have to be heavily edited to satisfy Henry's agents. The documents that resulted, whether altered or not, make it clear that Richard was universally regarded as an untrustworthy, unstable, tyrannical despot and Henry's accession was regarded with public relief.[3] This is not to say that such a view was the invention of chroniclers eager to satisfy the manipulative and spin-conscious Henry as to their loyalties, though the latter was a careful and shrewd politician who was always conscious of his image and made the most of his glamorous reputation as a crusader (against pagans in Lithuania, not in the usual Palestine), pilgrim to Jerusalem, and champion jouster. The facts speak for themselves and Richard was abandoned by almost all the landed elite in 1399 as Henry landed with a very small army – though the extent of dissatisfaction with Richard may have been played up after he lost power and it was safe and politically wise to deplore his 'misrule'. A backlash against Henry's expensive government and its unforeseen costly war against the major Welsh rebellion after 1400 – itself partly caused by Henry's initial mistakes and underestimation of his local foes – cannot explain the extent of Ricardian plots after 1399 or the fact that these often centred on the usually 'unpolitical' Church as well as the usual power-hungry nobles. The blatantly political execution by Richard of the ex-'Appellant' leader Richard Fitzalan, Earl of Arundel, in 1397, the suspicious death of arrested royal uncle and ex-'Appellant' Duke Thomas of Gloucester a few months later, and the banishments of their former colleagues Henry of Bolingbroke and Thomas Mowbray, Duke of Norfolk, in 1398 are ample evidence that Richard indulged in personal revenge for past humiliations as Edward II had done – and both suffered similar fates later.

Following Henry's dubiously legal disinheritance from his father John of Gaunt's legacy, the vast and profitable Duchy of Lancaster, in February 1399, the exiled Henry and his ally Thomas Fitzalan/Arundel (the sacked ex-archbishop of Canterbury and brother of the executed earl of Arundel) launched a risky invasion of England with a few hundred men once Richard had left for a campaign in Ireland. Unlike Isabella's invasion in 1326, the attacker did not have any major powers or a reasonably-sized and coherent body of foreign mercenaries to improve their chances; Henry's host in his exile was Richard's child-bride's father and his own ally, the sporadically insane King Charles VI of France, who had signed a controversial peace-treaty with Richard to halt the ongoing Anglo-French wars in 1396 and did not offer him any help. Richard's politically understandable but unwise confiscation of the huge Duchy of Lancaster (on the grounds that it had been legally, not illegally, taken from Henry's mother's ancestors by Edward II in 1322 so it should not have descended to them and hence to him) was a far more serious blow to his standing and financial prospects than his ten-year exile from England in 1398. His relationship with Richard, his contemporary, had been fraught for years with modern historians suggesting an element of jealousy on the unmilitary Richard's part for his heroic cousin, a first-class participant in tournaments and other favourite sports of the warlike nobility who – like Richard's father but not him – shared their lifestyle and standards. (It is not clear which of them was the elder; Ian Mortimer thinks it was Richard).[4] Back in 1381 Richard, aged fourteen, had failed to provide for the adequate manning of the gates of the Tower of London, refuge of the Court from the rampant 'mob rule' in London, as he rode out to confront the rebel army of the 'Peasants Revolt'. In his absence at a meeting with Wat Tyler a determined crowd had broken into the Tower, let in by the guards, and dragged out the Archbishop of Canterbury and Chancellor, Simon Sudbury (originator of the hated poll tax). He and the Treasurer had then been executed on Tower Hill; Prince Henry, as son of the equally hated Duke John of Lancaster, had been among the helpless Court refugees who the lynch-mob had considered killing and eventually spared. This may have given him a grudge against or contempt for the self-centred Richard, who had left him to his fate.

Henry's participation in the successful revolt of the 'Lords Appellant' against Richard's favourites and ministers in 1387 exposed him to the king's subsequent desire for revenge. Earl of Derby at the time and without any obvious political grudges apart from Richard's enmity towards his father, his participation was probably sought by the more senior 'Appellants' as the representative of his father (absent in Spain attempting to conquer Castile which had been seized by pro-French Henry of Trastamara from his half-brother King Peter, father of John of Gaunt's second wife Catherine). John was arguably Richard's heir, as his oldest surviving paternal uncle and the third surviving son of Edward III, although Richard had declared to Parliament in November 1385 that he regarded his heir as the under-age Roger Mortimer, grandson of John's late elder brother Lionel. This logically gave Henry (and John if he had been in England at the time of the 'Appellant' revolt) reason to back any attempt to rein in Richard by his magnates – the latter should use a sympathetic Parliament to reaffirm that John and Henry were the rightful heirs. Henry could bring in his and his father's substantial 'affinity' of tenants and retainers to fight in the rebel army; he thus helped to destroy an army being brought by royal 'favourite' Robert de Vere to rescue Richard at Radcot Bridge in December 1387. It is noticeable that Henry had not joined the initial rebel rally at Waltham Cross in November to demand that the royal 'favourites' be put on trial by Parliament, and he was at court in London when the rebel leadership arrived to put their requirements to Richard. He only joined the rebels as De Vere assembled his army in Cheshire (where Richard was Earl) to oppose them. He may have earned Richard's enmity that way, by preventing Richard's armed supporters from rescuing him from the 'Appellants' – and fighting against a royal army was technically treason, with the obsessive Richard being then and later keen to have any resistance to royal orders definitively ruled as treason by his courts and purging judges to make sure he received the verdicts which he wished.

Richard's naming of the rival (Mortimer) line of his father's elder brother Lionel as his heirs in 1385 threatened Henry's chances of kingship and may have been decisive in causing him to turn on Richard in 1387 to ensure that the new government backed his and his father's rights instead. Henry's participation may also have been to head off the threat that the rebels' 'Merciless Parliament' in spring 1388 would instead back his uncle Thomas, the new Duke of Gloucester, John's younger brother and a senior 'Appellant', as the heir or put him on the throne. It is only the chronicle of Whalley Abbey, however, which states that after the 'Appellants' took control of London in December 1387 Thomas and Henry quarrelled over who was to be the next king and Richard was temporarily 'suspended' from exercising his power.[5] If this was accurate or a rumour arising from a threat made to Richard by hs uncle Thomas, then it would arguably mean that in Richard's eyes the latter had committed treason and could be legally executed in 1397 so his violent death was not the act of a 'tyrant'. Having him deported from his home at Pleshy Castle in Essex to Calais then quietly strangled in an inn by the king's 'heavies' avoided the embarrassment of a public trial, where the royal duke would have to be tried by his peers and could be acquitted or let out embarrassing secrets.

Henry's part in the December 1387 coup placed him with the other rebels as an object of revenge for Richard as he reasserted his power in punishing the rebel leadership in 1397–8. He was initially exempted from the list of past 'rebels' accused of treason by Richard's loyalists in the 1397 Parliament amidst an apparent promise of safety,[6] but this is not decisive proof that Richard was then prepared to exempt him from punishment as he may have been biding his time. The king was even prepared to alienate his intended heir, his cousin Roger Mortimer, by ordering him to arrest his uncle Sir Thomas Mortimer, for helping to destroy De Vere's royalist army at Radcot Bridge in 1387; it is possible that Richard turned against Roger at this point, as one source claims that as of 1398 the king regarded either Henry or the more loyal and passive Duke Edmund of York's son Edward as his probable successor, not the Mortimers. Roger did not get a dukedom like other close aides, and may have annoyed Richard by his warm public reception at the Shrewsbury Parliament that year – a hint at popular backing if he turned on the king? Henry's confrontation with Richard this year followed a dramatic meeting on the road near Brentford with his fellow 'Appellant' Thomas Mowbray, Earl of Hereford (and soon to be Duke of Norfolk), who claimed that they were about to be singled out for punishment too and that Richard's arch-loyalists, led by his nephew Thomas Holland, had plotted to murder Henry and his father John of Gaunt. Richard had supposedly backed this plot but pulled out – echoing his apparent interest in a plan by his friends to murder John in 1385. The fact that Mowbray was then so terrified of the king's reaction to his confession that he denied he had ever said anything – even when this meant calling expert warrior Henry a liar and being challenged to a duel – shows the fear that Richard's unpredictability and temper were by then arousing among his closest allies. There was also the question of Mowbray's part in the murder of the arrested Duke Thomas of Gloucester while in his care at Calais in 1397. Richard had apparently ordered Mowbray, as Captain of Calais (where Gloucester had been sent on his arrest) to kill him in August, weeks before he died; Mowbray failed to do so and the king sent out some thuggish henchmen from his chamber with a second order in early September to ensure that he obeyed. This time Mowbray's servant John Hall and some others removed Gloucester from his cell in the town's castle to an inn and smothered him with a feather-bed, or so Hall claimed to Henry's Parliament in October 1399. (The MPs' shock at this shows that Gloucester was seen as a good character and royal victim despite his harsh and vindictive behaviour to the King's friends in 1387–8.) The incident apparently played on Mowbray's conscience, and he confessed about it to Henry as they met on the road near Brentford – but as he had now accused the King of having his uncle murdered he apparently later panicked and denied to the furious Richard that he had said anything. It led to a series of charges and denials, mutual accusations of treasonous slander between Mowbray and Henry, and the reputed plan by the panicking Mowbray to waylay and murder John of Gaunt (who Henry had told about Mowbray's revelations) en route to Parliament at Shrewsbury. It ended with the King's decision to call Henry and Mowbray to take part in a judicial trial by combat by a Court of Chivalry at Coventry in September 1398. At the last moment, the combat was called off – with Henry the better duellist so expected to win and thus be able to show that Mowbray was guilty (and that the king was guilty by association). Henry was banished for ten years and Mowbray for life.[7]

When Henry was first exiled after the dramatic aborted 'trial by battle' against Mowbray at Coventry all contemporaries knew this to be a punishment for a political crime – his part in the successful revolt of the 'Lords Ordainers' against Richard in 1387–8. But he still had his estates and titles and the prospect of succeeding his father, Duke John, as the greatest magnate in the kingdom after the king – and if the crown was to be inherited by male rather than female descent John and Henry were the childless Richard's heirs. Crucially, Richard's second wife, Isabella of France, was a girl of seven when they married in 1396

– the king would not have children for years. It has been suggested that both Henry and John expected him to be recalled in a few years, and he had a past predilection for travel (including a pilgrimage to Jerusalem) and overseas military service which he could resume as a lordly knight-errant. Depriving him of his right to the dukedom would impoverish and humiliate him and make him dependent on others' charity, quite apart from it being of dubious legality. Nor would it improve his treatment by and hospitality from foreign rulers nervous of incurring Richard's enmity. Accordingly he launched a sudden invasion of England while Richard was overseas in Ireland in July 1399, with a small group of his friends and clients and no support from his host in exile, Charles VI of France – Richard's father-in-law so with no interest in removing him. It seems that he deceived Charles as to his intentions, and at best had a small foreign contingent from Brittany – whose dowager duchess Joan he was to marry three years later and may already have met. The final decision to invade may have been due to Henry being encouraged by the deposed and exiled ex-Archbishop Thomas Arundel (Fitzalan) of York, who joined him in France shortly beforehand. Arundel was to be Henry's Lord Chancellor and chief minister on and off during his reign as well as being restored as archbishop and leader of the English church; the king's most ruthless supporter, he would go on to initiate burnings for heresy under Henry as king with the notorious statute 'De Heretico Comburendo' and would start to censor the official debates in and publications of the country's universities as a controlling chancellor of Oxford University. Arundel had lent his ecclesiastical sanction to the 'Appellants' in 1387–8 and been their choice for archbishop of York and then as Lord Chancellor, in which rank Richard had been forced to retain him for years; the king had clearly been awaiting his chance for revenge and was to condemn him in personal letters after his condemnation. After Henry had taken over the country in September 1399 he stood by the new strongman's side in Parliament as he claimed the crown, making it clear that such a claim had his backing and ignoring the arguably legally stronger claims of the under-age Edmund Mortimer.

Richard had weakened his position for ensuring support if Henry did invade by a typical act of haughty and autocratic decision-making – going back on the terms of Henry's original exile in 1398 with minimal explanation. If the king's cousin and a potential royal duke could be deprived of his rights by royal fiat, was anyone's title or lands safe from Richard? Thus Henry could argue and thus the elite could fear who would be next on the unstable King's list for retaliation. Indeed Henry carefully claimed to be returning to regain his estates (for which he had legal grounds) rather than to depose Richard; the usual legal excuse for rebellion of 'rescuing the King from his evil counsellors' could be deployed with a faction controlling office as against Henry III in 1264 and against Edward II in 1309, 1322, and 1326. It had been used against Richard himself by the 'Lords Appellant' in 1387–8. Given the structure of the kingdom's military machine – no 'standing army', and men being recruited for each campaign by their lords under royal licences – the reaction of the landed nobility was vital to both Henry and Richard. The precedent of 1326 suggested that an unpopular king relying on a narrow base of support could easily be deserted by their elite, and if Henry won Richard could go the same way as Edward II. The king had been spared such a fate in the 1387–8 rebellion and had subsequently killed or exiled all the leaders of the revolt. Backing Henry was likely to make him king or at least regent for the under-age Edmund Mortimer, with failure meaning the full penalties for treason from an increasingly vindictive Richard – though the Percys, blocking Henry's route in Yorkhire when he landed but then deserting to him, were later to claim that they had only supported Henry because they believed his public oath not to take the throne.[8]

Richard had taken a large army to Ireland, led by his own trusted bodyguard of Cheshire archers, but there were many magnates available to rally to his cause. One crucial issue is why the position of the government was so weak – and why the regent, the sluggish and politically marginal Duke Edmund of York (aged fifty-seven and with considerable military experience as a commander in France but no major victories to his credit) failed to react but passively awaited Henry's arrival, retreating west to the Bristol area. If only a few senior magnates – led by the Percys under the veteran Earl Henry of Northumberland and his son, Henry 'Hotspur', and brother Earl Thomas of Worcester – really supported Henry's landing, why did not more people rally to Richard's regent, York? Or to Richard himself as he belatedly returned from Ireland? The striking lack of resistance to Henry cannot be written off as simply fear. York had reason to oppose his nephew's invasion, with the succession to Richard in prospect if Henry was debarred from the throne by reason of his exile – as Richard may have already hinted.[9] He apparently knew Henry was at sea with hostile intent, though not where he was heading as he expected an invasion of the south or south-west. (Isabella had landed in Suffolk in 1326.) But when Henry landed and received the Percys' support he did not march forward to fight them but stayed inert at Bristol – unless this masks a failure to attract enough recruits – and as Henry approached he came to terms with him. His own son and heir, Edward of Aumale, was one of Richard's abruptly-elevated new peers, the 'duketti', as Duke of Surrey, and was with Richard in Ireland and could well be named as heir. Either he was aware he would have no support against Henry or he believed Henry had justice on his side. The speedy collapse of Richard's rule in 1399, as with the similar desertion of Edward II in 1326, shows that it was not just propaganda by the victors that they had popular opinion and at least the tacit support of most magnates on their side. The size of his army by the time he reached Bristol was clearly much greater than it had been when he landed in Yorkshire.[10]

Was Richard actually seen as a 'tyrant' and was his autocratic rule, backed by a cowed and/or complaisant judiciary, that controversial in 1397–9 given that his regime's heirs were attracting considerable support against Henry after 1400? The use of Richard's large new bodyguard from his earldom of Chester to intimidate Parliament in 1397 (they were stationed outside it in the palace yard at Westminster), his overhaul of the judiciary to promote the King's right to arbitary decisions, the punishment of the leaders of the successful attack on the king's party in 1387–8, and the promotion of 'low-born' royal friends to senior noble rank in 1397–9 may have been less feared or resented across the political 'nation' than Henry later alleged. The point of the king's massive creation of peers on 29 September 1397 was not so much to ennoble 'low-born' Royal toadies as to entrench Richard's closest allies in leading roles within the peerage, supplied with lands forfeited from the ruined 'Appellants'. Most of the creations were of existing peers or heirs of ancient blood with higher rank, e.g. Henry of Bolingbroke (Duke of Hereford, a title held as an earldom by his late wife's ancestors), Thomas Mowbray (Duke of Norfolk, a title held as an earldom by his grandmother's family), Thomas Percy (Earl of Worcester), the Duke of York's son Edward of Cambridge (Duke of Aumale, a title formerly associated as an earldom with the York title), John

Holland, Richard's half-brother (Duke of Exeter), John's nephew Thomas Holland (from earl of Huntingdon to Duke of Surrey), and Thomas Despenser (earl of Gloucester, a title held by his ancestors). The most controversial of them, royal chamberlain and ex-captain of Cherbourg Sir William Scrope, was the only 'self-made' courtier ennobled, and he was the eldest son of former Chancellor Lord Scrope. Sir John Beaufort, only recently made Earl of Somerset and now made Marquis of Dorset, was also elevated suspiciously fast but was the eldest illegitimate son of John of Gaunt and so of the royal blood.

Richard had also embarked on an unusually intensive programme of promoting royal power, which the new pomp and dignity of his appearances in state at court complemented.[11] Edward I and III had also appeared in appropriate majesty at ceremonial occasions and had hosted splendid courts, but more as chivalric military leaders in the tradition of the literary legend (then thought to be genuine) of King Arthur – and they had had closer personal relatonships with the great nobles, who they had led on the battlefield unlike Richard. His attack on the right of the judiciary to declare the law autonomous from royal reinterpretation and persecution of defiant judges shows that he had a concept of 'L'etat c'est moi' which was impressive and was supposed to be as guarantor of justice but was politically naive.[12] At the least, it indicates an obsession to put himself beyond the reach of legal control by his nobles, reacting to their use of Parliament to restrain him by going against his wishes to exile his favourites in 1386. Any judges who expressed reservations about carrying out his wishes met royal fury, not reluctant acceptance of their independence of thought – Richard could not contemplate any defiance. In terms of international academic and constitutional law he may have been influenced by contemporary writers who built up the concept of the supreme secular sovereign, the 'Emperor', as opposed to the all-too-fallible and divided Papacy; his first wife Anne had been sister of the Holy Roman Emperor-elect, King Wenceslas IV of Bohemia. (Wenceslas was to end up deposed too.) But this theory of rigid hierarchical rule was not practical politics in England, where the magnates' consent was essential. Did Richard make the same mistake of assuming that his magnates would obey his demands and accept his theorists' elevation of the royal office in all the circumstances that Charles I did? He was also interested in the sacral nature of the royal office and made much of his connection to the royal coronation site and necropolis at Westminster Abbey, even annexing the recently 'discovered' holy oil (said to have been sent down from Heaven via a dove to crown the kings of England like that of France) stored at the abbey and carrying a vial of it round his neck on his expeditions away from London. The abbot preferred to keep it safe in his treasury and there was a struggle over its possession – and ironically Richard never had the chance to be anointed with it like a proper 'holy' king at a coronation so it was first used by his usurping cousin, Henry. To his credit he was so fastidious in contrast to his 'rough and ready' nobles that he was said to have introduced the handkerchief to England and more certainly built a rare royal 'bathroom suite' on an island adjacent to his palace at Sheen, 'La Neyt'. He also famously commissioned the best surviving piece of contemporary art, the 'Wilton Diptych', which showed him as a teenager attended by Christ, the Virgin Mary, and angels plus three royal saints as he prayed.

Defenders of his reputation against Henry's propagandists may argue that he was seeking to build up the royal power – and the king's ability to act for the country's benefit – as a principled idealist, an idealist for national stability, and an opponent of defiant magnates, hoping to end the run of successful revolts against Royal authority. In his letters after the 1397–8 'purge' to his fellow-sovereigns, Duke Albert of Holland and Emperor Manuel Paleologus of the Byzantine Empire, he stressed that he had suppressed his factious and untrustworthy nobles to restore peace to his nation for his lifetime.[13] This is to his credit, and until 1397 he certainly lacked the vindictiveness (except to a few of his relatives) that Edward II possessed, though both men could be erratic and moody. But the personal is rarely separable from the theoretical in Late Medieval politics, and his vengeful actions towards his past coercers were clearly spite as much as of principle. The private murder of Gloucester, in particular, avoided any necessity of an embarrassing public trial – although he was a controversial figure and did not deserve much sympathy given his crude threats to Richard in 1387–8 and his insistence on the execution of Richard's tutor, Sir Simon Burley. At Arundel's trial in 1397 his alleged verbal insistence in 1387 to the king that Burley be killed was dragged up by Richard[14] – was this seen as his worst crime? The arbitrary extension of the terms of exile imposed on Henry of Bolingbroke and Thomas Mowbray in 1398–9 duly unnerved his enemies and stimulated the decision to remove him.

Contemporary writers stressed the king's lack of commonsense and reliance on a coterie of 'unworthy' and resented advisers, with some hints being made about the sexual implications of his excessive fondness for and lavishing of honours on certain supporters.[15] An insecure need for emotional 'dependence' on trusted figures is as likely an explanation as suppressed homosexuality, which Henry of Bolingbroke or his ruthless allies like Archbishop Arundel (deprived of his see and his brother executed by Richard) would have been capable of exploiting in 1399 if feasible. Unlike his father and grandfather, Richard had been brought up until the age of ten away from Court in the household of his ailing father, mostly at Berkhamsted well away from London – he did not know his elite contemporaries on easy terms as a boy, as Edward III and the 'Black Prince' did. His isolation, firstly away from London and then in the unique role of King where deference was required to him, plausibly increased if not caused his distancing from the great nobles and a corresponding reliance on a small coterie of friends, above all in 1382–6 Robert De Vere – who unlike Edward II's Gaveston was from the old Anglo-Norman nobility although equally resented as the object of special trust and lavish grants of lands, titles and offices. Nor were women absent from or marginalised at his court, as to some degree at Edward II's court. It seems that he was quick to turn on friends who seemed to betray him, and reluctant to forgive; Thomas Mowbray had been one of his early intimates but was never to regain this status after he joined the 'Appellants' in 1387–8. This indicates emotional insecurity rather than homosexuality, and Richard is less easily accused of the latter than Edward II. Richard's reliance on and excessive grants to his mother Countess Joan of Kent's kin, the Hollands (descendants of her first marriage), can be paralleled with Henry III's dependence on his mother Isabella's Poitevin relatives and his French wife Eleanor's family. In all cases, the King trusted his personal dependants rather than the independently-landed aristocratic barons, and was turned on by a relative who he had elevated to honours but who could not trust him.

The deposition of Richard II, 1399

Ireland was currently divided between a smallish region of Anglo-Norman settlement and direct control by the royal government in Dublin, the 'Pale' in the east and south-east; a land of mixed Anglo-Norman and Gaelic lords and mostly Gaelic lower classes beyond that which was technically loyal to Dublin but mostly in the hands of autonomous warlords who were only sporadically reliable; and usually independent and anti-English Gaelic lords, the 'native Irish' as they were called. Some of the Anglo-Norman provincial magnates who had huge regional estates and private armies of English and/or Gaelic tenants, both within and outside the 'Pale', eg the Butlers of Ormonde in Munster and the Fitzgeralds of Kildare (Meath within the 'Pale') and of Desmond (south-west Munster, outside the 'Pale'), were usually loyal and Anglicised and were called upon to help out the government and take senior office in Dublin from time to time; others were not. All of them militarily overshadowed the under-resourced Dublin regime, and technically all of Ireland had been granted to the kings of England by the Pope in the mid-twelfth century so the king had been its overlord since the Anglo-Norman invasion of 1169–70. But only Henry II (in 1171) and John (as prince in 1185 and king in 1210) had ever bothered to go there and campaign to secure their position, and the area under English control had shrunk drastically since the chaos and autonomist Gaelic revolts of the 1310s (led by King Robert Bruce of Scots and his brother Edward, who had claimed the kingship of Ireland as descended from the ancient kings of Leinster). To complicate matters, some of the main English noble dynasties also held blocs of land and titles in Ireland and had their own private armies there – including the Mortimers, as heirs of the De Lacys of Trim in Meath. Edward III had married off his second surviving son and intended governor of Ireland, Duke Lionel of Clarence (d 1368), to the heiress of the extinct Anglo-Norman earldom of Ulster in the north – and that bloc of lands had now also descended to the Mortimers via Roger Mortimer's (d 1398) father's marriage to Lionel's daughter and heiress Philippa.

Richard had previously bestowed the governorship of Ireland, for life, with an unprecedented Marquessate, on his favourite Robert de Vere in 1385 – 'contracting out' the problem to a loyal family connection as Edward III had done, but not to one with any lands in (and thus a call on local loyalty from) Ireland. The De Vere grant was greeted with hostility in both England and Ireland, and was cancelled at the favourite's fall.[15] Richard then led an expedition there in person after his first wife Anne of Bohemia died in 1394,[16] claiming to Duke Philip of Burgundy in a letter that the purpose was to punish rebels and restore good government and justice. His interest was commendable after a century and a half of royal neglect, though the recent shock death of his wife probably meant he was anxious to find distraction away from London. The expedition, of around 7–8000 men, had clear military superiority over the ill-armed Irish 'kerns' of the local tribal Irish dynasts and duly achieved the submission of Art MacMurrough, principal rebel lord of Leinster, and of the leading O'Neills of Ulster.[17] By the end of his expedition he had obtained the submission of all the Irish dynasts within reach of his military power in south-east Ireland, showing politic mercy to the 'rebel Irish' (ie. those lords of non-English descent traditionally subject to his ancestors), alienated by past misgovernment, to coax them away from alliance with the 'wild Irish' (i.e. those never subject to English rule). Treating the Anglo-Irish barons, descendants of the twelfth–thirteenth-century settlers (some of them semi-Hibernicised in culture), and the ethnically Irish lords as equal parts of the 'lordship of Ireland' showed political sense. It helped to cut costs by avoiding endless warfare for the bankrupt government in Dublin – and Richard's itineraries show that he generally spent more time outside southern England than most thirteenth- and fourteenth-century kings so he was imaginatively interested in his outlying dominions. The literary fabulations of Arthurian enthusiasts since Geoffrey of Monmouth had built up a picture of the King of England as a sort of 'emperor' within the British Isles which no doubt appealed to Richard. In summer 1399 he returned to Ireland rather than resting on his laurels after his crushing of the 'Appellants' – and left his kingdom open for Henry to invade. Art MacMurrough and the Dublin government were at war again, and Richard had removed his cousin Roger Mortimer as Lord Lieutenant, replacing him with his nephew and favourite Edward of Cambridge (Duke of Aumale), on 26 July 1398. In June 1399 Richard arrived at Waterford to lead his second expedition against MacMurrough, but this time could not corner him into surrendering. The news of Henry's landing in England then caused the expedition to be abandoned.

As Henry invaded England with a few hundred men as summer 1399 approached, leading aristocrats may have been unwilling to oppose an experienced and tough campaigner – a veteran of the brutal Teutonic Knights' wars against the Lithuanians, who had legal right on his side as long as he claimed to be pursuing his duchy not the crown. The latter claim was not made until he had Richard in his power, as his Percy allies later complained. Once he had landed in Yorkshire at the end of June, he apparently swore that he had only returned to secure his legal rights to the Duchy of Lancaster.[18] The location of his oath (or oaths) was not clear – Bridlington, Knaresborogh, or Doncaster? – though he may have sworn more than one. He was supposed to have sworn either not to claim the Crown at all or to hand it over to the 'worthiest' candidate – which could mean himself if his peers judged him worthy. He also swore not to levy the oppressive taxation that Richard had done, which he more definitely violated under the needs of war in 1401. Some magnates who joined him may have expected Richard to be placed under restraint, as he had been in 1387–8 only now permanently, or to be removed in favour of his presumed heir Edmund Mortimer.[19] The problem of restraining a monarch with a council given special legal powers was of the resultant reaction when the king recovered his freedom of action – as shown by Edward II's recall of the banished Gaveston and his and Richard's hunting down of the nobles who had led their humiliation. But given that Edmund Mortimer was aged eight, if he was put on the throne there would be a long regency. Henry was the rightful claimant to that as the nearest male kin, being son of the next of Edward III's sons to Edmund's ancestor. The previous personal 'Governorship' of an under-age new King, Edward III, had gone to his nearest male kinsman, Earl Henry of Lancaster, while the boy's mother Isabella had been effective regent (assisted by her lover Roger Mortimer). Richard's regent while he was overseas in Ireland, his surviving uncle Edmund, Duke of York, was incapable of – or unwilling to? – organise resistance and remained inert in the south-west as Henry marched southwards. His inaction was decisive. It is even possible that the fact that Richard had made him regent gave him hopes of securing the succession, the role of regent normally going to the male heir – though the 'rightful' heir as Richard saw him, Edmund Mortimer, was too young to be regent in 1399 so a substitute had been needed. The next choice of regent after Edmund of York, his son the new Duke of Aumale, had been sent to Ireland in 1398 and so was unavailable.

Richard delayed his sailing home from Ireland for a crucial two weeks or so, while his position in England collapsed as the unhindered Henry crossed the midlands. The Duke of York, unable to raise an army around

Gloucester and Bristol, gave up and came to terms with him at Berkeley Castle on 27 July. The leading Ricardian ministers Bagot and Bushy were seized and executed as Bristol, the main port in the west of England and key to the south-west, defected, and tenants in the Welsh Marches failed to muster for the king. By the time Richard returned directly to Pembrokeshire around 14 July – and landed in an isolated part of Wales, far from the centres of power in England – Henry had already gained control of most of England. The king advanced east to reach Whitland on 29 July and Carmarthen on the 31st, and according to the monastic chronicler Thomas Walsingham was initially looking forward to fighting Henry.[20] Lack of local support condemned him to abandon a direct march against Henry's positions around Bristol, though it is unclear if he knew that the port had fallen before he decided on a change of tactics. The latter seems to have doomed him as it entailed abandoning his troops for a quiet and unobtrusive journey with a small escort north to join up with his presumed army in the north, which he may have expected to be more loyal than his current limited support in South Wales. Its quixotic nature may be another example of his moodiness and instability of character – or just due to reasonable fears that his current troops would not stand up to Henry's men but desert. He made a slow journey north through difficult country along the western Welsh coast to attempt to link up with remaining loyalists in the north under the third Earl of Salisbury, who he expected to be around Caernarfon or Conwy castles. According to the Dieulacres Abbey chronicler he abandoned his army to travel with only fifteen companions (including the Despenser earl of Gloucester and York's son, Edward of Aumale), possibly for speed or else through fear of betrayal. When his Steward, Thomas Percy, earl of Worcester (brother of the Earl of Northumberland), found that he had gone from the southern army's camp he realised that the king would lose his throne, broke his rod of office as was done when a monarch died, and tearfully suggested that the bemused royal army disperse. One writer who was with Salisbury claims that Richard disguised himself as a priest, suggesting that fear of arrest was his main motive. He was out of touch with his continually deteriorating position within England, and ended up trapped with Salisbury at Conwy Castle as the superior rebel army led by earl Henry Percy of Northumberland, Worcester's elder brother, blocked his route. Henry arrived at Chester to join them after a hasty journey up the Welsh Marches from Bristol. Arriving at Conwy around 15 August to find Northumberland a few miles ahead of him blocking the way east, Richard agreed to open negotiations. His first envoys (his Holland half-brother Exeter and nephew Edward of Aumale) were sent to Henry at Chester but detained there.[22] As of this point, Salisbury's army had suffered desertions, so fighting was not an option. Richard still had the ability to flee before or after Northumberland and ex-Archbishop Arundel arrived to see him at Conwy Castle with Henry's terms (probably on 12 August). He may well have been tricked into surrendering with a false promise that he would preserve his throne, whether or not the Percys were being honest later in assuring that Henry had told them that Richard would not be deposed. Whether Henry was being honest at the time in his oath not to depose Richard is impossible to know, as Richard's deposition followed the captive King making threats to have his revenge later. But Henry would have known from experience that Richard was untrustworthy before that.

Northumberland and Arundel apparently swore to Richard that he would preserve his dignities, and the claim by pro-Henrician sources that the king offered to abdicate at this point have been 'rubbished' by modern analysts. The more neutral sources, eg the French eye-witness Jean Creton, claim that Northumberland merely required Richard to accept a Parliament presided over by Henry plus the trials of five leading supporters, including the Dukes of Aumale (Edward, York's son) and Exeter and the Earl of Salisbury. The Earl also swore that Henry would keep his word on this[23] – though as Parliament had required Edward II to abdicate in similar circumstances in 1327 it was obvious that Richard could be deposed later by this means. Richard duly emerged from Conwy Castle to accompany Northumberland to a meeting over dinner at his base, Rhuddlan east of the river Conwy. Only when he was away from the walls did an armed contingent of Percy retainers emerge from a nearby valley and take him captive. Confined at Flint Castle, he was said to have realised that he was doomed when he saw Henry's army approaching.[24] It was naïve of him to think that he would be given a second chance to go back on his word after he had promisd to forgive the 'Lords Appellant' for their actions in 1387–8 then arrested, exiled or murdered them; nor had he honourably kept the laws imposed on him at that point but had had them and any restraint of the king declared illegal.

At the best he could be expected to be reduced to a powerless figurehead for far longer this time – presumably either by a Lords Ordainer-style committee of peers or even a regent such as Henry. This may have been what Northumberland expected to happen, if he was sincere in believing that Richard would keep his throne. In any event, it was disastrous that after an initially polite welcome to his captor Henry, Richard went back on his submissive behaviour as he was being escorted to London under guard. He was reported to have boasted (in another mood-swing?) that he would not consider himself bound by any promises that he gave to Henry, who would be punished later.[25] This is known to the chroniclers, so it is apparent that Henry was told about it and made the most of it on his arrival at the London Parliament to urge the other peers to depose the unreliable king. Henry, unlike Queen Isabella with her husband Edward II in 1326, had his victim brought to London to abdicate publicly – so that a larger group of nobles could witness the act and it could be done quicker than had been possible with Edward II.

The assembly of the lords spiritual and temporal at Westminster Hall on 30 September did see the claims to the throne of York and his sons, Edward of Aumale and Richard of Cambridge, formally raised – but only after the king's abdication had been announced and Henry had made his claim first. According to French witness Jean Creton (more reliable than a Henrican partisan) the lords did not speak up for York and his family, and acclaimed Henry instead. It would have been a brave man to stand out against the clear intention of the assembly with the current Archbishop of York (Richard Scrope) and the soon-to-be-restored ex-Archbishop of Canterbury (Thomas Arundel) flanking Henry to show Church support for him.[26] Edmund Mortimer's name was not mentioned – and ironically Scrope was later to be executed by Henry in 1405, for leading an anti-tax rebellion in Yorkshire and putting up placards calling on Henry to be deposed in favour of the legitimate king, Edmund Mortimer. It is possible that the York family's hopes and their thwarting led to the equivocal attitude of Edward of Aumale to Henry IV's regime – though Edward had other reasons to revolt as Henry required him to hand back the Dukedom of Aumale which Richard had given him. Edward joined the subsequent Ricardian plot by 'hard-line' ex-courtiers to murder Henry and his sons at Windsor at New Year 1400, only to swiftly change his mind and inform the king who thus fled the castle in time to London and escaped assassination. York was never charged, and may even have acted as a 'double agent' once he had decided to change sides – he certainly told his fellow-plotters as they took over Windsor that Henry was coming with a large army (an exaggeration) and panicked them into fleeing so Henry may have instructed him to do this.

Richard II's death – murder or suicide?

The fate of the deposed king was always likely to be unpleasant, though notably Henry did not dispose of his other potential challengers, Edmund Mortimer and his younger brother, when he had them in custody in 1400–05 – even after assorted plots had been raised in their name and they had been abducted by rebel agents in February 1405 in a failed attempt to get them to safety in rebellious Wales. (This is in sharp contrast to what is generally assumed to have happened to the 'Princes in the Tower' in 1483.) As long as Richard was alive there was a danger of his partisans or other enemies of Henry rescuing him, although even if he was killed these could – and did – just transfer their allegiance to the Mortimer brothers instead. Thus Henry had the motive for killing Richard and he was certainly calculating and ruthless enough, and in 1405 he was to go as far as to execute Archbishop Scrope of York for rebellion in defiance of the supposed immunity of the clergy from lay prosecution. Even Henry II had not executed an archbishop in cold blood, with the murder of Archbishop (St) Thomas Becket linked to rash royal words spoken in a rage about his supposed treachery and the disloyalty of the King's employees in not ridding the realm of their master's upstart enemy. Henry IV executed an archbishop in cold blood after a brief trial,[27] and he deliberately ignored the pleas of his close ally Archbishop Arundel not to do it and when the chief justice, William Gascoigne, refused to pass sentence he found another judge to do it. Afterwards his sudden onset of a serious illness and eventual collapse with a debilitating skin complaint plus loss of muscular power seems to have been regarded in the popular mind as divine vengeance for his wickedness.[28] Henry was assumed to have leprosy, was in a coma for some days in 1408, and by the time of his final decline in 1412–13 (still in his mid-forties) was unable to walk or ride. His physical collapse is one of the main royal medical mysteries of the medieval period, and its causes are still unclear due to its mixture of symptoms and uneven progress. His initial collapse with a 'burning sensation' in his skin and probable giddiness during a storm shortly after Scrope's execution[29] was probably connected to an early manifestation of his later skin-condition, but he was soon recovered fully and his writing was unaffected which argues against a stroke; and after a period of uncertain health he had another collapse and was unconscious for days in 1408 but recovered again, though less fully. His skin-problems then returned and became chronic, and he seems to have gradually declined in his mobility and energy and by 1412 had lost his ability to walk – but how his problems interacted and whether there was one underlying cause is still unclear. Politically, his eldest son Henry held the regime steady in 1410–12 and its internal feuding in 1412 may have been exaggerated by gossip; but it was a major blow to his reputation as his illness was assumed to be a judgement of God on his misdeeds.

It is not clear if he did kill Richard, directly or by deliberate neglect, but the decisive event in making this outcome a distinct possibility was the plot that was now launched by Richard's partisans to overthrow him. This was as a result of the new regime's politically popular but divisive prosecution in autumn 1399 of what it called the 'Counter-Appellants' – the Ricardian stalwarts who had led the prosecution and 'unjust' punishments of the 'Appellants' in 1397. Arundel had been convicted and executed in dubious circumstances despite his having been pardoned – twice – for his coercing the king in 1387–8; his brother the archbishop had been sacked and exiled; the ageing earl of Warwick had been tried, forced to beg for mercy from the king, and exiled to the Isle of Man; Thomas of Gloucester had never even been tried but had been secretly murdered; and Henry of Bolingbroke (now King) and the later Duke of Norfolk, Thomas Mowbray, had been pardoned but later exiled on dubious evidence. A clique of the ex-king's ministers had charges drawn up against them over their actions in 1397–8 by the new Parliament, and on 21 October demands were made to try Richard too by the Commons. Henry asked the Lords for advice on the ex-king's fate, and eventually on their advice imprisonment for life under the guard of trusted persons but no trial was agreed.[30] On 29 October 1399 Richard was taken from the Tower in secrecy, in disguise, by an armed escort,[31] and (like Edward II in 1327) was taken around the country with no clear evidence of where exactly he was emerging. One version has it that he was first taken to

Gravesend in Kent, and then, disguised as a forester, to isolated Leeds Castle inland; he ended up in the North, in Pontefract Castle, Yorkshire, some time before Christmas.[32]

On 29 October 1399 the trial of the 'Counter-Appellants' for the illegal 1397 prosecutions, killing the Duke of Gloucester, and confiscating Henry's inheritance illegally in 1399 were launched. They pleaded coercion by Richard and his ally William Scrope, the by now executed earl of Wiltshire. To the embarrassment of the new regime, the arrested Ricardian minister William Bagot – regarded by snobbish contemporary observers and Henricans as especially guilty and expendable due to his sudden elevation to high social status and presumed greed for wealth – went 'off message' and refused to submit to his fate tamely. Instead he alleged at his public questioning by Parliament that it had been Edward of York who had proposed that Richard kill off the earls of Arundel and Warwick, the Duke of Gloucester, and Henry in 1397–8 to secure the Ricardian regime from its main foes and Bagot had argued the King out of doing this and so saved the current King's life. In other words, it had been Edward of York, not him, who had committed the worst treasons – and Edward, like Mowbray when accused of embarrassing and treasonable revelations by Henry in 1398, denied it. Instead he challenged Bagot to a duel in front of the House of Lords, and when asked why he had approved so many illegal acts by King Richard he embarrassingly asked the Lords 'Is there any one among you all who, if King Richard had demanded a certain thing from you, would have dared to disagree with him or not complied with his order?' This was clearly seen as the truth – and a revealing comment on the fear that the paranoid King had inspired – but Bagot had clearly been 'lined up' as an expendable sacrificial victim to the wrath of Richard's opponents and as he accused more 1399 defectors (including Surrey and Exeter) of equal complicity to himself they challenged him to duels too. The regime had to 'shut down' the shouting-match, reassure Edward of York and the others who Bagot had challenged that they had no need to fight and were believed innocent of treason, and adjourn the enquiry. However one of Henry's senior allies who had been victimized in 1397 by Richard, Lord Cobham, was still noisily out for revenge no matter what trouble it stirred up and persuaded the Lords that as the 'Counter-Appellants' had proudly called themselves the childless Richard's 'foster-children' they must be punished with their 'foster-father' for the sake of common justice.[33]

The accused lords swore that they had not known about or approved of Gloucester's murder and had only taken part in the punitive Parliament of 1397 out of fear of Richard, and the House of Lords passed the question of judgement back to the King with a recommendation for mercy. On 3 November they were announced by Chief Justice Thirning as guilty, and had their lives spared but were stripped of the titles and lands which Richard had given them in 1397. The duke of Aumale (ie Edward of York, earl of Cambridge), Surrey (ie Thomas Holland, earl of Kent, Richard II's nephew) and Exeter (ie John Holland, earl of Huntingdon, Richard's half-brother) were stripped of their 1397 titles as illegally granted and resumed their previous ones. John Beaufort (earl of Somerset), the new King's half-brother, lost his marquessate of Dorset and Thomas Despenser loses his earldom of Gloucester. Their 1397–99 grants of lands were confiscated and they were told that any attempt to restore Richard II would incur the penalties for treason. Among the accused Ricardian prelates, Arcbishop Arundel's 'illegal' replacement at Canterbury, Roger Walden, lost his office to the latter and was not prosecuted further; nor was Richard's sacked treasurer, Bishop Guy Mone of St Davids, who after a decent interval (1402) was given his job back by Henry. Various other bishops who had assisted Richard as Privy Councillors were also kept on. Bagot got off with a term of imprisonment, but the executed Earl of Wiltshire (William Scrope) and the similarly 'targeted' lower-class minister William Bushy/ Bussy, the latter a defected former employee of Henry's, were posthumously condemned and had their property seized. All persons were invited to submit petitions for miscarriages of justice and other crimes committed under Richard, for justice to be done.[34]

Henry was clearly aiming at an uneasy balance between punishing the agents of 'royal despotism' and not alienating senior nobles who had supported Richard – and only lower-class gentry ministers such as Bushy were executed. But the country was deeply split over the mixture of royal repression in 1397–9 and revolution in 1399 – perhaps more so than it had been in 1326, as then the undoubted heir had taken over but there was no definitive law on the royal succession in this era and it could be argued that Edmund Mortimer had a better claim to be king than Henry. If candidates could be ruled out of contention as claiming the throne by female descent (as Edmund did, his grandmother Philippa being Lionel of Clarence's daughter), then what of the English claim to France which came via King Charles IV's sister Isabella, Edward III's mother? In 1199 a boy claimant to the throne, King Richard I's deceased next brother Geoffrey's son Arthur of Brittany, had been set aside in favour of the adult John, the younger brother of Richard and Geoffrey – but this had never been legally confirmed as the established practice in England. Richard still had his unreconciled supporters, led by some of his ex-courtiers and his half-brother John Holland, but their enemies had wanted them purged more brutally for the 'illegal' royal executions and banishments in 1397–9. Henry soon received threatening anonymous letters for allowing the 'Counter-Appellants' to live. But his forcing these resented Ricardian nominees to give up a significant part of their gains produced a larger pro-Ricardian party ready to attempt a coup. Richard's nephew the earl of Kent (Thomas Holland) and his brother Huntingdon (John Holland) and their allies planned to slaughter Henry and his sons en masse over the Christmas holidays at Windsor (probably on Epiphany, 6 January 1400) and then restore Richard to the throne. The disgraced ex-earl of Gloucester, Thomas Despenser, and the young third earl of Salisbury (who has been barred by Parliament from petitioning the King for injustices committed in the 1390s as he was a Ricardian) joined in, along with the sacked ex-archbishop of Canterbury, Roger Walden, abbot William Colchester of Westminster Abbey (favoured by Richard), and the ex-king's clerk Richard Maudelyn, who later impersonated him. But on 4 January 1400, as the conspirators assembled at Kingston-upon-Thames, the King was tipped off at the last minute about the Windsor murder-plot and fled to London with his sons. The most likely informant was the Duke of York's son Edward (ex-duke of Aumale), though it may have been carelessness not betrayal. One (French) story has it that Edward accidentally left a sealed document mentioning the plot on the duke's dinner-table the previous evening and his father read it and persuaded him to tell the king; another says a royal henchman heard from a London prostitute what her plotter client had recently told her. Edward was not charged, which may be suggestive. The king reached London in the evening, collected troops with Lord Mayor Knolles who he found setting out to warn him of a rebel gathering, spent the night at the Tower, and sent a warning to archbishop Arundel who was nearing Kingston en route to Windsor but fled to his late brother's castle at Reigate.

The rebels entered Windsor in a hurry hours after Henry had left to find no king, proclaimed Richard restored, and proceeded to Richard's young wife Isabella's residence nearby at Sonning to secure her support. The king, riding on Windsor with his troops next morning, sent Edward of York (pretending to be still a rebel) to tell his 'colleagues' that all was discovered and they must flee his large army; the rebels broke up and fled to Oxford. It is noticeable that the plotters thought it better to rise in Richard's name than that of the less politically controversial Edmund Mortimer, Henry's ignored rival for the throne at the time of the deposition of Richard, who they could plausibly claim had been denied his rights. Salisbury and Despenser headed for Cirencester (en route to the Marches, Wales or abroad?) with Lord Lumley but Salisbury and Lumley were arrested there by the locals on arrival on 6 January, locked in the abbey, and when they tried to escape on the 8th were beheaded by a mob. Despenser was arrested and lynched in Cardiff on the 13th, and Huntingdon/Exeter failed to raise his lands in Devon, sailed to Essex, failed to get the earl of Oxford (a relative of Richard's late favourite Robert de Vere, d 1392) to protect him at Hadley Castle, hid near Pleshy castle in Essex, but was caught. He was handed over to the king's mother-in-law the Countess of Hereford (sister-in-law of his 1397 victim Gloucester) at Pleshy, and was soon seized and executed too. Henry arrived in pursuit of the fleeing rebels at Oxford on the 11th, and on the 12th assorted arrested 'traitors' were tried there and 26 or 27 were beheaded. This ended the chaotic but still dangerous rebellion and on the 16th Archbishop Arundel led a thanksgiving procession in London.[34]

As the plot was linked to a possible rescue of Richard II, it probably doomed him and it is usually assumed that the ruthless Henry now decided to make sure that the surviving Ricardians had no live symbol to rally around. A French source (*La Traison et Mort de Richard II*) has Henry send Sir Piers Exton to Pontefract on 6 January to kill him, ie at the height of the rebellion when he could still be rescued. The murderer then sets about Richard in his cell with six other assassins, and although Richard seizes an axe from one of them he is overpowered and bludgeoned to death. He is then buried at Pontefract – which is inaccurate. In fact, Exton cannot be traced though the name may hide some other Henrican official; this is most likely to have been Henry's adviser and former fellow-Crusader, Sir Peter Bucton or Buxton. In the story the king tells 'Exton' to go to Pontefract and dispose of Richard as he is raising his troops in London on 6 January ready to march on rebel-held Windsor, a logical time to act with the outcome of the rebellion still unclear and a bid to rescue Richard feared. Ian Mortimer suggests that perhaps Bucton/Buxton was told to be ready to kill Richard if Pontefract was attacked, not to act at once on his arrival, which would explain how Richard appears to have been alive for some weeks after this. It was probably Sir Thomas Swynford, son of Henry's late stepmother Katherine Swynford (John of Gaunt's mistress and third wife, and mother of his Beaufort children) who was in charge of Richard in January 1400, and it was him who despatched the 'official' news of the ex-king's death to London on 14 February as listed in the official administrative *Close Rolls*. The 'Exton murder by violence' story was the one which Shakespeare used for his play *King Richard II* so it achieved a spurious authority – and the Shakespearian dramatization of a group of noble conspirators deposing a 'tyrant' was seen as so inflammatory even 200 years after the event that Queen Elizabeth I regarded the play with distaste and tried to ban it; and the 1601 Essex Conspiracy plotters attended a performance before their revolt to try to inspire themselves. Other French chronicles also refer to violent murder in the aftermath of the failed January uprising,[35] but the French government – with which Richard had signed a peace-treaty in 1396 despite the preference of many nobles for continuing the lucrative wars – had every reason to fear the military intentions of Henry IV, who was spreading claims that he was the heroic King foretold to reconquer all of Aquitaine (his late father John's duchy) from France. An invasion from England was to be expected from the feared and skillful jousting-champion Henry with his international connections, and the more he could be portrayed as a murderous usurper and Ricardian resistance be inspired the better.

It is more likely that Richard was killed – or died by his own hand? – later than this, and more convincing evidence has him still alive in February. A royal Council meeting document of c. 4 February refers to a debate on guarding him closely if he is still alive[36] – so was this unclear to the councillors due to King Henry's extreme secrecy over what was happening at Pontefract? Some modern commentators, eg Joel Burden in 2003, have suggested that this unusual wording was a hint to the king by embarrassed councillors that if he wanted to take steps to liquidate Richard and solve this 'security problem' they would not object. The ex-king's death was reported to Charles VI of France at the end of January 1400, as he referred to him as dead in his 29 January letter of confirmation of the current Anglo-French truce to the English ambassadors in Paris which they then sent on to London. It was delivered by the ambassadors' messenger William Faryngdon to the Council on 9 February.[37] It may have been inspired by the story that reached the French chroniclers about 'Piers Exton' being told to do the killing at the height of the January 1400 rebellion. Even if it relied on rumour it suggests some expectation and acceptance that Richard was dead – and might have reassured the Council and king that if the French believed Richard to be dead they could go ahead and kill him without fear of reprisal. By that reckoning, if Faryngdon arrived in London a few days before the Council meeting and told the king the news from Paris in private he could have ordered Richard to be killed then (ie c. 7 February). Richard was known to be dead at Pontefract by 17 February, when a royal squire was sent there to view his body and bring it to London;[38] this followed the despatch of a squire to London from Pontefract to report the ex-king's death on 14 February by Sir Thomas Swynford. Contemporary chronicler Adam of Usk dated his death at the end of the month (possibly due to news only leaking out then).[39] Other contemporary chronicles gave the date as around 14 February.

The cause of death is less clear, though Richard's body could be seen in public afterwards on its arrival in London so no obvious violence occurred (unlike with Edward II) and the possibility arises that he starved himself to death in despair rather than being murdered by starvation by his captors. An official chronicle of the reigns of Richard and Henry states that Richard starved himself to death.[40] Thomas Walsingham wrote that he had starved himself as a result of depression after the failure of the January 1400 plot, then tried to eat but could not and had a fatal organ failure.[41] Others claim he was killed by others by starvation. This is presumably the accepted version as of 1400; the Evesham chronicle says that he was said to have refused food but some reports had it that he was deliberately starved and Adam of Usk says that he mourned his downfall to the point of death but was also tormented by being starved by his custodian Swynford.[42] The *Brut* blames his guards and the Percys' rebel manifesto of 1403 claims that Richard was starved to death on Henry's orders, over fifteen days.[43] The Percies were in the best position to know the truth as Henry's closest supporters and as major lords in the Yorkshire region, and notably they did not attempt to claim that Richard had escaped in their declarations during their 1403 rebellion though this was widely believed and there was a pretender to his identity, the 'Mammet', at large in Scotland.

The body was displayed at St Paul's Cathedral on 6–7 March for public obsequies and buried out of the way of a potential 'martyr' cult at King's Langley in Hertfordshire, near a royal country manor.[44] The bishop of Lichfield and several important abbots attended, but no lay lords; it was clearly a 'low-key' affair. Henry V, once Richard's well-treated ward and hostage during his father's exile in 1398–9, seems to have felt some guilt for the ex-king's death and out-of-the-way burial and moved the remains to a grander tomb in Westminster Abbey with a public ceremony in 1413.[45] The date of death was given as 14 February 1400, but his survival was widely rumoured after 1400 and was connected to the appearances of imitators sponsored by the current king's foes – most notably Richard Maudelyn, the 'Mammet'.

Richard was clearly an unstable and deeply suspicious character given to conflicting emotions and wild plans as early as 1385 when he was eighteen, given the bizarre plan to murder John of Gaunt which he was at least presumed to have approved. Nor did he 'sideline' the apparent leader of the plot, his close friend Robert de Vere, then as a potential political disaster – or cease giving him unusually large amounts of honours and offices. After the so-called 'Wonderful Parliament' took control of the political agenda from him at Westminster in 1386 (possibly urged on by John of Gaunt and Thomas of Gloucester behind the scenes) Richard threatened to 'go on strike' and refuse to approve their legislation, to no avail. In 1397–9, as we have seen, he endeavoured to strike down his enemies by a mixture of legal persecution and outright murder, and he was still threatening Henry with due vengeance after his arrest at Flint in North Wales – which gave his cousin every reason to argue for his permanent removal. In view of all this an outbreak of deep depression and starving himself to death was possible, if less likely than foul play. But whereas the plotters intending to free Edward II had been a small group of his committed partisans in 1327 and his half-brother in 1329–30 and nobody ever seriously attempted to put him back on his throne, Richard attracted ever more implausible claims of his survival even when his death was more certain (though still secret and so open to wild rumours that it was faked). There now emerged a network of friars apparently spreading rumours of Richard's survival through 1400–02, with arrests following; they were aided by the 'Prophecy of the Six Kings' (dated around 1312?) that a King of England identifiable as Richard II would lose his throne to a ravening 'wolf' and then recover it. One arrested friar told Henry to his face that the Prophecy would be fulfilled as Richard returned to fight and destroy him.[46] The Prophecy could then be moulded to fit circumstances as events changed; in 1403 the earl of Northumberland and his son 'Hotspur' quarrelled with Henry and launched their own rebellion so they could be identified as the 'Dragon from the North' who would join with the heraldic beasts of the west (ie the rebel Welsh) and Ireland (ie the Mortimers who had estates there) to overthrow the usurper. The involvement of so many churchmen, from an 'activist' wing of the clergy who often included both learned men and devout ascetics, suggests that – as with the involvement of Franciscan friar thinkers like Adam Marsh and idealist bishops like Robert Grosseteste and Walter and Thomas Cantelupe with 'reformer' Simon de Montfort's cause in the mid-thirteenth-century – the sheer illegality of Henry's usurpation and the flagrant deposition of the current King (who unlike Edward II was not morally suspect) infuriated them. These sort of medieval prophecies had a habit of being self-fulfilling as people fitted past events into their terms and expected the outstanding parts of them to be carried out; the prophecy was thus a useful weapon for Richard's enemies whether or not he was actually alive. In more prosaic terms, people of some education argued openly that Henry's government was illegal; one arrested Franciscan friar in June 1402 (Roger Frisby) was bold enough to tell the King to his face that it was illegal to force Richard to abdicate against his will.[47] All the offenders were hanged at Tyburn – once Henry could find a jury to convict them, which took several attempts. Nor was the succession in 1399 as clear-cut as in 1327, and as people of high birth and repute had challenged it on the battlefield within four months of Henry's accession this emboldened more to do so.

Given Richard's pacific attitude to France and Henry's apparent desire for war with them, French help could be expected for any troublemakers, and from autumn 1400 they had another ally in Wales where one of Richard's former (probable) partisans, Owain GlynDwr the heir of the ancient royal line of Powys, rose in a successful 'national' rebellion. But the main case of a pretender to Richard's identity emerged in Scotland, which had had its own dangerous military confrontation with Henry in summer 1400 as he unsuccessfully demanded that its King Robert III (second of the Stewart line and with the birth-name 'John') do homage to him for his kingdom. The ageing and ailing King, a sexagenarian depressive with a lame leg who later called himself the unluckiest of men, was by this time eclipsed in power by his vigorous younger brother and 'Governor' (regent) Duke Robert of Albany, a ruthless character with his own predatory ambitions who had been fighting over power with the King's elder son David, Duke of Rothesay, since 1398. Like King Richard, the arrogant and luckless David was a young man of many talents who mishandled the country's elite and ended up feared for his gangster-like marauding and interned by Duke Robert in 1401 'for his own safety' while trying to take control of the property of the see of St Andrews in Fife. Locked up in Robert's Falkland Castle, like Richard he then mysteriously starved to death (aged twenty-four), leaving only the King's eight-year-old son Prince James between Duke Robert and the throne. The Duke was clearly capable of extreme measures in protecting his country and his own interests, and some time in late 1401 a pretender to Richard's identity who resembled him closely, known popularly as 'The Mammet' (a contemporary word for 'puppet'), emerged in Scotland and was recognized by the regime as the rightful king of England. According to what Duke Robert's warlike ally Earl Archibald of Douglas told the French when he headed to France that November-December to seek a military alliance, 'Richard' had been discovered hiding in the guise of a servant in the kitchens of 'Lord of the Isles' Donald Macdonald, head of the eponymous clan and lord of most of the Hebrides.[48] Donald, descended from a semi-autonomous dynasty of mixed 'Viking' and Gaelic inheritance that had ruled the Hebrides and Argyll/Lorn since the times of Somerled 'the Mighty' (d 1164), was the son of his predecessor 'Lord of the Isles' John Macdonald (d 1386) by King Robert III's sister Euphemia, and so was of the close royal kin though very much his own man and frequently at war with or defying his nominal overlords the Stewart kings. Whether or not either Robert of Albany or his ally Douglas had sent the pretender out of the way of any pro-Henrican agents or assassins until they were ready to use him or he was a Macdonald client, he now came in useful in stirring up trouble in England to keep Henry busy and ensure that he had no time to invade Scotland again. He has sometimes been identified with a previous Ricardian lookalike' called Richard Maudelyn who the 'Epiphany Rising' rebels in January 1400 paraded dressed in royal armour as 'Richard' during their revolt, but the latter was apparently captured and hanged in London afterwards so this is unlikely. The French chronicler Jean de Creton, former Ricardian household member and witness of the royal deposition of September 1399, was sent off to Edinburgh to see the 'Mammet' and judge if he was genuine, probably as a result of Douglas' embassy to Paris winning the backing of semi-insane King Charles' powerful and Anglophobic younger brother Duke Louis of Orleans who was planning a war. (As the French had officially accepted Richard as dead in early 1400 and had even arranged for his widow Isabella to return home to seek a new French husband, recognizing him as alive in 1402 had its problems.) While Douglas was helping to muster a French fleet at Harfleur in the Seine estuary to sail to Scotland and aid an attack on England, De Creton interviewed the 'Mammet' – and concluded that he was a fake. By September 1402 he was back in Paris reporting his opinions.[49] But the 1402 Scots attack on England went ahead, to meet a crushing defeat at the battle of Homildon Hill where Douglas and the Governor's son Murdach were captured and many of their troops killed – resulting in a quarrel over the resulting ransoms between King Henry and the battle's Percy victors and a Percy revolt in 1403. This time the rebellion, which was defeated at the battle of Shrewsbury, was in the name of Edmund Mortimer, as was the subsequent 'Triple Alliance' plan between the earl of Northumberland, Owain GlynDwr, and Edmund in 1405. The rumours of Richard's survival continued, but the senior anti-Lancastrian plotters now seem to have given up on producing him (or a convincing enough fake) and moved on to support Mortimer, who had the advantage of lacking Richard's controversial record for autocracy and executions. But due to a mixture of muddle, rumour and high politics Richard had been for a time more popular when he was already dead than when he was alive.

Chapter 4

The 'Princes in the Tower': Who Killed Them, if Anyone?

The background

The fate of Edward V and his brother Richard, Duke of York, the 'Princes in the Tower', remains as much a mystery as it was five hundred years ago, with a whole industry of rival conspiracy theories and connected controversy over the character and culpability of their uncle Richard III (the discovery of whose remains at Leicester in 2012 added to the modern interest in it). Richard III did have a 'crookback' as in Tudor propaganda, but was the latter correct about him being a serial killer too? The twelve-year-old ex-king Edward V, who had succeeded on his father's surprise death at the age of 40 on 9 April 1483, and his brother were last definitely seen alive some weeks after Edward's deposition on 25 June. Edward had been in the Tower – probably at the royal apartments on the south side of the main keep, the 'White Tower' – since his arrival in London on 5 May. He had been intercepted en route to London from his residence at Ludlow Castle on 1 May by his uncle and later supplanter Richard, Duke of Gloucester, who had been nominated as 'Protector' of the realm in Edward IV's will but alleged that the boy's mother Queen Elizabeth Woodville and her partisans were planning to get the new king to London for a quick coronation in order to argue that a crowned king did not need a Protectorate. The precedent was Henry VI, titularly adult from his coronation in 1429 aged seven-and-a-half though controlled by a council from 1422 until 1437 – though on that occasion there had been no need for a 'Protector' and the new king's uncle Duke Humphrey of Gloucester had been refused that role.[1] They would then take over the government for their own benefit, contrary to the late King's intentions. In fact, it is not clear exactly what legal powers (full authority for himself as regent or just first among equals on a council who all had votes on policy, as in 1422?) Edward intended for Richard.

From the propaganda which Richard later put out when seizing power in the Parliamentary Act *Titulus Regius*, he was allegedly concerned at the Woodville family's immorality, grasping habits, and bad influence on the late king and feared for their control of the government. Indeed, they were blamed for driving Edward IV to his death aged forty by loose living and gluttony – a plausible charge given that Edward was recorded as being noticeably overweight as early as 1475 by the French envoy Philippe de Commignes at the 'summit meeting' between Edward and Louis XI at Picquigny.[2] Edward had not only died at forty but had shown little signs of his old vigour in recent years, most noticeably in the dispute with Scotland since 1480 when his brother Richard had been left to command the invasion of 1482. The royal court was riven by a feud between the king's close friend and Chamberlain, Lord Hastings, and the king's stepson the Marquis of Dorset, his wife Elizabeth Woodville's elder son by her first husband, suggesting that Edward IV could not control his relatives and demand that they show public respect to each other. Nor was there any indication that Edward was formulating a response to the serious diplomatic reverse he had suffered in 1482, when Louis – who had effectively bribed him to abandon his invasion in 1475, a disappointment to royal advisers like the belligerent Richard – had abandoned the betrothal of his son Dauphin Charles to Edward's eldest daughter. The unmilitary Louis had been careful to buy off Edward at Picquigny as a serious threat, but now ignored him in his 'rapprochement' with his old enemy, Edward's ally Maximilian of Habsburg (ruler of the Low Countries, England's principal trading-partner). Edward had been left without an ally by Louis' blatant move in 1482, but so far had not responded. Was this due to laziness and preoccupation with court diversions, what Richard – now proved right in refusing to take part in the celebrations with the French in 1475 – would have called Woodville-influenced debauchery? In fact, a sluggish royal response to rising crisis had also been apparent from Edward in facing the domestic threat from his angry cousin, the Earl of Warwick, in 1468–9 – the latter had been showing his antagonism to Edward's wife and her kin for years but was able to stage a revolt and march on the royal court without Edward having set spies to watch him, having enough troops on call, or joining the latter once Warwick was approaching. He had been taken by surprise again by the attack on him by Warwick's brother John Neville as the now-exiled

Earl invaded in October 1470, and with no troops handy had ended up fleeing the country. Nor had he quickly arrested his unstable next brother, Duke George of Clarence, for months in 1477 as the latter made ominous noises about wanting the succession and staged a 'kangaroo court' to deal with one of his late wife's ex-maids who he believed had poisoned her. Edward thus did not often react quickly to crises. This flaw in failing to anticipate a potential threat or react quickly to it as it emerged probably increased the danger to Edward's sons in 1483, by means of the king not 'balancing' the power of Richard against other great nobles just in case he was removed from the scene before the Prince of Wales was an adult. Richard had been unswervingly loyal to Edward in the crises of 1469–78, unlike Clarence – but he could still be a threat to Edward's sons later.

The new king's uncle and guardian Anthony Woodville, Earl Rivers (brother of Queen Elizabeth Woodville), evidently did not expect trouble from Richard in April 1483 though according to an important source for events that spring and early summer, the Italian observer in London Dominci Mancini, the Council had blocked Edward IV's intended terms for a full regency by Richard (ie with him having semi- Royal legal powers) in favour of him having only one vote on a regency Council of equals. This was supposed to be out of fear that if Richard had full powers he would usurp the throne, and was coupled with a plan to crown Edward V as early as 4 May. By implication, the coronation would take place before Richard could arrive in London from his Yorkshire estates and interfere with whatever the queen and her allies were planning to do – to seize power and set aside Edward IV's will, Richard subsequently alleged. As Richard was in no hurry to get to London until he was told of the timetable unofficially by Hastings and then left York in haste, this backs up Richard's later complaint that he had not been told of the date and the Council's majority (presumably led by the queen from her panic when he found out and intervened) was intending to carry out the coronation without him. The Croyland Abbey 'continuation' chronicler, based in the fens but usually well-informed, states that the queen (and presumably her son by her first marriage, the Marquis of Dorset, and her brother Sir Edward Woodville) wanted Edward V and Rivers to bring a large army to London with them and Edward IV's close friend and chamberlain, Lord Hastings, stopped this and had it limited to 2,000 men. Presumably the larger army proposal was a plan either to keep Richard out of London by force – and intimidate the Council and the Londoners into accepting a Woodville take-over – or at least to be ready should anyone challenge a Woodville take-over. But if this was the intention, Rivers does not seem to have been part of the plot – or alternatively he thought his sister's plans excessive and Richard to be no threat. He did not leave Ludlow with Edward V in a hurry (ie within a few days of the news of Edward IV's death reaching Ludlow), which should have been the case if he intended to get to London before Richard arrived from the more distant York and then to assist a coup as advised by the Woodvilles in London. News of Edward IV's death on 9 April reached the isolated Welsh Marches town in five or six days, probably on 14 April; Rivers had time to move the Royal entourage quicker than he did and as Hastings had persuaded the Council to limit Rivers' entourage to 2,000 men he did not have to wait for an assembly of the Marcher lords and their men to form up a larger army for him to use. His delay until the 24th in leaving Ludlow suggests that, contrary to Richard's claims circulated in London in May, he was not involved in the queen's alleged plan to stage an early coronation (4 May) and avoid the supposed need for a 'Protectorate' (ie a regency with full powers for one man). Certainly he was not ready to leave Ludlow in a hurry – which argues against the modern suggestion that he and the Queen had slowly poisoned Edward IV in order to run a lucrative regency. He had to be urged to make haste by her son by her first marriage, the Marquis of Dorset, and was clearly not intending to arrive in London by Dorset's intended date of 1 May.

Apparently the queen's attempt on 11 April to get the Council to agree to Edward V and Rivers bringing a large force to London, which other councillors blocked, had so alarmed Hastings that he threatened to withdraw to his governorship of Calais (where he had troops of his own) rather than co-operate with it.[3] The governorship of Calais had been used to defy a previous government, when the Yorkists defied Henry VI from there in 1460 – and used it to re-invade England – and the governor had a large, coherent body of standing troops, which the king did not. (At this date there was no regular army, only local retainers raised for specific campaigns by their lords when required.) Possibly Hastings feared that if a large 'Woodville army' took over London, Dorset would use it to arrest him. When the plan for a large army of Welsh Marcher retainers advancing from Ludlow with Rivers was abandoned and the force limited to 2,000 men Hastings sent in haste to Richard to warn him to hurry to London and stop the 'plot'; from what Richard's partisans circulated in May it seems that there was supposed to be a Woodville plan to ambush Richard en route to London.[4] The crucial Council debates of April 1483 are known to us from two sources – the continuation of the 'Croyland (Abbey) Chronicle', written in the fenland in 1486, and the account written up in December 1483 by the Italian visitor Dominic Mancini, who was in London that spring and summer. What they guessed or reported from hearsay is unclear. Mancini claims that Richard wrote to the Council pointing out his services as Edward IV's principal military lieutenant in the 1470s, in which role he had run his war on Scotland in 1480–2, and asking that he be appointed 'Protector' – as supposedly promised in Edward's will.[5] It is not clear if this was what Edward had promised him earlier (verbally or in writing?), and whether or not Hastings told him of this only now. In any event the Council ignored his request – which might have been expected to draw a military response from him, though if Rivers was so warned he was slow to react. This was however in line with the Council in 1422 refusing the role of Protector to Duke Humphrey, and was not in itself a hostile act.

Richard duly set out from Middleham Castle north-west of York for London on 20 April, with only 300 men (presumably more could not be collected quickly), but accepted an offer from Henry Stafford, Duke of Buckingham, who was based in his Marcher lordship at Brecon, to meet him en route; Buckingham also had around 300 men. Buckingham, descended in the female line from Edward III's youngest son Duke Thomas of Gloucester (murdered 1397) so with his own remote claim to the throne, was married to Elizabeth Woodville's younger sister Catherine but was not a 'Woodville ally' and was supposed to resent having been forced by Edward IV to marry a woman of lower social status than himself. They arranged to meet at Northampton, on the main road south-east across the Midlands, on 29 April – and when Rivers was informed he agreed to join the rendezvous. When Richard's and Buckingham's forces arrived on the 29th Rivers had already moved on to Stony Stratford, several miles ahead. If this breach of the agreement was intended to avoid Richard, as the latter seems to have suspected, it was not very effective as Richard could easily catch the royal party up by a forced ride and Rivers did not have his men on alert to repulse an attack as subsequent events showed.

More likely is Rivers' own explanation sent to Richard, that he did not want all three armed parties to try to secure lodgings in one small town. He did not try to escape or fight, but rode over to Richard's lodgings in Northampton to join him for dinner. Next morning he woke up to find his inn surrounded by troops, and he and other senior Woodville agents – his nephew Richard Grey, the queen's younger son by her first marriage and Dorset's full brother, and the chamberlain Sir Thomas Vaughan, seized on the 30th at Stony Stratford – were arrested by Richard and sent to prison in Yorkshire. The king was secured at Stony Stratford as he was mounting up to ride on to London. The way events unfolded suggests that, as the king's party was caught unawares by Richard's arrival at Stony Stratford, Rivers had told them to set out on the 30th without waiting for his own return. Was Rivers just nervous of the potential for a clash between the two armies, or did he expect the king's party to keep a day or two's ride ahead of Richard all the way to London and enable him to link up with Dorset's men there? The king's party still outnumbered those of Richard and Buckingham by around two to one, but without Rivers' leadership they put up no resistance and the soldiers obeyed Richard's orders to disperse and go home. Edward had to complete his journey with Richard's men. Richard informed the king that he had 'rescued' him from a plot to take control of the government by the Woodvilles, but was not believed. According to Dominic Mancini, not a witness but in London in the spring and summer of 1483 and so able to talk to members of the royal entourage, Richard and Buckingham complained that the Woodvilles had ruined Edward IV's health with riotous living and were not fit to take charge of his son. Buckingham also sneered that a woman, namely the queen (his wife's sister), should not take charge of a regency as Elizabeth was proposing to do. Edward defended his right to rely on his mother's family, to no avail.[6]

On news of the capture of Edward and his Woodville escort the queen and her remaining children took refuge in the Sanctuary at Westminster Abbey, apart from her eldest son Dorset who with her brother Sir Edward Woodville fled the capital. The queen had been driven into this bolt-hole before, when her husband was overthrown by her father's killer the Earl of Warwick in October 1470 in favour of the previously deposed Henry VI, and had given birth to Edward V there on 2 November. This time she was supposed to have broken down the connecting wall between

Palace and sanctuary to move trunks loaded with her goods into safety quicker. Sir Edward Woodville seized part of the late King's treasure and control of the fleet, at least according to what Mancini heard – though in a recent study of Richard's reign Michael Hicks has pointed out that Edward died in debt, his jewels having to be sold to pay for the funeral, so it is not clear where this 'treasure' came from.[7] If the money raised to wage the intended Scottish campaign in 1483 was meant, this was not the 'Royal treasure', a phrase suggesting Edward's personal fortune; indeed, Sir Edward Woodville (as the naval commander) was entitled to use military financial resources. Was the damning implication that the Woodvilles had embezzled the king's personal fortune a piece of post-coup Ricardian propaganda?

The Lord Chancellor, septuagenarian Archbishop Rotherham of York, had some explaining to do when Richard arrived about why he had handed over the Great Seal to the queen in sanctuary rather than kept it ready to give to Richard; he was around seventy and may have been confused but was clearly amenable to Woodville pressure. He changed his mind after a night to consider it and retrieved the Great Seal, but when Hastings wrote to Richard informing him Richard had him dismissed. The Archbishop of Canterbury, Thomas Bourchier (Richard's great-uncle and also related to Buckingham) took the Seal until a new Chancellor was appointed.[8] The Royal party arrived in London for a state entry on 4 May, and the new 'Protector' displayed cartloads of alleged weaponry and armour seized from Rivers' force on his arrival in London, to demonstrate the latter's warlike intentions. Mancini wrote that the explanation for the weaponry was not accepted by the public, and that the arms had been stored in London for use in the next Scots war, and Sir Thomas More's account of c.1513 alleged that people said that the arms would have not been sealed up in barrels if the Woodvilles anticipated using them.[9] (If they were a Woodville stockpile, why had Sir Edward not removed most of them on his ships?) According to the 1486 *Croyland Chronicle* Richard led the taking of oaths of fealty to Edward V by the lords spiritual and temporal, and on 10 May the Council confirmed Richard as 'Protector'. The Chronicle and Mancini agree that there was relief in London at the peaceful outcome, and that Richard treated Edward with all due respect as his sovereign. Edward stayed at the Bishop of London's palace in the City until the Council agreed that he should move to the Tower in mid-May, apparently at Buckingham's suggestion, and Richard joined his mother Cecily Neville at the York family residence, Baynard's Castle (near the mouth of the Fleet River). His subsequent move to Crosby Hall in June was probably due to a need for more space when his wife Anne Neville and her household arrived from York, rather than anything more sinister such as his intention to revive the story of his mother's alleged affair with the archer Blaybourne and claim Edward IV was illegitimate. The coronation was postponed until 24 June, later changed to 22 June – logical enough in order to ensure a good attendance and so greater legitimacy for it. Meanwhile the Anglo-Portuguese naval and merchant adventurer Sir Edward Brampton (Duarte Brandao), a favourite of both Edward IV and Richard, was empowered by the Council to pursue Sir Edward Woodville and succeeded in persuading all but two of his captains to abandon him; the other rebels fled to Brittany.[10] The most prominent opponent of the English regime residing in Brittany, albeit under close supervision from Duke Francis' officers so not able to plot with the new arrivals unhindered, was the Lancastrian claimant to the English throne, Henry VI's nephew Henry Tudor.

Weeks of seeming calm followed, with Richard and the rest of the Council working together ahead of Edward V's planned coronation on 22 June but with evident tensions behind the scenes and the likelihood that some of the Council did not trust Richard's intentions over the throne. It was proposed that Richard's Protectorship should continue after the coronation – a break with precedent, as the formal powers of the last governorship for a minority, Duke Humphrey of Gloucester's, not as formal Protector but as head of a co-equal council, had ended with his ward Henry VI's coronation. That had been in 1429 when he was not yet eight, and Edward was twelve; but Henry had remained subject to effective political tutelage by a Council led by Humphrey until his majority in 1437 aged fifteen. Edward III had not needed a 'political' as opposed to a personal guardianship at his accession aged fourteen, but had been informally under Isabella's and Mortimer's control until his coup against them in October 1330 aged seventeen. His personal guardian, his nearest male kinsman Earl Henry of Lancaster, had not headed the Council.

The likeliest explanation for the Council's agreement to Richard's plan is a reasonable desire to avoid open political conflict with the vengeful Woodvilles once the coronation was over, whatever the personal advantages of a long regency for a power-hungry Richard. There was also the constant reminder for Richard of the fate that had befallen his predecessor Duke Humphrey, undermined by enemies at court once his nephew had reached his majority and arrested suddenly in January 1447 (whereupon he died equally suddenly). Given the somewhat anxious and ultra-suspicious tone of those few letters of Richard during this crisis that we possess (eg to his officials in York asking them to send him extra troops) and his constant harping on about Woodville immorality, it is likely that he was paranoid – with reason or not? – about the danger that he could go the way of Humphrey, the previous Duke of Gloucester disposed of by the men (and women?) around his gullible royal nephew. The nature of the plots and counter-plots of May-June 1483 is obscure and has been clouded by Richard's own 'spin' after his coup on 13 June, which alleged that Lord Hastings had reconciled with his recent foe Dorset through mutual hostility to him. There had been secret messages sent from Hastings to the queen in sanctuary. But it is clear that even if Richard exaggerated the nature of the resistance he was not trusted by many of the late king's senior advisers. A crucial point of debate, as will be explored later, is the date at which the Council considered the allegation that Edward V's parents had not been legally married so the new king was illegitimate and would have to be replaced. Who revealed this, why, and when? Was this discussed in a meeting of the 'lords spiritual and temporal' (ie more of the elite than the Council, so summoned for a special and urgent political purpose?) on or near 9 June? (The question of what this meeting discussed and if it included the revelation of the Edward IV/Eleanor Butler 'pre-contract' that invalidated Edward V's claim to the throne is also complicated by the question of the exact date of the meeting; sceptics argue that the statement in a letter of 9 June by the well-connected Simon Stallworth that there was no important recent news implies that the meeting had not discussed anything important.) Was the story of the new king being illegitimate a 'put-up job' by the ambitious Richard to secure the throne for himself, and was it this which so alarmed Hastings that he was prepared to ally to his ex-foes, the queen and Dorset? Was the allegation that he was plotting with them true, or was it invented or at least exaggerated by Richard?

A recent book by Peter Hancock on the seizure and execution of Hastings also draws attention to the role of one of Hastings' junior allies, the rising Northamptonshire lawyer William Catesby – who was soon to be satirised as one of Richard's inner circle, the 'Cat', in William Collingbourne's famous 1484 rhyme about 'The Rat, the Cat, and Lovell our dog'. Sir Thomas More's abandoned 'hostile' biography of Richard in c.1510 claimed that Richard had used Catesby to approach Hastings about an alliance in pursuit of his plans (ie to depose Edward V) but Hastings not only rejected this overture but used such disturbing language about Richard that the alarmed Catesby reported this to Richard – implicitly, as evidence that Hastings would oppose him physically so he had to be destroyed. In that case it could have been the violent rejection of Richard's overture that tipped Richard over the brink into suddenly arresting and killing Hastings, not (or not only) the evidence/gossip of Hastings dallying with the hostile queen via Mistress Shore. As far as More was concerned, the devious and power-mad Richard was the real plotter and now decided Hastings would stand in his way, and as far as modern apologists of Richard are concerned Richard was the innocent party fearing a Woodville plot. But could the ambitious Catesby have exaggerated Hastings' hostility to persuade Richard to destroy him, thus enabling himself to reap rewards from the paranoid Richard as the Protector/future king's loyal henchman? In the event, Catesby did quickly acquire from Richard both the Chief Forestership of Rockingham Forest in his home county and the Chancellorship of the Exchequer, two lucrative offices held by Hastings.

In any event, Richard suddenly seized and executed Hastings and arrested Lord Stanley, Archbishop Rotherham, and Bishop Morton of Ely at a Council meeting in the Tower on 13 June – not a full Council meeting, as some councillors were meeting separately at Westminster at the same time. This fact of two separate meetings has been used to suggest that Richard planned the 'coup' and summoned those councillors who he suspected to the Tower for a showdown but kept others away so he could deal wth his enemies on their own. The accusations issued to the public afterwards (which found their way into Mancini's and the *Croyland Chronicler*'s contemporary accounts) that the accused had been meeting secretly in recent days may be genuine and reflect what Richard feared they were up to – but not necessarily that their meetings were a plot, only that he either believed this or used it as an excuse. There has also been modern disagreement over whether it was significant that it was only the later account by Polydore Vergil, after Richard's fall in 1485 (not Mancini's 1483 story), that mentioned Richard's arrest of the by then King Henry VII's stepfather Lord Stanley on 13 June. Was this correcting an oversight in earlier accounts, or did Stanley seek to play up – or even invent? – the tyrant's targeting of him on 13 June once Richard was dead and disgraced, to show that he had been patriotically plotting to overthrow Richard at the time? Or would inaccurately putting Stanley on the 13 June 'hit list' to promote his reputation after 1485 have been too blatant, even for such a master of spin? In any case, the meeting ended in a dramatic scene with Richard's retainers storming into the council-chamber in the White Tower at a pre-arranged signal by him. Apparently he had been genially discussing sending out for some strawberries from Bishop Morton's gardens for refreshment one minute and shouting about a plot the next, after a brief interval when he left the room – which has enabled his apologists to claim that in the interval he had received some new message (or documentation) about a genuine plot by one or more of the accused. But as the retainers who stormed in were clearly pre-positioned he had decided on the arrests earlier even if the execution was a surprise move decided on the spot. According to the post-1485 Vergil account Stanley, possibly thinking he was to be killed by the armed henchmen, put up a fight and was injured and overpowered.

The scuffles around the table and the immediate execution of Hastings outside afterwards, said to be over a log on Tower Green,[11] were unusual even for brutal late mediaeval high politics, where dissident ministers were more likely to face a 'show-trial' or – frequently fatal – imprisonment in a distant castle as Richard II's foes had done in 1397–8. Even by Richard's own lurid account his enemies had not been about to murder him and thus required instant justice before their followers could rescue them; the drama was clearly intended to terrorise his critics into acquiescence with his plans. The fact that he did not follow usual precedent in imprisoning Hastings is the clearest riposte to the claims of earnest Ricardians that he was the man of honour and morality that he portrayed himself during his reign, incapable of killing his nephews. Technically he was head of the Council and 'regent' so in the king's legal position and an attempt to overthrow or murder him would count as treason and be punishable by death, and he was Constable of England so he could carry out executions – but hardly without some form of 'court' (even a brief one). The late king had executed captive Lancastrians captured in battle at Tewkesbury in May 1471, with Richard at his side, but they appear to have had some sort of brief judicial procedure rather than being executed within minutes. Richard's execution of the captive Rivers and Sir Richard Grey – the queen's brother and second son – at isolated Pontefract Castle in Yorkshire a few days later were also not necessary given that they were locked away in Yorkshire, were unlikely to be rescued, and had not had any formal trial, though they may have appeared before a makeshift tribunal headed by the Earl of Northumberland. The charges laid at this trial were certainly never publicised, which suggests secrecy and flimsy evidence – even if Rivers had been involved in Elizabeth Woodville's plan to deny Richard the Protectorship, he had not made any obvious threat to Richard's life and his executed companions' 'crimes' had never been listed. Richard's father-in-law Warwick had similarly executed the queen's father and another of her brothers without any apparent judicial procedure in the course of a violent coup in 1469 – did this and the May 1471 executions at Tewkesbury act as Richard's precedents for thinking he could get away with acts of blatant terror?

On 16 June Richard sent his emissaries to the Sanctuary to require the queen to hand over Prince Richard to join the new king, making it clear that if she did not do so he would be seized by force. (Richard and his brothers had violated sanctuary before, at Tewkesbury Abbey after the nearby battle in May 1471 to seize and execute Lancastrian leaders.) She did as she was told, with Archbishop Bourchier – as head of the Church, a valuable guarantor of the boy's safety, and also a remote royol cousin – taking charge of him to hand him to Richard and join his brother.[12] Six days later the boys' bastardy was publicly proclaimed in a surprise sermon by the Lord Mayor of London's brother Friar Shaa/Shaw at Paul's Cross, though Mancini (who says that the sermon alleged that Edward IV was not legally king as he was a bastard) and the *Croyland Chronicler* (who says that Edward V was cited as a bastard due to his father's 'pre-contract' to Eleanor Butler, nee Talbot, before he married Elizabeth Woodville) disagree on the nature of the accusation. According to Mancini, after Edward IV had been announced as a bastard the Duke of Buckingham addressed an assembly of the leading men of London and repeated the charge, adding that anyone could see that Edward IV had not resembled his 'father', Duke Richard of York (a small man whereas Edward had been over six feet tall), but Richard did resemble the late duke. This political shock – which cannot have been welcome to Edward IV's and Richard's mother Duchess Cecily of York if it indeed accused her of adultery – was followed by Edward V's deposition on 24 June. A deputation of leading citizens – no doubt stage-managed – then waited on Richard next day at his city residence, Crosby Place, to request him to assume the throne. As early as 10 June he had been writing to York asking for the urgent despatch of an armed force to London to help him against plotters, with exaggerated language about the queen and her kin planning to murder him and Buckingham and overthrow the realm's men of honour[13] which is typical of his reliance on a 'moral' tone combined with paranoia in his public utterances. At the least, it indicates a mixture of serious personal insecurity and a readiness to resort to semi-religious language plus spin demonizing his opponents – which is probably evidence of an unstable element in his character. These troops were duly used to intimidate opposition in the capital. In a significant settling of what appear to be old grudges, Edward IV's most well-known mistress 'Jane' (really Elizabeth) Shore was forced to do public penance as a whore after being accused of being the go-between who had brought her lovers Hastings and Dorset to co-operate in the recent 'plot'.[14] In another example of repeated use of a moral tone plus bearing grudges, Richard later wrote angrily to his new chancellor Bishop Russell about the obtuseness of his solicitor Thomas Lynom in proposing to marry 'Jane' who he regarded as wicked and immoral. The marriage went ahead despite the king's anger.

The boys were not at Richard's coronation on 6 July according to the usual story, though Horace Walpole's investigation of the evidence in the 1760s was to turn up a Royal Wardrobe account for the costume intended to be worn by the 'Lord Edward, son of Edward the Fourth' at the coronation. This was explained away by others as being a left-over order for robes for Edward V's cancelled coronation, but in that case it would have called him 'King' not 'Lord' and the same roll referred to the 'Queen', i.e. Richard's wife Anne. Possibly Edward did attend the coronation; he was apparently expected to do so from this evidence. The boys could still be seen playing in the Tower's internal gardens some time during the summer, according to the *Great Chronicle* – though it only dates this vaguely to the Lord Mayoralty of John Shaa/Shaw which ended in October so it is not decisive as to timing.[15] They were then 'gradually withdrawn' into the inner apartments with Richard's own retainers in charge of them; thus wrote the Italian visitor Dominic Mancini, who compiled his account from stories he had heard during his stay in London without giving precise dates or sources. He wrote it up after returning home in December, so some 'post facto' guesswork or muddle is possible. He wrote that this process of debarring Edward's former attendants began after Hastings was executed on 13 June. The 'inner apartments' probably mean the White Tower rather than the normal royal apartments around the courtyard to its south; access to the latter was more easy. They were seen less and less frequently at the windows – until they were not seen at all.[16] It is likely that there were genuine plots by Woodville partisans to free them which Richard took as an excuse for his action; a letter of his from his 'progress' at Minster Lovell on 29 July to Bishop Russell, the Chancellor, refers to some serious but unspecified enterprise by unnamed persons of which he will have heard.[17] The plot was clearly too sensitive to be mentioned in a letter which might go astray, so it probably involved overthrowing Richard. In August a series of judicial investigations were carried out in the city into a plan formed in London to storm the Tower and rescue the Princes,[18] but it is not clear if this was by Woodville partisans sent by the queen-mother or a spontaneous local plan. In either case, Richard had reasons to keep the boys closely guarded by his 'trusties' and remove their previous attendants.

They were rumoured to be dead in London before Mancini left London in late July 1483 (five weeks after Richard's coup) as he wrote that he had seen people he talked to in London bursting into tears about their probable fate after they ceased to be seen.[19] The murder was rumoured on the continent by Christmas. The Neville protégé panegyricist John Rous, writing in Warwickshire, later named the date of the killing as three months after Richard seized Edward V, i.e. early August.[20] The first formal accusation of murder was made by the French Chancellor, Guillaume de Rochefort, in a speech to the Estates-General in the new year of 1484. He knew Mancini's fellow-Roman and patron Angelo Cato (Archbishop of Vienne), who asked Mancini to write his account; and as the latter had by then received Mancini's account it is possible that he owed his information to them.[21] As France was under a stable regency for a king of Edward V's age he could score a diplomatic 'point' that French regencies did not end in regicide by ambitious uncles. Louis XI also seems to have heard something about possible murder of the boys before he died on 30 August 1483,[22] though the source for this detail was written later. In England, the *Great Chronicle* reported that the murder was widely rumoured at Easter 1484 but rumours had been circulating in summer 1483.[23] The boys were presumed to be alive by the landed gentry in the south-east in September 1483, as the rebellion then by Edward IV's former supporters – including an impressive thirty-three JPs, three sheriffs, and Richard's own brother-in-law St Leger – was carried out in their name, but rumours of their murder at Richard's hands were circulating at that point. Co-ordinated with action by the boys' fugitive half-brother Dorset and uncle Sir Edward Woodville, the revolt was intended to restore Edward V. The rebels were forced to act earlier than the planned 12 October, probably due to a leak of their plans to Richard – who seems to have heard rumours of a plot as early as 29 July if the letter he wrote to Bishop Russell then can be interpreted thus. The risings in the south-west occurred slightly later than those in the south-east so Richard did not have to face both at once. His principal lieutenant John Howard, granted Prince Richard's Dukedom of Norfolk at the end of June, was able to divert the rebels in Kent from London; the loyalists could then move on to tackle risings in Wiltshire, Dorset and Devon.

But the next stage of the rebellion, by Richard III's disloyal ex-ally Henry Stafford, Duke of Buckingham, in South Wales a few weeks later, brought Henry Tudor into play as the new candidate for the throne. Henry was the son of the senior surviving Lancastrian claimant, Margaret Beaufort – the wife of Lord Stanley, the greatest lord in Lancashire and one of the anti-Ricardian Councillors arrested on 13 June. Daughter of John Beaufort, Marquis of Somerset (died 1444), she had been first married – at the age of thirteen – to Henry VI's half-brother Edmund Tudor, son of Henry V's widow Catherine de Valois by her former servant Owen Tudor. (Catherine's secret marriage, the first major late medieval royal misalliance, had been conducted privately away from court but was accepted by the 'Establishment' as being legal, unlike Edward IV's similarly secret marriage in 1483–5.) Margaret had been widowed before Henry was born, as Edmund had been sent to South Wales to re-impose royal authority there against the plans of local pro-Yorkist magnates and had been captured and died of the plague after a period in custody, technically after his release. Stanley was her second Yorkist husband since then, and had loyally supported Edward IV in 1471 despite being brother-in-law to his foe Warwick 'the Kingmaker'. He had however failed to aid Edward when Warwick revolted in 1470, and was to earn a reputation for treachery over his blatantly equivocal conduct on the battlefield of Bosworth in 1485.

It is uncertain whether Stanley or Margaret was the prime mover in their participation in the presumed plot against Richard on 13 June 1483, and as suggested above it is also possible that Stanley played up his involvement after 1485 in order to show how valiantly he had resisted the 'tyrant' in 1483. This is not to say that he was never involved in any move in June 1483 to resist Richard's alleged threat to Edward V's crown, merely that the depth of his involvement – and thus his wife's – is unclear. All that is clear is that if they were arrested Stanley was soon released and Margaret was entrusted to him as surety for her future good behaviour. (Apart from Jane/Elizabeth Shore, Richard usually treated women chivalrously.) So is the story of his being attacked by Richard's lackeys in the famous scuffle in the Council Chamber in the White Tower that day, which only appeared after 1485, untrustworthy due to its late emergence; did the Stanleys play it up to show that their enmity to Richard and betrayal of him in 1485 was his fault, not theirs? And was Polydore Vergil's version, that Richard backed off punishing him as this would add more enemies to an already extensive list, also post-1485 'Stanley spin' promoted by the then 'back in favour' Stanley? But as of late summer 1483 Margaret, if not her husband, was plotting (again?). Her own claim to the throne was dubious, ironically on the same grounds as that which Richard was to use against Edward V. Her grandfather John Beaufort, eldest son of John of Gaunt by his third marriage (to Katherine Swynford, Chaucer's sister-in-law) and half-brother to Henry IV, had been born illegitimate while John was married to another woman, Princess Catherine of Castile. They had been excluded from the throne at the time of John and Katherine's belated marriage in 1396. The Beaufort/Tudor claim to the throne was weak, and it was therefore surprising that the Yorkist loyalists of Edward IV's line should link up with this claim unless they believed their own candidates to be dead. The sources agree that Buckingham rose in October in Tudor's name, despite an apparent meeting just before his revolt with the Queen's refugee brother Bishop Lionel Woodville who could be expected to be acting for the Princes. Sir Thomas More alleged that he was persuaded into acting for Tudor by his captive Bishop Morton of Ely, another hostile Councillor arrested by Richard on 13 June and now in Buckingham's custody – and More's chief informant would have been Morton himself who More had served as a young man. The *Croyland Chronicler*, writing earlier than More (1486), also mentions Morton as persuading Buckingham to revolt and to do so in Tudor's name.[24]

There is no apparent indication as to why Edward V's cause was quietly dropped. The date when his cause was transformed into Tudor's is unclear too, with no indication which rival – Edward V or Tudor – was proclaimed by the Cornish rebels at Bodmin. If the later evidence that Edward IV had considered marrying off his eldest daughter Elizabeth to Tudor around 1476 is accurate, it is possible that he would have been willing to sail to England to aid a rebellion in her family's favour even before he was the preferred candidate for the throne.[25] Alternatively, the idea was just a means of luring Henry home and persuading his host Duke Francis that he could be handed over safely; Henry did not trust Edward and took sanctuary until Duke Francis agreed he could stay in Brittany. Apart from assisting in any plot to weaken the House of York, he could already have been hoping for Elizabeth's hand and a powerful role at the court of a restored but under-age Edward V. As Henry Tudor won the next round of rebellion against Richard in 1485 and was then in a position to control the publication of 'official' histories, he could well have banned any reference to the fact that in September-October 1483 he had sailed to join in the revolt in Edward V's name and only became the candidate for the throne when rumours of the Princes' deaths reached the rebels. Alternatively, it is possible that his mother Lady Margaret promised Elizabeth Woodville and her family to back Edward V, but was planning to double-cross her by spreading rumours that the boys were dead so the rebels should proclaim Henry as king instead. If Margaret's henchmen and other Tudor partisans did spread the rumours, this is not proof that they had anything to do with the boys' disappearance – but the rumours could not be contradicted by any Woodville partisans having proof of the boys' survival.

The fact that Henry Tudor and emissaries from Elizabeth Woodville's faction in London seem to have reached an agreement late that year on a joint strategy against Richard centring on Henry marrying the boys' eldest sister, Princess Elizabeth – which Henry swore to do at Rennes cathedral at Christmas 1483 – would indicate that both parties believed the Princes to be dead and Elizabeth thus to be the Yorkist heiress. Elizabeth Woodville's belated agreement with Richard in 1484, leading to her emergence from sanctuary with her daughters, is no proof that she regarded Richard as innocent of murder – rather, she could not stay in Westminster Abbey indefinitely and had to come to terms.[26] As it was, her action in coming to terms with Richard was to be used by Henry Tudor as an excuse for disgracing her in 1487 – who from his apparent keenness to use this pretext may have thought she had betrayed him. This was harsh. Richard may not have killed the Princes, but he had executed her brother Earl Rivers and her second son Sir Richard Grey – leaders of the escort intercepted at Stony Stratford – in June 1483 so there is no question of this marking a reconciliation between them.

What remains puzzling is why in 1485 Elizabeth Woodville advised her eldest son, the Marquis of Dorset, to abandon Henry Tudor's cause and accept the offer of a pardon from Richard – who in 1483 had violently criticised him as a debauchee who had helped to ruin Edward IV's health and who had executed his brother Richard. Dorset was convinced enough to try to slip away from the Tudor headquarters in France, but was caught and forced to return.[27] Presumably he had been convinced by his mother to abandon Henry as a losing cause – but why would either of them trust Richard? Elizabeth Woodville had no reason to support Richard against Henry, unless she was hoping that he would marry her eldest daughter Elizabeth (seen as a strong possibility in spring 1485 and possibly backed by the princess herself unless she was really after a Portuguese match) and use that as an opportunity for a family reconciliation. But why trust Richard's promises? Elizabeth Woodville may have been unaware that Richard's advisers William Catesby and Sir Richard Ratcliffe had warned him that an 'incestuous' marriage could cause a revolt among his invaluable northern supporters, as stated by the *Croyland Chronicle* (which accused Richard of lying and his Council of knowing he was lying when he told them that the thought of the marriage had never entered his head). But the king's public oath in spring 1485 that he was not going to marry his niece[28] – who was then sent well away from court, to Sheriff Hutton castle near York – should have put paid to hopes of this alliance for the foreseeable future. Richard also nearly managed to persuade the ailing Duke Francis of Brittany's scheming chief minister, Pierre Landois, to get a warrant issued for Henry Tudor's arrest and extradition, which would have stymied his invasion plans. But Tudor was tipped off and fled to France in time, apparently following a warning from the exiled Bishop Morton in Flanders (who may have relied on a Council 'leak' in London from Sir Thomas Stanley, Henry's stepfather, as the plan was highly secret).

Richard III – was his usurpation legal and did it make him kill his predecessor?

The usual murderer is cited as Richard, who had physical custody of the boys in the Tower of London and had been at pains to depose Edward in June 1483 rather than just taking over the regency. As the new king's nearest male relative he had a just claim to the latter, whether or not Edward IV's will had appointed him 'Protector' – Henry VI's paternal uncles had taken over his regency in 1422. It is not clear if Edward's will had appointed Richard as the new king's full 'Protector', with the same legal powers to carry out political business as the king, or just as his personal guardian; Richard claimed the former. The fact that the will was not published must be suspicious, though the political chaos of May-June 1483 could explain the fact; Richard was not to be trusted on other matters and may have sought to imply that Edward had given him more powers than he had in fact done. The creation of a full legal Protectorate for a boy already aged twelve was surely such a large step that if Edward had clearly done so in a specific, retrievable document Richard and his allies of May 1483 (including Hastings) would have felt obliged to publicise it, if only to leading citizens. They did not – so was the real will suppressed as useless to Richard's propaganda?

The notion of a full 'Protectorate', giving control of the government to the incumbent, on behalf of a boy already aged twelve in April 1483 is unprovable and had no precedent. (It had not been mentioned in Edward's previous will, drawn up before his expedition to France in 1475 when the Prince was only four.) Edward III had not needed a 'Protector' at fourteen in January 1327, with the government only unofficially controlled by his mother Isabella (who had possession of the royal seal to validate orders) and her lover and the king having a legal 'guardian' – his closest male kin, the Earl of Lancaster – not a Protector. On this occasion, Isabella and Mortimer clearly did not want their foe Lancaster – later dismissed at their behest after trying to gain physical possession of Edward – possessing any political power. Even in August 1422 the accession of a baby of eight months had not led to such drastic action on behalf of either of his father's adult and competent brothers. The Council had rejected the terminology of a 'Protectorate' for the regency of Henry VI's younger uncle Duke Humphrey of Gloucester, who was to rule within England while his older brother Bedford did so in France, in order to give equal powers to all the regency council jointly. The term 'Protector' for Richard's regency was apparently given in a letter to him by Lord Hastings once Edward IV was dead, informing him of the terms of the royal will and the 'Woodville plot' to set it aside; but what powers did it entail? Richard later had Hastings – the only other person who had seen it? – executed so he could not confirm the details to later enquirers.

Richard might have shown the letter to the Council when he arrived in London to justify his arrest of Rivers' group and Hastings confirmed the details, or that they had read the late king's will for themselves once its 'suppressor' Elizabeth Woodville was out of the way in sanctuary. But this is not certain; the large armed escort who arrived with Richard, and Hastings' acquiescence in his actions, would have intimidated any ministers who wanted to question their version of events. The royal will was not publicised during May 1483; the public had to take Richard's word for the contents. But even if Edward IV did intend his brother to be 'Protector' as opposed to being the new king's personal guardian as Lancaster had been to Edward III, this may only have been intended to cover the few weeks until the coronation. Given the immanent quarrel between Richard and Hastings, and Hastings' closeness to Edward IV, it is possible that the late king had intended the Protectorate to last only to the coronation and that Hastings backed this; too late, he found out that Richard had other ideas.

Richard's second coup: the 'pre-contract' story emerges

Richard had the right to be Edward V's guardian. This was not a politically secure position, as Edward III's guardian Lancaster had found in 1327–8 – he was denied power by the queen-mother and her lover Roger Mortimer and when he tried to take personal custody of the new King was blocked by military force. The late King's brother, Edmund, Earl of Kent, ended up executed in 1330 for attempting to overthrow the new regime. Richard would have been aware of these precedents, and of the suspicious death of Henry VI's politically neutered uncle Humphrey, the last Duke of Gloucester before him – in 1447. But claiming the throne was another matter, particularly as it was on the novel basis of Edward IV not having been married legally to Elizabeth Woodville. Nothing had been heard of this claim until now – at least publicly, as it may explain the suicidal bravado of Richard's brother George, Duke of Clarence, in claiming to be Edward IV's rightful heir in 1477. Given the instability and sporadic greed for power of the unstable Clarence, however, other historians have long been sceptical about whether Clarence 'needed' such concrete evidence of his being cheated of his rights to challenge his elder brother. Already pardoned for joining in his father-in-law Warwick's revolts in 1469–70 and then backing Henry VI against Edward in 1470–1 in return for being made his heir, Clarence had saved himself from punishment by deserting back to Edward on the latter's return in March 1471. In typically treacherous fashion, he had been allegedly bringing his south-western levies to the south Midlands to rescue Warwick (based at Coventry) from the advancing Edward when he joined up with the latter instead, probably at Burford in the Cotswolds, but it is unclear if he had already been in contact with Edward secretly (via their mother Cecily or their sister Duchess Margaret of Burgundy?). His armed retainers had been needed by Edward to fight the experienced and well-supported Warwick and ex-Queen Margaret's French troops in 1471 so his pardon was inevitable, but he had then chosen to challenge Edward again in 1477 and hint that the king's sons were not the legal heirs. According to the near-contemporary accounts of Dominic Mancini and Polydore Vergil, he had been using astrologers to predict that Edward IV's successor would be 'G' (ie George, himself – though in the event a surprise twist meant that the real successor was 'G' for 'Richard of Gloucester'). He may have been unhinged by his wife Isabel Neville's recent death in childbirth in 1476 as he had one of her gentlewomen, Ankarette Twynho, seized and executed for supposedly killing her by poison, intimidating the jury which he summoned into finding her guilty. But his conduct was bizarre

The Rufus Stone, as set up in 1745 near Malwood and Stoney Cross Plain, New Forest. But how accurate is the tradition that King William II was killed here? (© *Maigheach – geal/Creative Commons*)

New Forest landscape close to the Rufus Stone site. Ideal for a lurking assassin with a bow? (© *Peter Facey/Creative Commons*)

Winchester Cathedral where the 'accidentally killed' king was hastily buried while his brother seized the Treasury and headed for London to be crowned. (© *Tim Venning*)

Hereford marketplace; site of the gruesome execution of the captured royal favourite Hugh Despenser the younger by Queen Isabella in 1326. (© *Tim Venning*)

Berkeley Castle. Gloucestershire. Site of the supposed secret murder – or escape? – of the deposed king Edward II in 1327. (© *Philip Halling/Creative Commons*)

The courtyard of Berkeley Castle, which the ex-king would have had to cross (and then negotiate the walls and moat) if he really escaped from his cell before Roger Mortimer's assassins arrived. (© *Chris Gunns/Creative Commons*)

Corfe Castle, Dorset. According to the mysterious 'Fieschi Letter' the escaped king, turned hermit, hid out here in 1329 – and others believed this story too. (© *Tim Venning*)

The Great Hall ruins in the keep, Corfe Castle. 'Edward II' was supposedly seen dining here two years after his 'death' – but was this a scam to trap his would-be rescuers? (© *Tim Venning*)

Conwy Castle, North Wales, where Richard II was tricked into surrendering by the Percy allies of his rebel cousin Henry of Bolingbroke in 1399. (© *Jeff Buck/ Creative Commons*)

Pontefract Castle ruins, Yorkshire. The site of Richard II's imprisonment and probable death in early 1400 – was it murder or suicide? (© *Betty Longbottom/Creative Commons*)

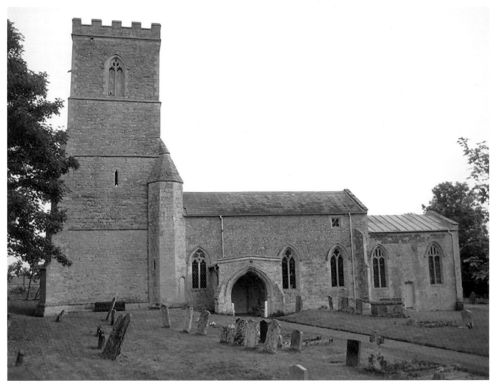

Church of St Mary the Virgin, Grafton Regis, Northamptonshire. The parish church adjacent to the manor-house of Edward IV's secret wife, Elizabeth Woodville – why did he not marry her there openly in 1464? (© *Nigel Cox/ Creative Commons*)

Battlefield of Tewkesbury, 1471 – the 'Bloody Meadow'. Site of Edward IV's final military triumph and the capture for execution of Prince Edward of Wales, later presumed to be Richard III's first victim. (© *Philip Halling/ Creative Commons*)

Apartments of the future Edward V at Ludlow Castle, Shropshire. After his accession and interception by Richard en route to London he disappeared in the Tower of London – but who killed him if anyone? (© *Tim Venning*)

Bloody (originally Garden) Tower, the Tower of London. Shown to visitors since the Victorian period as the site of the murder of the 'Princes', but on no reliable evidence. (© *Christine Matthews/Creative Commons*)

The White Tower, Tower of London. Site of Richard III's more proveable act of extreme violence, the arrest and execution without trial of Lord Hastings. (© *Richard Croft/ Creative Commons*)

The chapel of St Peter ad Vincula in the Tower. A possible site for the burial of the Princes, as claimed in 1494 – but why was this not made public to thwart pretenders? (© *Chris Gunns/Creative Commons*)

given his near-ruin in 1471, and ended with him in the Tower sentenced
to death for treason. Demurring at a public act of fratricide, Edward IV
supposedly had him drowned in a butt of his favourite Malmsey wine
(from Monemvasia in Greece). It was later alleged, in Hall's *Chronicle* in
the 1540s, that it was Richard who had done the killing without royal
permission – as Edward IV's next brother Clarence was the legal heir
to the throne if Edward's marriage was invalidated, Richard needed to
remove him. Mancini says that Richard was furious and depressed at
Clarence's death and vowed to avenge it, presumably on the Woodvilles
– and Richard's sympathetic modern biographer Paul Murray Kendall
believed that words in Richard's 1484 letter to the Earl of Desmond
sympathising with him over and allowing him to seek redresss for his late
father's execution in 1468 (supposedly arranged by the Woodvilles) imply
that Richard regarded Clarence as another victim of the queen. More
hints that Clarence's removal was not unwelcome to Richard, as relieving
him of a rival, while stressing that nothing about his attitude was known
for certain, but Polydore Vergil and the *Croyland Chronicler* firmly blame
Edward IV alone.[29] Even if Richard was dismayed at Clarence's fall, he
still made the most of it in acquiring his lands and titles for himself and
his son Edward (the Earldom of Salisbury for the latter).

Did Clarence receive hints about Edward's marital legal problems,
probably from Robert Stillington, Bishop of Bath and Wells and twice
Edward IV's Lord Chancellor? He was supposed in 1483 to have carried
out the king's previous marital 'pre-contract' – a term usually assumed
by modern interpreters to be a nuptial betrothal ceremony and as such
as fully legal as a marriage, but possibly in contemporary terms implying
a formal marriage ceremony as in the fourteenth- and fifteenth-century
a 'betrothal' (often a ceremony between two under-age partners who
could not live together and consummate the marriage yet) was not legally
distinct from a marriage. For that matter, even stating an intention to
take marital vows before witnesses – without a full legal ceremony –
was then seen as binding, and any subsequent vows taken with another
woman in the participants' lifetimes as illegal. The alleged 'Edward's
pre-1464 betrothal to another woman' did not have to have had a priest
present to be legal. The contract was with Eleanor Butler, nee Talbot,
daughter of the late John Talbot, Earl of Shrewsbury (killed in battle
in Gascony in 1453) and widow of Sir Ralph Butler, in the early-mid

1460s. At the time Stillington was Keeper of the Privy Seal, and thus was responsible for assisting with confidential royal business; as a cleric he could carry out a private ceremony of betrothal. He was also distantly related to Eleanor, which could explain More's statement that he found out about the secret relationship (as her cousin or her 'confessor'?) and persuaded her and Edward to regularise it as marriage to halt their 'sin'. His subsequent grants of the Bishopric of Bath and Wells (1465) and Lord Chancellorship (1467) could be taken as a reward or 'pay-off'. This is possible, though such advancement was normal for a competent and trusted Royal Household cleric. Also important is Stillington's mysterious arrest in spring at the time of Clarence's killing; he had apparently issued words prejudicial to the King, which in the context of that spring's events means in support of Clarence.[30] The duke had been using the services of an astrologer who maintained that Edward's successor's name would begin with 'G', not 'E' (Edward V), so this could mean that Clarence believed he was the king's rightful heir – as Edward V was a bastard. There is an argument that the date of Stillington's arrest, which followed Clarence's trial in January 1478 not Clarence's arrest, means it was not directly related to the charges – surely if it was, Edward IV would have arrested him earlier to provide proof? But it may be that Edward did not find out until early 1478 that Clarence had acquired his information about the 'pre-contract' from Stillington, and acted then. As first commented on by Edward's 1640 biographer Habington, presumably the story had not got out in 1469 or 1470–1 or else the queen's and her Woodville kin's foe Warwick and Edward's children's rival Clarence would have used it to have the Edward/ Elizabeth Woodville marriage invalidated then.

Clarence had been involved with plots to remove Edward and boost his chances of succeeding him twice, as seen above. He had deserted Edward during his prospective father-in-law Warwick's revolt in 1470, fleeing England with him to marry Isabel Neville overseas (in English – held Calais) after defying Edward's orders not to marry Isabel, and had then linked up with Warwick's new allies, the Lancastrians. He would have needed a major reason to do this, given that they had killed his father, the Duke of York, and brother Edmund at the battle of Wakefield in December 1460. Greed for the throne was the apparent reason which is usually cited, as Clarence had been Edward's heir until the birth of his daughter Elizabeth in 1466 – and still had an arguable case as the best successor in place of a girl, female succession never having occurred yet in England. Presumably he acted to halt Elizabeth replacing him as heir, with the queen's pregnancy that year adding to the threat to him if a son was born (which duly occurred on 2 November). The birth of a boy occurred after he had helped Warwick to depose Edward, but could be anticipated as a reasonable possibility before then; the fertile queen had already had two sons by her first marriage. It is still argued as to whether Clarence had a promise of the succession to the throne from Warwick and the Lancastrians after Henry VI's son in return for his deserting Edward.[31] Warwick had no reason to back the alternative candidate, the deposed Henry VI's exiled teenage son Prince Edward – the latter's mother Margaret of Anjou was his arch-foe, who was not directly responsible for the death of his father (the Earl of Salisbury) along with the Duke of York, Warwick's uncle by marriage, at Wakefield but had gloried in it afterwards. Warwick might well have backed Clarence, his son-in-law, not Margaret's son as Henry's heir, and Clarence logically expected this when they decided to revolt. But it is probable that when the exiled Warwick was persuaded by Louis XI of France to come to terms with Margaret after his flight the queen insisted on him backing her son's claim in return.

The queen would undoubtedly have insisted on her son's reinstatement as heir once the Lancastrians were back in power, so Clarence was making a massive gamble in deciding to ally with her faction. Was it just down to inordinate ambition and greed, or was he incensed by Edward displacing him as heir? And was he so incensed in 1469–70 because even then he had heard rumours that Edward had illegally married Elizabeth Woodville and their children were illegitimate, but he could not prove it so he kept quiet? The fact that the Edward-Eleanor 'pre-contract' was not cited as evidence by Clarence and Warwick after Edward's deposition argues that neither of them had firm enough proof to act at this point. Instead, Warwick resorted to a claim that Elizabeth and her mother, the Dowager Duchess of Bedford, had ensnared Edward by witchcraft and there was a story circulated that Edward himself was illegitimate due to his mother having an affair with an archer, Blaybourne.[32] Modern investigation of Edward's father Duke Richard's itinerary in Normandy at the presumed time of Edward's conception in 1441 has implied that the boy's mother might have had the chance to have an illicit liaison as the Duke was not with her all the time. It would seem that the 'pre-contract'/betrothal ceremony was never known for certain by Warwick, or he would have used it during his period in power in October 1470 – March 1471. But that is not proof that it was a later invention; Eleanor herself appears to have died in a Norwich convent in June 1468 and Stillington, as the only witness, may have preferred to keep out of trouble. He had been dismissed as Lord Chancellor at the restoration of Henry VI, and had no reason to seek to help the Lancastrians. The 'pre-contract' or 'first marriage' story – true or not – may have been around in 1477, and Richard thus did not invent it in 1483. But this remains guesswork, though logically plausible, and is denied by some modern historians.

The confusion about the pre-contract is heightened by the fact that one major authority for the events of June 1483, Thomas More – probably informed by his patron Archbishop Morton, at the time Bishop of Ely and arrested in Richard's Council coup of 13 June – names the other party to it as Edward's mistress from 1462–3, Elizabeth 'Lucy' (nee Wayte), not the late Earl of Shrewsbury's widowed daughter Eleanor Butler, *nee* Talbot.[33] (To add to the confusion Elizabeth Lucy, whose stepmother's lands adjoined some of Eleanor's so she may have known her, was a widow like Eleanor and Elizabeth Woodville – did Edward have a habit of pursuing young widows?) That 'mistake' has been used as an indication that the story was invented in 1483, as More should have identified Eleanor as the other party – there is no other indication of Edward marrying Elizabeth Lucy. If there had been such a plausible story concerning her as Edward's 'real' wife, her son Arthur would hardly have been treated with trust in 1509–40 by the suspicious Henry VIII – who executed one claimant to the throne, the Earl of Suffolk, in 1513 and a rumoured claimant, Edward Stafford, Duke of Buckingham, in 1521. It is probably due to a simple slip on More's part, as Elizabeth was known to be Edward's mistress before his marriage in 1464 with the resulting son, Arthur Plantagenet, being prominent at Henry VIII's Court at the time when More was writing (c. 1510). But it is clear that the public announcement of the pre-contract in a sermon at Paul's Cross in London by the Lord Mayor's brother, Friar Ralph Shaa, on 22 June[34] was not clear – or precise? – enough to be remembered accurately years later. (See later article on the question of the Eleanor Butler marriage.)

Even though Henry VII was clearly politically embarrassed by any claims that his wife had been illegitimate and thus destroyed all known copies of the act confirming this (*Titulus Regius*) in 1485, enough people would have attended the sermon – at London's premier 'open-air' place for services – or heard about it to recall its tenor for More around twenty-five years later. Even if the shock of the unexpected news had meant that the listeners did not remember precisely who Edward IV had been pre-contracted to, senior figures who More knew would have had two years to read and memorise copies of '*Titulus Regius*' – and note the name of the person involved – before Henry VII destroyed the act. Some modern historians, such as Alison Weir, assume that despite Clarence's bizarre behaviour and veiled hints in 1477 Richard invented the pre-contract story in a hurry in 1483 as a means of removing Edward V from the throne, and thus constructed it between his coup in early May and the Council arrests and execution on 13 June. Richard's written instructions to his followers in Yorkshire to send reinforcements to him in London on 10 and 11 June referred in urgent if not paranoid terms to a plot by the Woodvilles to 'utterly destroy' him and his ally Buckingham, plus confidential information on this which Sir Richard Ratcliffe would explain by word of mouth.[35] This evidently referred to the conspiracy which he claimed to have uncovered on the 13th, and has been taken as evidence of his intention to stage a coup when these reinforcements arrived. But even if the latter set out for London at once they would have been hard-pressed to arrive by the date then set for Edward V's coronation (25 June), and they were never expected to be in London by the time Richard struck on the 13th. He may have been intending to use them to intimidate the post-coronation Parliament and/or been genuinely in fear of his life after what had happened to Clarence in 1478, and it is clear that whatever he planned at this stage was overtaken by events.

Logically, the letters show that he expected to stage some military action to disarm the queen's faction – and Hastings too? – later in June, but was rushed into precipitate action earlier. The fact that he killed Hastings on the spot may be due to his nervousness that he had not enough troops available to be sure of defeating Hastings' own retainers if they joined the queen's in a revolt; he killed Hastings to prevent this threat. What is not clear is if he always intended to use the reinforcements to depose Edward V as well as to arrest the queen's adherents (Archbishop

Rotherham, Bishop Morton, and Lord Stanley) and Hastings. What panicked him into acting before his men arrived in London?

The fact that Hastings, Edward IV's Lord Chamberlain and closest friend, had explicitly backed Richard against the Woodvilles in May but then switched to intriguing with them in early June shows that he came to fear Richard's intentions during this period. The 'plot' (as Richard saw it) would have taken a week or two to mature at least, whether or not all the details Richard gave were accurate. The contemporary witness Dominic Mancini reported that Londoners doubted that Hastings would really have used Edward IV's mistress Elizabeth (later called 'Jane' by eighteenth-century writers) Shore as a 'go-between' with Elizabeth Woodville in the Westminster Abbey sanctuary, as Richard alleged.[36] Would the queen not have seen this use of her rival as an insult? Or were circumstances so desperate that she did not object? The latter is possible if she was now aware that Richard aimed to dethrone her son – in which case that scenario was already being discussed in early June. It is possible that a secret important meeting of senior political figures as early as 9 or 10 June was called to discuss the revelation (or invention) of the pre-contract rather than it coming out ten days or so later. This is Sir Clement Markham's interpretation of the meeting, on uncertain evidence.[37] His belief that Bishop Stillington brought learned 'doctors (of the law), proctors etc' to the meeting to lay written evidence of the Butler precontract and its invalidating the new king's legitimacy and right to rule relies on a statement by the 1540s chronicler Hall that these men had been consulted, which does not specifically state that they were called in at this meeting. The identification of Stillington as the source of the precontract story was first made by the Frenchman Philippe de Commignes, an intimate of King Louis XI but not present in London in 1483, rather than by the 'man on the spot' Dominic Mancini – so although Victorian historian James Gairdner (in his *History of the Life and Reign of Richard III*, 1898) believed that Stillington was both responsible and honest some modern experts such as Charles Ross claim that it was all a 'put-up job' by Richard. There is also the question of an apparent reference in the 'Hilary Term' 1486 legal records of London by the lawyers who were then investigating the Ricardian Act of Parliament '*Titulus Regius*' (which declared Edward V and his siblings bastards on account of the 'Eleanor Butler pre-contract/marriage') to 'the Bishop of Bath and

Wells' (Stillington) as the 'author'. P.W. Hammond and others have cited this as proof that Stillington was known as the originator of the pre-contract/marriage story in 1486 independently of Mancini's story, but sceptics reply that the term 'author' might only refer to Stillington as the author of the Act *Titulus Regius*.

A formal revelation to the Council and/or other senior lords by Stillington – and his 'experts'? – on or around 9 June and Richard's resultant suggestion that he now receive the Crown would have given a warning of Richard's intentions to those who doubted Stillington's story or what Richard made of it. This would have caused the manoeuvres against him on the Council by Hastings, Dorset, and Morton to which he reacted violently on the 13th. The timescale sounds short, however for a suddenly anxious Hastings to get his new lover Mistress Shore to contact her ex-lover Dorset's mother the queen and arrange a link-up with Richard's enemies Stanley and Morton, so was Richard already showing signs of wanting the Crown? It does not exclude the possibility of the Peter Hancock version cited earlier, ie that when Richard made an approach to Hastings for help (in this scenario, regarding bastardising Edward V) an alarmed Hastings refused to have anything to do with it and warned the queen and Dorset of what was intended. Richard did not however suddenly decide to deal with his 'enemies' halfway through the 13 June meeting and call in his 'heavies' rather than having been thinking about it since c.9 June, as his retainers (led by his ally John Howard's son Thomas) were already waiting outside the room earlier. This suggests that he intended arrests then, even if his sudden change of mood to violence was not feigned but was a result of hearing some new information in an interval during the discussions.

Whether or not the Eleanor Butler claim was behind it, drastic political realignments occurred (or were feared by Richard as likely to occur) in the early days of June. Before the crucial Council meeting on 13 June Hastings had reversed his alliance with Richard which was more unlikely than the ex-Lancastrian Morton or the devious Stanley plotting. In mid-April Hastings had saved his chances of securing the Protectorship – he had written to him urging him to hurry to London and forestall a plot to prevent the Protectorship by the Woodville clan. Hastings and Elizabeth's son Dorset had been on extremely bad terms for months and Edward IV attempted a reconciliaton as he was dying. But now Hastings allegedly got in touch with the queen in sanctuary through the medium of Edward IV's mistress Elizabeth/'Jane' Shore, which would indicate that he feared a plan to deprive her son of the throne by his current ally Richard. Only extreme danger would have led to Hastings being prepared to link up with his old foe Dorset, now in hiding. Alternatively, as More claimed c. 1510, Richard's approach to Hastings via Catesby was rebuffed – though possibly an ambitious Catesby exaggerated Hastings' reaction in order to destroy him. In retaliation Richard, evidently tipped off (as his modern admirers claim) or else letting his paranoia run rampant, seems to have arranged two separate meetings for members of the Council on 13 June, one at Westminster and one (with his alleged enemies included in the list of invitees) at the Tower. This suggests either a pre-arranged plan to arrest or kill the latter, or at least an intention to question them on their own without other councillors there who might object. He called armed retainers (who were clearly stationed outside ready to act on a signal) into the Council meeting at the Tower on 13 June, apparently as the meeting resumed after a brief interlude – and had Hastings dragged out and beheaded (over a log outside?) without any attempt at a trial. The men had been waiting outside for the signal, a shout of 'Treason!' by Richard, and the post-1485 version of events by Polydore Vergil states that in the confusion of the scuffle Lord Stanley was also attacked but resisted. This is not mentioned by sources writing while Richard was alive – as seen earlier, it may suggest spin by Stanley after 1485 to play up his role in the plot. One major revision to this version was proposed by Alison Hanham, who has endeavoured to interpet an apparent anomaly of dating in the Mercers' Company records to show that Hastings was alive on the 20th so the coup was a week later than thought, giving even less time before Richard seized the throne. This would have meant that Hastings was reacting to Richard's seizure of Prince Richard from sanctuary and so had more reasons to fear Richard's plans for the boys, but is now thought unlikely.[38]

Killing a political opponent in the heat of the moment in battle was normal practice for dealing with trapped foes, and captured enemies had been dragged out of sanctuary afterwards (the Duke of Somerset at Tewkesbury) or killed after capture (the Duke of York and possibly his son Rutland, at Wakefield in 1460). But even during the intense family feuds among the top nobility of 1455–71 a degree of decorum had been usually observed when there was no armed clash underway – the Lancastrian leaders arrested hiding in Tewkesbury Abbey after the battle had been given some sort of a trial, albeit a summary one with a foreordained verdict. The fact that some of the Council – none of them arrested in the plot – were summoned by Richard to meet away from the Tower on the 13th, with the Ricardian ally Bishop Russell at Westminster, may show that Richard did not want them arguing over his right to execute the 'traitor' Hastings on the spot. As none of them were to be arrested he trusted them politically, but he clearly wanted them out of his way. Hastings' summary execution and the imprisonment of other 'plotting' councillors (including Bishop Morton and possibly Richard's later nemesis Lord Stanley) went beyond the usual limits of behaviour, and was clearly designed to terrorise the potential opposition to his coup. The public reaction to this seemingly unprovoked murder in London was one of extreme fear and resentment, as shown by the accounts of Mancini (who wrote that many believed Richard had made up the story of a plot to excuse the killing) and the *Great Chronicle*.[39] In the public reaction, Hastings was regarded as a man of noble qualities, generous and honourable, who had naively trusted the unscrupulous Richard – and Mancini stated his own judgement on the irony that a 'friend' not a known foe had brought Hastings down and clearly regarded him as innocent. After this proof of Richard's exceptional brutality and clear reliance on terror to intimidate his foes – which his defenders such as Paul Murray Kendall choose to sidestep – it was natural to suspect that he had gone on to murder his predecessor and the latter's next heir, though even his successor evidently did not know the exact truth. Henry VII resorted to unspecific and undateable allegations of infanticide in his indictment of Richard after he took the throne in 1485[40] when he could have been expected to play up the crime to show up his late rival and decrease the chances that the surviving Yorkists would set up a pretender as one of the boys. It is not clear if any reference was made to Richard's crimes including infanticide in his challenger's speech to his men at the battle of Bosworth either.[41]

The Ricardians – a chain of defenders of Richard III's memory – have long sought to deny that he would kill his nephews, not least on the grounds that infanticide and of his close relatives was worse than the usual cold brutality shown to adult rivals in late Plantagenet politics. It would have been an unthinkable sin for someone who made such play of his piety and loyalty as Richard, and as the boys had been bastardised they were no threat anyway. Killing a deposed adult sovereign like Edward II, Richard II, or Henry VI was not that unusual or reviled, and usually the victim had been unpopular (at least among a section of the nobility) in order to be deposed in the first place. Even then, a sense of political realism did not preclude a degree of 'fairness' in the public response; the one deposed king who might be held innocent of personal misrule, the mentally feeble Henry VI, had attracted posthumous sympathy since Edward IV had had him eliminated in May 1471. Richard was to promote – or at least tolerate – the king's growing cult and stage a reconciliatory reburial of his remains at St George's Chapel, Windsor.[42] He was clearly aware of the popular devotion to his brother's victim and sought to be seen to atone for the evident murder, so why would he risk probable equal devotion to the 'martyred' Edward V by killing him? Or was he so obsessed with his own security that he ignored the possible consequences as less dangerous to him than leaving the ex-king alive to be rescued by a Woodville plot?

Richard III's reputation, his defenders and their alternative explanations

Unlike any other reviled English sovereign such as King John – who probably killed his own nephew and rival for the throne, Arthur, in secrecy in 1203 – Richard has even attracted a society devoted to his cause. The extent of the obloquy unleashed on Richard was bound to cause some reaction over the less proveable claims against him. Right from 1485 Richard had been the evident victim of a political campaign to denigrate him and make Henry VII seem the heroic rescuer of England, as when the former Yorkist loyalist John Rous revised the original (pre-1485) version of his chronicle of the Earls of Warwick – and apparently its illustrations too – to make Richard into a tyrant around 1490. This Warwickshire chantry priest had published his first version of the Earldom's history in 1483, at the time of Richard's accession. As an employee of the family of Richard's wife Anne Neville (daughter of the Warwick heiress, the Kingmaker's wife), known to Anne personally, and eulogist of their historic record, Rous was unable to attack Anne's husband in her lifetime had he known any damaging stories. But once she died in March 1485, preceded by her son, he was at liberty to revise his earlier encomium of Richard – and it appears that he was indignant at how Richard had treated her in her last months. He removed all his favourable references of Richard from the revised copy of his Warwick family chronicle, and replaced his drawing of Richard with one of Anne Neville's first husband Prince Edward, son of Henry VI – a suitable candidate for post-1485 promotion as a victim of Yorkist murder after the battle of Tewkesbury in 1471. But he went further than prudent time-serving for the new regime, in presenting Richard as a hump-backed monster who had been born with teeth and hair after two years in the womb and alleging that he had poisoned Anne and killed Henry VI.[43] In fact, there is early mention of Richard having a 'crook back' independent of 'Tudor propaganda' like Rous' work – in a lawsuit brought against a citizen of York after Bosworth for 'slandering' the late King in this manner – and the discovery of Richard's skeleton buried at the site of the Grey Friars Church in Leicester in 2012 has shown that he did have a twisted spine by 1485. So did Rous collect contemporary gossip?

The anonymous author of the Croyland Abbey *Chronicle* continuation, writing in 1486, was not doing so under royal orders at court so he was not a Tudor propagandist; indeed he may have been Richard's ex-Chancellor, Bishop John Russell of Lincoln, though this is now thought to be unlikely. At any rate he had access to public opinions in London, not just in the Fens; possibly he obtained his news from visiting clerics' gossip. (Henry VII's close ally John Morton was Bishop of Ely, though under arrest at Brecon, not at home in summer 1483.) Yet he endorsed the view that Richard had been guilty of gross bad faith to his brother's sons who he had been supposed to protect, without specifically saying that he killed them, and accused him of deceitful dissimulation to his peers about his intentions in May-June 1483. The seizure of Edward V's uncle Rivers and his companions at Stony Stratford as well as the killing of Hastings was denounced, showing no belief in Richard's excuses about Woodville plots. Nor did the chronicler believe in the truth of the claim about Edward IV's pre-contract/marriage to Eleanor Butler or illegitimacy. He even made the assertion that Henry VII – arch-enemy of possible Croyland chronicler Russell's late patron – was an angel of deliverance, which goes beyond politic flattery of his new employer. This is usually taken these days as evidence of his being a Tudor propagandist, though it may just reflect genuine relief after Augsut 1485 that the devious and sporadically violent Richard (whose arrests and execution of 'plotters' on 13 June 1483 had caused panic in London) had been removed so the elite could feel that their heads were safe. Whoever the chronicler was, he had access to knowledge of Council debates during 1483 – and he was sceptical of Richard's claims to the throne. The 'unofficial' but still deeply hostile view of Richard's reign and motives was continued by the relevant section of the *Great Chronicle of London* for 1483 and two lesser works, the chronicle known (from its early seventeenth-century Cotton Library classification) as 'Vitellius A XVI' and Robert Fabyn's chronicle. The modern editors of the *Great Chronicle* (published 1938) reckoned that the relevant section was written before 1501–2 and was also written by Fabyn, who died in 1513. They all agree on Richard as a treacherous power-seeker and believe that he murdered the Princes, while lacking direct evidence; the *Great Chronicle* however suffers from inaccuracies, such as placing Buckingham's autumn 1483 rebellion after Anne Neville's death (March 1485). It lamented that Richard might have ended his days in honour had he kept his promise to safeguard Edward IV's sons, but instead let greed and ambition overcome his scruples. (At this stage there is no hint, as later, that he coveted the throne before Edward IV died.)

Already Henry's victory was seen as divine punishment for Richard's sins, and Richard's fate after his death in battle (being paraded naked through the streets of Leicester and supposedly denied Christian burial) as deserved retribution.[44] In fact, as the discovery of Richard's body under a car-park on the site of the Grey Friars church in Leicester in 2012 shows, the late king was given a suitable if 'low-key' burial in a 'high status' church – and was not exhumed and thrown in the nearby river at the Reformation either.[45] It is also possible that poetic references by anti-Ricardian Welsh bards such as Lewis Glyn Cothi and David Llywd, backers of Henry VII's invasion in summer 1485, to Richard murdering his predecessor were composed before Bosworth as part of Henry's propaganda to encourage recruitment as he marched across Wales.[46] As they were categorised as 'prophecies' they presumably predated Bosworth – though this would only show that the story was current then. Possibly Dr Lewis Caerleon, Elizabeth Woodville's and Margaret Beaufort's physician who according to Polydore Vergil carried the crucial messages between them in autumn 1483 to arrange the 'Henry Tudor/Elizabeth of York' betrothal, and/or some of Buckingham's fellow-rebels in the autumn spread the story of royal murder – but as propaganda or as truth?

The first royal Tudor historiographer who published an account of the late king's reign and Henry's triumph, Bernard Andre, could be dismissed as a Court hack delivering the 'official' line, not a serious historian. He duly presented Richard as a satanic monster and Henry as the angel who saved England from his tyranny. But the first major historian to write a complete account of the reign in *Anglica Historia* (c. 1513, published 1534), the Italian scholar Polydore Vergil, was not so clearly doing the bidding of the court. A respected humanist and not a direct royal protégé despite subsequent Ricardian complaints, he came to England in 1502 as an employee of the papal tax-collector Adriano de'Castelli. He had limited connections with the court, though he said that Henry VII had asked him to compile his work, and his (minor) preferments awarded in the seven years until Henry died appear to have come as Castelli's assistant, not as a historian. He wrote his official dedication of the work to Henry VIII in 1513 in anticipation of future patronage, but received no such support and was at odds with Henry's principal minister Cardinal Wolsey throughout the next fifteen years or so. He claimed to have assiduously interviewed all the main surviving witnesses to events of the 1480s, and complained of the lack of chronicles to consult for this era unlike for the period pre-1450. His account dealt with fifteenth-century history in general, so he was not writing a specific polemic aimed at Richard's usurpation. He portrayed Richard as a deceitful and ambition-crazed murderer who hid his real intentions beneath a hypocritical image of justice (which Shakespeare took up), and made snide references to his low stature and scowling countenance. He did not believe in the alleged 'plot' discovered on 13 June 1483, which would indicate that this is the story he heard at court in the 1500s from surviving witnesses.[47] His version of the killing of the Princes stated that the fact of their deaths was agreed but he had not been able to find out who had done the deed and how, which seems to reflect the genuine uncertainty about it in the 1490s. The ending of an era of bloody civil war by Henry in 1485 required a portrayal of the preceding regime as particularly unpleasant to justify his usurpation. But this is not to say, as Ricardians have done, that the real Richard was not a controversial and feared ruler and there was no widespread sense of relief at his downfall. The City of London chronicles, written at arms' length from court, and Vergil all agree on dismissing Richard's excuses for his actions.

The principled Catholic 'martyr' Sir Thomas More, Lord Chancellor to Henry VIII, provided a particularly damning portrait of Richard in his moralistic biography of c.1510, apparently never completed. Debate has raged over whether this work could be called deliberate Tudor propaganda to vilify Richard (Paul Murray Kendall et al.), a primarily literary moral tale, not a strictly historical chronicle (Alison Hanham), or a lawyerly accurate picture of the view of Richard at the Early Tudor court (R.S. Sylvester).[48] It has been noted that More treated Edward IV's reign, the just and peaceful prelude to an unanticipated tyranny, in the manner of Tacitus' comparison of the reigns of Augustus and Tiberius. The latter was portrayed by Tacitus as hiding his evil intentions under a public pretence of honesty and good governance, like Richard. More's invention of long 'set-piece' speeches whose details he could not have known about, such as Edward IV's on his deathbed and Buckingham's to the London citizens on 24 June 1483, is reminiscent of the style of Thucydides in his account of the Peloponnesian Wars. Thus, he was consciously using approved literary models – and writing literature, not factual history? He also made assumptions without evidence from contemporary sources, such as that Richard secretly sought the throne even before Edward IV's death. He broke off his work at the account of Buckingham's rebellion, so we cannot know how he intended to deal with the final section of Richard's reign; his reasons for doing so are disputed but as of c.1510 Buckingham's son and heir was a powerful court peer who it would have been unwise to offend. Did More decide not to risk this by mentioning the awkward theory that Buckingham had really wanted the throne for himself, not Henry, in 1483? If More abandoned his work sooner than falsely flatter the duke, this would imply that he intended to write an 'honest' work not a piece of propaganda. His source for the events of mid-June 1483 was probably Bishop Morton, in whose household he served as a boy; and his famous account of the 13 June Council meeting has Richard asking Morton to send him some strawberries from his garden minutes before arresting him in the coup, which only Morton is likely to have bothered to remember.

This established a long-standing popular image of Richard as an arch-villain unique among English sovereigns, which remained the usual image into the seventeenth- and eighteenth-century. The dramatic licence used by Shakespeare in his play was particularly notable, if based on a respectable 'historical' source in the form of Edward Hall's 1548 chronicle of *The Union of the Two Illustre Families of York and Lancaster*. The latter had its own pro-Tudor agenda, seeking to present a picture of vicious civil wars and court feuds which the saintly Henry VII had ended;Richard was the monster who had symbolised all the worst excesses of the pre-1485 strife. The main sources for Hall's work were More (whose account was taken over verbatim) and Vergil, with extra histrionic flourishes about Richard's cruelty and greed for power, though he conceded (with the London chronicles) that Richard had been courageous and a successful war-leader who could have achieved much for good. Shakespeare then developed his play from this picture, following Hall in presenting the usurpation as the final act of a drama of inter-family feuding between York and Lancaster that led to its resolution by Henry VII. 'Richard III' was thus the final play of Shakespeare's series on the reigns of the kings since 1399, with Henry IV's illegal usurpation in that year as the 'original sin' which had to be paid for in bloody conflict. The loyal Elizabethan political message of the series of plays was that rebellion is never justified – except, of course, the one by Henry VII to save England from an exceptionally wicked and infanticidal usurper. The hunchbacked villain of Shakesepeare's play, who had been unfeasibly long in the womb and been born with a deformity, owed his origins to Vergil's portrait, accentuated by More, but was now taken to extremes. He could never have carried out Richard's real-life feats on the battlefield – and the long list of murders attributed to this 'serial killer' was extended from logical victims like the Princes to the less likely Henry VI and Clarence.

As early as the 1610s Richard received a more sympathetic account from Sir George Buck, Master of the Revels to James I and so with access to State documents. (Buck had had an ancestor who fought for Richard at Bosworth, which probably inspired his unusual decision to defend the king.) Buck, whose original work was published in a truncated version by his nephew in 1646 but has been reconstructed in a modern edition (1979), knew the great manuscript-collector Sir Robert Cotton and had access to his Westminster library. The manuscripts found there included the *Croyland Chronicle*. His findings apparently included evidence that Richard's niece Princess Elizabeth had written to the Duke of Norfolk supporting her proposed marriage to her uncle. This implied that Elizabeth had not believed that Richard had killed her brothers, though the letter may only refer to Richard's plans to betroth her to Portuguese King John II's cousin and heir Manuel. If she was keen on it, was she anxious to be out of England because of the violent deaths of her relatives – and which ones, at whose hands? Buck also made claims that he had found an old manuscript that implicated Bishop Morton in the killing of the princes, but did not transcribe or identify it so this story has not been seriously considered in the modern era. Sir William Cornwallis' *Encomium of Richard III* in 1617 was more of a literary exercise in opposing the established version of events than a serious historical investigation.[49] In 1767 Horace Walpole wrote his *Historic Doubts on the Life and Reign of Richard III*, attacking the 'established' Tudor verdict on his crimes though defending Richard on the grounds that he had no logical motive for infanticide rather than with new evidence. He abused More's evident lack of veracity and exaggerations, and claimed to be analysing the evidence with the modern advantages of a non-committed spectator from the 'Age of Reason'. He had no axe to grind, so to speak, and could take a more accurate view than that possible when Richard's reputation had to be denigrated for political reasons by the Tudors. He reasoned that no sensible political actor would have behaved in such a violent and bloodthirsty manner – only to change his mind for a revised edition in 1792, when the French Revolution had showed him what power-crazed ambition could lead to.[50]

The veracity of the post-1485 chroniclers was defended by Sir James Gairdner, a veteran investigator of the fifteenth-century records, in his particularly hostile biography of 1898. But after that the trend among historians was more in the king's favour. In 1906 Sir Clements Markham, Gairdner's main critic and a notable member of the Royal Geographic Society and patron of explorers, went as far as to accuse Henry VII of the murder of the Princes and present More's patron Cardinal Morton as the sinister 'mastermind' behind his anti-Ricardian campaign.[51] Markham, notably, was a wealthy polymath and naval administrator who was primarily a geographer rather than a historian, though his wide interests led him to write eighteen biographies. For the man who hand-picked Captain Scott for the 1911–12 Polar expedition, Richard's actions showed his heroism – and this *Boy's Own Paper*-style hero could not possibly have behaved in the underhand ways alleged by More and Vergil. He ludicrously compared Richard to Sir Galahad, which implied that all the charges laid by Richard against Hastings and the Woodvilles must have been true and skated over what such a paragon was doing executing people without trial. He also naively assumed that Richard could have kept the Princes alive in the Tower until August 1485 without any gossip getting out to that effect, enabling Henry VII to find them there and murder them instead, and did not explain adequately why in that case Richard had not either produced them to silence his accusers (eg the French) in 1484 or sent them off to the safer Sheriff Hutton in Yorkshire with his other under-age ward, Clarence's son the Earl of Warwick, in summer 1485. The 'revisionist' views exemplified by Markham were enshrined in a permanent campaign by the 'Richard III Society', founded in England in 1924 with an American offshoot.

In the mid- and late twentieth-century both historians and novelists (e.g. Josephine Tey in *The Daughter of Time, 1951*, and Rosemary Hawley Jarman in *We Speak No Treason, 1971*) were generally Ricardian and played up his just rule and seemingly honourable conduct. The latter was particularly hostile to the Woodvilles, who were presented as grasping and dishonourable. Sharon Penman in *The Sunne in Splendour* had Elizabeth Woodville finding out that Clarence knew of Edward IV's pre-contract to Eleanor Butler and persuading Edward to have him killed, and Buckingham murdering the Princes behind Richard's back expecting to be rewarded. The Woodvilles had denied Richard his right to the throne and sought to murder him, and he had only attacked them in self-defence.[52] Henry VII became seen as a master of fraudulent propaganda who blackened Richard's name, with Richard's openly 'moral' stance on various political issues seen as reflecting his real character, not as devious spin. Richard's exhaustive but partisan biographer Paul Murray Kendall (1955) was at pains to point out all the king's wise and just actions as sovereign[53] – which did not however cause overwhelming enthusiasm for his cause in 1485. In the 1980s there was even a 'Trial of Richard III' on television, using an approximation of the modern judicial process, which found him innocent – though 'Not Proven' would have been a more considered verdict given the ambiguities of the evidence after 500 years. The verdict was not likely to be 'Guilty' unless More's circumstantial evidence – written thirty years later – was taken as fact or the alleged bodies of the victims in Westminster Abbey were proven by 'DNA' evidence to belong to the Princes.

The crucial legal argument for his innocence – as used by Josephine Tey and the 'trial' – has been that the boys were no threat to Richard as they had been bastardised in law and so were ineligible for the throne. But in the fifteenth-century laws were frequently reversed for political reasons by Parliament, as had been the attainder of Richard (and Edward IV) by Henry VI's regime in 1471, and the bastardy statute was equally vulnerable. Richard's own statutory claim to the throne by bastardising Edward IV's children, the *Titulus Regius*, also illegitimised Henry VII's new queen, the boys' elder sister – so in 1485 he had it reversed and expunged from the records. This piece of re-writing was so thorough that if one copy of the contents had not survived in the Croyland Abbey records historians could not have reconstructed the Act.[54] If this is not 'rewriting history' for a devious political motive, what is? Henry's extreme action could be used to attack his motives and defend Richard's actions in bastardising his nephews and nieces – if the act had to be expunged from the national memory by Henry, perhaps he knew that he could not destroy it adequately using legal arguments. Surely, if it had been seen as ridiculous in 1483–5 that Edward IV could have had a secret 'wife' before 1464, Henry would have had no need to take such drastic measures? He had the alleged only witness to the marriage, Bishop Stillington, in custody, but did not use him to denounce it.

The fact remains that the boys were never seen again after they vanished into the inner fastnesses of the Tower in early July 1483. Both Mancini and the informants of Sir Thomas More agree that Richard moved the boys from the usual royal apartments around the courtyard which were to be demolished in Charles II's reign, to some more secluded 'inner' rooms, probably in the White Tower. The traditional site of the murder, the Bloody Tower which was then known as the Garden Tower, has no historical plausibility – it was not part of the royal apartments. But this could have been to guard against a kidnap attempt instead of being a preparation for a quiet murder. Mancini reported that a visitor from Edward IV's household, Dr Argentine, said that Edward V feared for his life.[55] This has been explained away as resulting from physical illness, not fear of Richard – which is unlikely given that the ex-king had seen his uncle and half-brother seized by surprise by a seemingly friendly Richard on their way to London in May 1483. They had now been executed, and Edward would have been aware of what had happened to ex-king Henry VI in the Tower in May 1471. Even if Edward V was possibly ill with some disease of the jaw (osteomyelitis?), as indicated by the evidence of the jaw of the elder body found in 1674 and medically examined in 1933, he would hardly have died within weeks.[56] Mancini's account refers to him praying for his safety like a victim expecting sacrifice, indicating a fear of physical violence from the new king. His younger brother Richard, Duke of York, was perfectly healthy. Nor is it certain that the bodies found in 1674 were those of the Princes, despite their being approximately the right ages and found in a logical location. (See below.)

Dominic Mancini, unlike Sir Thomas More, was a contemporary and a foreigner with no reason to support any one cause in the 1483–5 struggle for power; this should make his account more credible. He may not have been able to speak English, but he was able to acquire a good deal of confidential information – including about Council matters – and wrote a personal 'portrait' of Edward V's abilities which he probably heard from members of his household (Dr. Argentine?). Anti-Ricardian or not, he reported faithfully the pro-Richard claim that Richard had been incensed by the Woodvilles' part in Clarence's downfall and had waited to have his revenge. It is clear that he believed Richard to be acting out of ambition in a deliberate, calculated plot to seize power and to be dissimulating when he alleged he was only saving himself from plotters in mid-June 1483. Mancini also says that there was distrust and panic in London at the seizure of Edward V on 4 May, and alarm and anger at Richard's assumption of the throne – which fits in with the number of loyal Yorkist royal household figures involved in the rebellion. His 'outsider' status has meant that Ricardian critics have claimed that he could not understand English well enough to produce a balanced assessment of public opinion in 1483. However the contemporary verdict on Richard as a murderous usurper and probable regicide was shared by another foreigner with even less reason than Mancini to denigrate Richard, the Spaniard Diego de Varela who met Spanish merchants returning from England in March 1486 and wrote that Richard was believed to have killed the Princes.[57] The unknown Croyland Abbey chronicler, apparently a royal councillor and ex-ambassador, who composed the 'Second Continuation' of the original chronicle (covering Richard's reign) in 1486 – a figure with good sources of information – was unequivocal about Richard's ruthless ambition.

The 'official version' of the killing – but was it out of character for Richard?

According to the written accounts of the murder by Polydore Vergil (c.1513) and Sir Thomas More (c.1510), Richard III supposedly decided suddenly to protect his position while he was on his post-coronation tour – either at Warwick in mid-August, as More has it, or at York. The Constable of the Tower, Sir Richard Brackenbury, refused to do the murder, and Richard sought a discreet and ruthless agent to carry it out. Richard's exasperated exclamation that he could do with a reliable 'hit-man' who would do what he was told is reminiscent of Henry II's alleged call for someone to rid him of the 'turbulent priest' Becket – and how could More know what Richard had said unless the alleged sole witness, who he does not name, told him? Sir James Tyrrell was recommended – though More must be wrong in claiming that Richard was unaware of him until this occasion – and was allowed to take over control of the Tower for a night from Brackenbury by royal orders. (The Royal Household records show that Tyrrell did visit London from the royal household at York at the beginning of September 1483).[58] The story has some implausibilities, not least regarding Tyrell being unknown to the king at the time, but such a decision was not entirely out of character for Richard. He had already shown his total disregard for convention by his recent execution of Lord Hastings without trial on 13 June, having him dragged out of a Council meeting by his henchmen and beheaded outside in a clear act of terror to frighten other councillors into going along with his impending coup. His speedy confiscation of the younger Prince's aristocratic titles for his followers was equally blatant, if no worse than Edward IV's declaring the Countess of Warwick (Richard's and Clarence's mother-in-law) to be legally dead in 1471 so he could give her estates to them. One hopeful theory claimed that as Richard's ally John Howard received the Prince's Dukedom of Norfolk he was a candidate as the killer. In this cause, even the appearance of an order for quicklime in Norfolk's accounts could be interpreted as him seeking a way to get rid of the bodies.[59]

Nor is it clear that Richard's motives were totally honourable on other occasions. The most obvious is his action in seeking the hand of Anne Neville in 1471/2, even if they had grown up together at her father Warwick's base at Middleham Castle. Anne had been shamelessly married off by her father to Henry VI's son Edward in his reconciliation with his former arch-enemy Margaret of Anjou (who had killed his own father, the Earl of Salisbury, in 1460), in 1470. Edward was as unpleasant a character as Richard, an appropriate son for the 'Tigress of Anjou', who as a teenager had asked for some Yorkist prisoners to be executed in front of him as a favour – but this is no indication that Ricardians are correct that Anne would have preferred to marry Richard. If they were as devotedly in love as portrayed by the romancers, how come the accounts in early 1485 of court unease at his neglect of her over that Christmas festivities when she was fatally ill in winter 1484–5?[60] It is argued that this was not the action of a loving husband, who would surely have been too grief-stricken to enjoy flirting with his niece Princess Elizabeth, but of a calculating political gambler looking for his next wife. Alternatively, it may just reflect his ruthless need to consider the future and even his being in denial that Anne's condition was that bad – and he did stay at Westminster Palace with her for most of her illness in January-March 1485 apart from one trip to Windsor.

His earlier alleged murders have also been dredged up, though none of these were cited against him in the 1480s rather than after a couple of decades of Tudor rule by which time myths could grow up. *Hall's Chronicle* of 1547 and its use by Shakespeare have created a story of Richard as a serial killer murdering his way to the throne, starting off with his brother's predecessor Henry VI's son Prince Edward – the eighteen-year-old first husband of his wife Anne Neville. Edward was killed in uncertain circumstances while fleeing from the battlefield at Tewkesbury after Edward IV's victory there on 4 May 1471, though the first accounts did not name any killers and gave the impression that it was done in the pursuit rather than an execution. It has been more recently claimed that the Tudor account of his being taken alive and killed in cold blood (by Richard and Clarence?) after the battle, perhaps after he was dragged before Edward IV and defied him, may have been accurate. Anne was captured by Edward IV's troops with her mother-in-law Margaret of Anjou and her entourage afterwards at a nearby 'poor religious house', probably Little Malvern Priory, and on 7 May was granted a pardon by Edward IV at Tewkesbury. She was placed in the care of her sister Isabel and brother-in-law Clarence, presumably at their house in the City of London.

Anne now had a half-share of the claim to Warwick's estates, which would duly go to her next husband – and Clarence was later supposed to have hidden her away at a City of London cookshop disguised as a maid to prevent fortune-seekers finding her and thus reducing his wife's share of the Warwick properties. Richard ended up engaged to her in 1471/2 but had a long and acrimonious row with Clarence over the inheritance, as recorded by the *Paston Letters*.[61] He clearly had no intention of waiving his claims on the properties even for the politically necessary cause of improving relations with Clarence, as the tension between the two men over Clarence's resistance to giving half the estates to Anne shows. It was however the equally acquisitive Edward IV who had the idea of illegally declaring Anne and Isabel's mother, the heiress to the Beauchamp Earls of Warwick (extinct 1446), legally dead in 1473 so all her lands could go to her daughters' husbands – a blatant breach of law. Richard and Anne's marriage may not have been the love-match that Kendall or assorted novelists would prefer, and even in the pre-1485 writings of the Yorkist loyalist John Rous (who turned violently against Richard for his 1490 version of events) critics have detected unease at Richard's lust for Anne's estates. The story later arose that Anne was hidden at a cookshop in the city to keep her away from Richard, whether unwillingly is unclear. Either she, or Richard once he had traced her, was responsible for her subsequent flight to the sanctuary of the church of St Martin-le-Grand, near St Paul's – presumably to keep her from kidnap and a forced marriage. But was the abductor she feared Richard or Clarence?

Richard's courting of Anne was clearly linked to her estates, and at this distance it is impossible to prove that love may have been involved – unlikely though the latter was as an overwhelming motive for a fifteenth-century prince arranging his marriage. Anne eventually came without a cash dowry and this did not halt the proceedings; but was Clarence refusing to pay up so Richard had to give way? There was also the question of Richard and Anne being first cousins, which under canon law meant that they had to acquire a Papal dispensation to marry. Such matches were more common, for nakedly political reasons, among European royal houses (e.g. in Spain and Portugal) than in England. The problem had not stopped Clarence from marrying his first cousin, Anne's sister, in 1470, though the objecting Edward had endeavoured to halt it in order to break up the feared political alliance of Clarence and Anne's potentially rebellious father Warwick. But it appears that even if a dispensation was acquired by Richard and Anne in 1472(?), it was legally challengeable and Michael Hicks argues that it might have been advisable to gain a second and more clear-cut Papal dispensation – which was not done. When Anne was dying in early 1485 there were rumours that the marriage would be cancelled so Richard could remarry, suggesting that the insecure Richard was in a hurry to do this and was determined not to wait until his wife died as this could take too long. The embassy from England's ally Portugal which was in London to discuss Richard remarrying to their princess Joanna/Juana was there while Anne was still alive (and departed shortly after she died), suggesting that at the least he was ruthless – or practical – enough to want to secure heirs so that he ignored decorum by waiting for Anne to die naturally (which could take months with the marriage itself then taking another year or so to arrange). Alternatively, her decline was so swift that her doctors had told him she would die within weeks so he was starting the negotiations early – and gave his enemies a weapon to use of accusing him of wanting to be rid of her. 'Tudor agents' were already active in London, as seen by the execution of William Collingbourne for his famous rhyme about his ministers 'The Rat (ie Richard Ratcliffe), The Cat (ie William Catesby), and 'Lovell our dog' (Francis, Lord Lovell), so did they invent the 'poison' story? In this unsavoury political atmosphere, rumours that he was poisoning Anne to hasten her demise were probably inevitable not least if the Portuguese visitors' purpose leaked out. They are not that likely to have been true, given Richard's obsessive sense of piety and honour and the fact that Anne was dying anyway. But they were seen as believable, with the *Croyland Chronicler* (writing in 1486) recording them and saying that Richard's advisers warned him that if he married his niece soon after Anne died the latter's pro-Neville loyalists would say it proved that he had murdered Anne.[62] This says much about public fears of Richard's character even in the loyal north.

The charge laid against him of killing Henry VI is also unprovable, except that the ex-king (aged 49) was in no noticeable ill-health when Edward IV's army arrived in London on 21 May and yet he died the following night. Officially Henry was said to have died of 'pure displeasure and melancholy' at the news of his partisans' defeat and his son's killing at Tewkesbury,[63] but such an extreme reaction is unlikely from a man seen as unresponsive or docile at his last public appearance months earlier. It is probable that Edward ordered him to be killed to prevent any further rebellions in his favour, and as Constable of the Tower Richard may have supervised the murder – traditionally carried out in the private oratory at the Wakefield Tower while Henry was at prayers. In Richard's favour there is no contemporary indication that he was guilty of seeking Clarence's death in 1477–8 as Edward Hall in 1548 (and thence Shakespeare) alleged. He himself claimed in a letter of 1483 to the Earl of Desmond that Clarence had been brought down unjustly like Desmond's father, a Woodville victim – though this may have been self-justification after the event. It has been noticed that at the time (late 1477) Richard was quick to acquire some of Clarence's Warwick lands – Ogmore in South Wales – before the duke was condemned, let alone killed.

In June 1483 Richard had Edward V's maternal uncle Earl Rivers, the boy's half-brother Richard Grey, and a relative, Chamberlain Sir Thomas Vaughan – the trio in charge of Edward V who were arrested by Richard and Buckingham at Stoney Stratford as they took over the king – all executed in custody. They had been supposedly colluding with Elizabeth Woodville and her allies in London in a 'Woodville plot' to deny Richard the Protectorship by hurrying Edward to London for an early coronation, though Rivers' lack of haste argues against this. None of them were an immanent political threat. It has been argued that Rivers was on good terms with Richard as of April 1483, not an implacable enemy, as he asked him to act as co-guarantor in a legal case, and his lack of haste in heading for London before Richard intercepted him shows his lack of concern. If Dorset and the queen feared Richard and sought to cozen him out of the protectorship, as Mancini reports, Rivers did not share this fear to the same extent. Indeed, sceptics argue that Mancini's reports on the reasons behind the manoeuvres of 9–30 April 1483 derive from what Richard put about on his arrival in London – i.e that he had acted to halt a treacherous Wooodville plot. It is surely going too far to claim that this 'plot' only existed in his imagination or was a post-30 April justification for an unprovoked attack on Rivers' party; if the queen and her relatives had nothing to fear, why their attempt to hurry Edward to

London with a large escort? The flight of the Queen into sanctuary and Sir Edward Woodville with the fleet might have been due to panic at the attack on Rivers, not guilt that their plot had been foiled. But the alleged Council clashes and Hastings' appeals to Richard were not figments of Richard's imagination; as of May 1483 this story was being backed up by Hastings too, whatever his later conversion to the Queen's cause. Richard seems to have been a master of 'black' propaganda and was constantly vilifying the Woodvilles for debauchery from June 1483 to the words used in the Act *Titlulus Regius* in early 1484. But the Mancini account of his harsh words about them to Edward V's face at Stony Stratford on 30 April was not evidence 'controlled' by Richard; it was clearly what Mancini had heard from those present, in either Edward V's or (less likely) Richard's entourage. Richard therefore used this line consistently from the time of Edward IV's death, and Hastings went along with it at first – out of dislike of his alleged court foe Dorset, the queen's son?

The story Mancini presents of tension in the early 1480s between Richard, absent in the north and effectively at odds with the court, and a dominant Woodville clique in London, was clearly what was being said to him in the streets of London in summer 1483. He was not just collecting Ricardian propaganda, and had many other sources including Edward V's physician Dr Argentine. Did his account of Richard's confrontation with Edward V in Stony Stratford on the morning of 30 April 1483 come from Edward himself, via the doctor? But the general picture of a clique of drunken, lecherous Woodvilles leading Edward IV to his death clearly reflects what Richard himself wished to put out – as he showed in the propaganda used when Edward V was deposed and in his Act of *Titulus Regius* in 1484. The constant harping on Court depravity – reflected in having Mistress Shore paraded through the streets as a whore – shows Richard as both an obsessive moralist and a master of spin. His moral virtues were shown as justifying his seizure of power, and the Mancini account of his dislike of Edward IV's marriage and belief that the Woodvilles had destroyed Clarence in 1478 are at odds with the historical record. When Richard had two chances to wreck the marriage and drive out Woodville influence by backing Warwick and Clarence in 1469 and 1470 he did not do so; and he swiftly joined in the appropriation of Clarence's lands in 1477–8.

Naked power was clearly more important to him on these occasions, and it is possible that he exaggerated his earlier dislike of the Woodvilles from May 1483 as *post facto* justification of his actions then. As with Richard's action in bringing an army of his northern tenants into London in June to back up his coup, Richard was clearly as ruthless as most contemporary politicians but even more fond of violent intimidation than almost all of them. Such an impulsive and ruthless man as Richard seems to have been was arguably capable of reacting to a threat of a plot to rescue the Princes as figureheads for a revolt in July or August 1483 with the same sudden brutality as he did to Hastings or Rivers. Now that Richard's remains have been discovered at the site of the Grey Friars Church in Leicester (where they were buried unceremoniously after Bosworth) and identified by DNA we can see that he did have a curved spine, due to a medical condition, and that this element of Tudor propaganda was based on reality.[64] By extension, did his medical condition add to latent paranoia and a sense of alienation from Edward IV's licentious Court, and encourage his religiosity and sense of sin? Is this an unexpected explanation for his sporadic ferocity and obsessiveness?

Not only the 'official' Tudor historians writing to please the new regime after 1485, such as Polydore Vergil and (in the most detail) Shakespeare's main source Sir Thomas More, made the contemporary accusations against Richard. Robert Fabyn, a chronicler of c.1500, the independent *London Chronicle* of around the same date, and at least one Welsh bard of the late 1480s referred to him as the killer. A diplomatic visitor to London on behalf of Ferdinand and Isabella of Spain also referred to public belief of Richard's guilt in a letter of March 1486. The most reliable contemporary source, the 'second continuation' of the Croyland Abbey chronicle which may have been supplied with information for the 1480s by the senior minister Bishop Russell (as argued by J.R. Myres in 1954), has a poem allegedly written by an unknown poet which refers obliquely to Richard 'suppressing' ('oprimet') his nephews.[65] Whether or not this is code for the story of suffocation by Richard's hirelings which More presents, or just a general term for their secret removal, it is presumably as much as Richard's one-time ally Russell would reveal – or knew? – of the matter. As such Richard can be presumed to bear official responsibility for the boys' disappearance while in his care, whether or not he issued the actual orders for their killing. Hopeful Ricardians have however claimed that if they were killed at all it was by an over-eager courtier keen to do him a service – or by one particular ally with his own dubious motives (see below).

Was Buckingham the killer – and if so, on whose behalf?

It is possible that Henry Stafford, Duke of Buckingham – a hugely-ambitious direct descendant of Edward III's youngest son, who had already gained massive amounts of land and office from Richard for assisting him against Edward V's maternal family in April/May 1483 – was the murderer, either on Richard's behalf or on his own. He is the favourite candidate of Dr Richard Green as the killer, citing the contemporary claim that Buckingham was supposed to have given 'advice' in the murder.[66] The varied meanings of the word in the fifteenth-century could be interpreted in the modern sense, as implying that he advised Richard to do it, or as saying that he was the 'means' of murder i.e. the killer. The main surprise about Buckingham is the fact that he staged his own revolt that autumn despite all the rewards Richard had given him. He had been made chief justice and chamberlain of North and South Wales and given custody of all the royal castles and estates in Wales (fifty-three in all) in May, along with supervision of and the duty of raising troops from Herefordshire, Shropshire, Devon, Wiltshire, and Somerset – an unparalleled grant of authority showing Richard's trust in him or lack of alternative aristocratic allies. After Hastings' execution the latter's supporters were said to have transferred their allegiance to him[67] – presumably as a less offensive patron than their late master's killer, Richard. Given Hastings' role as Edward IV's closest ally, they would have been anxious for the cause of Edward's sons – and assumed that Buckingham, married to Elizabeth Woodville's sister, would defend his wife's nephew Edward V's cause? Instead, on 24 June Buckingham spoke up for Richard's claim to the throne (already put to the City of London on the 22nd by Friar Ralph Shaa) in an address to the Lord Mayor and leading citizens. It is probable that he made the argument on the grounds of Edward IV's 'illegitimacy' rather than Edward V's, indicating that he was more certain on this ground than on that of the pre-contract. An account of his speech says that he argued that six-foot Edward IV had not looked like his undersized father, the Duke of York, but Richard did – and Richard then appeared at a window to remind the citizens of that fact. The implication was that Richard's mother Cecily Neville had been unfaithful to her husband in Normandy in 1441–2 (with the archer Blaybourne), an allegation which Richard seems to have tolerated to his mother's outrage.

Buckingham could not reasonably hope for more from backing a restored Edward V or a new Tudor king, so why revolt? His apparent ambition and evident lack of scruples in betraying Richard in 1483 after receiving huge rewards is not sufficient proof that he had a Machiavellian plan to murder the boys – his own potential rivals for the throne – and blame it on Richard. Writing an early Tudor history of Richard's reign c.1510 with the advantage of personal access as a youth to his employer Cardinal Morton who had been arrested by Richard in June 1483 and placed in Buckingham's custody, More claimed that Buckingham had been so horrified at news of the murders in July 1483 that he decided to revolt before Richard liquidated him too,[68] and that Morton persuaded him to back Tudor. The 1543 London publication of Hardyng's *Chronicle* by Richard Grafton gave a version of More's account that added on more detail of what Morton allegedly discussed with Buckingham, but his source is unknown – though it might have been notes by Morton himself that had been used by Morton's ex-employee More. Polydore Vergil c.1510, by contrast, traced the duke's decision to revolt to Richard angrily refusing Buckingham's demands in July 1483 for all the inheritance of his ancestress the Duchess of Gloucester's sister the Duchess of Hereford, wife of King Henry IV – the two women being the daughters and heiresses of the last of the De Bohuns, lords of Brecon. (The Hereford half of the inheritance had gone to the House of Lancaster, Henry IV's family.) This may also rely on Buckingham's own account, presumably told to Bishop Morton and by him to Henry VII's court (or direct to Vergil) as well as to More. Given what Richard had already done to people such as Hastings, fearing that the paranoid king would turn on him next is not an impossible assumption for Buckingham to make in July/August 1483 – though the word of the master intriguer Morton cannot be taken as proof for Buckingham's motives. Morton may have persuaded Buckingham that he was in danger, or the greedy Buckingham decided to overthrow Richard for his own benefit while assuring Morton that it was for Henry Tudor's cause. Morton died in 1500, so he must have handed over any information to More years before More wrote the book if he was the latter's (or Grafton's) source. More's son-in-law Rastell claimed this version of More's book to be inaccurate and his own 1557 version to be correct.

Buckingham's accusers commenced with the account in the Low Countries of the anonymous *Divisie Chronicle* of c. 1517, which given its location may have picked up on stories connected to the Perkin Warbeck plot. They preferred to assert that either he murdered the boys to do the hesitant Richard a service, failed to win his gratitude, and revolted in panic at what Richard would do to him, or that he killed them to blacken Richard's name as part of his master-plan to gain the throne. Morton's presence in Buckingham's custody at Brecon as he launched his revolt in September 1483 is intriguing, but – as with Buckingham – it is impossible to be able to do more than guess at his motives or the extent of his involvement nearly 540 years later. As mentioned, 1610s author Sir George Buck's naming of him as a possible killer of the Princes relies on unnamed evidence. Morton may have just spurred on an already panicking or greedy Buckingham, after being told of the planned rebellion by one of Margaret Beaufort's agents. But that has not stopped some Ricardians claiming that he could have done more – ie encouraged Buckingham to carry out the murder while he was in the Duke's custody after his arrest.[69] This would further his secret 'Lancastrian' sympathies for the Tudor cause by helping to start a civil war among the Yorkist leadership from which Henry Tudor could then benefit. Alternatively, Morton might have been egged on by Henry Tudor's mother, Lady Margaret Beaufort, who was to be a prime mover in the autumn 1483 rebellion and used her physician Dr Lewis of Caerleon and Windsor cleric Dr Christopher Urswick to send messages to other participants.

But just because Morton was a die-hard Lancastrian in 1470–1 and re-emerged as one in 1483 is no proof that he had this sort of master strategy in mind to use Buckingham for Henry Tudor's cause. Morton had been with Queen Margaret of Anjou and Anne Neville when Edward IV had seized them after the battle of Tewkesbury in 1471, but was soon re-employed by him. He was arrested by Richard in his Council coup of 13 June 1483, putting him as a partisan of either Hastings or of the Woodvilles; it is not clear if he was then working with his post-1485 ally, Henry Tudor's mother Margaret Beaufort, whose husband Lord

Stanley was also arrested then. He may have been working on behalf of the 'Woodville' cause of restoring Edward V or his brother in June-September 1483, and fled to Tudor in late 1483 because he had heard that the Princes were dead and had no other candidate left to support against Richard.

Morton's close links with Tudor's mother Margaret Beaufort – accused of being party to the rebellion by Richard – hint at her involvement, and it is possible that her husband Lord Stanley (arrested in June but soon reinstated by Richard) or another senior figure had enabled Margaret, and hence Morton, to find out some rumours of murder from the new King's entourage. Margaret, as her son's ally at Court, was the most likely means of arranging the messages to Queen-Mother Elizabeth Woodville that autumn which preceded Henry Tudor's Christmas announcement that he would marry Princess Elizabeth. The go-between was supposed to have been her physician, Dr Lewis Caerleon. According to subsequent post-1485 stories from the Stanleys, Edward IV had considered neutralising the exiled Lancastrian claimant Henry Tudor by offering him his eldest daughter earlier, c. 1476; the plan thus had the implicit backing of the late king. Margaret and senior clerics at Edward's court had discussed the legal problem over the two being fourth cousins. This may have been exaggerated after 1485 to add to the marriage's acceptability – and Edward IV was keen to lure Henry back to England to put this pretender under guard (or even kill him?) so he may have been insincere about the marriage plan. Henry did not believe it at the time, and when his host Duke Francis of Brittany briefly supported it he took sanctuary so he could not be handed over to the king's envoys. But if Margaret Beaufort or another court contact told Elizabeth Woodville that the boys were dead around September-October 1483, that would induce her to accept that her daughter was now the legal rival to Richard for the throne, and thus to engage her to Henry Tudor. This does not mean that the story of a murder was invented to fool Elizabeth; the boys had to be known to be missing or Morton and Margaret Beaufort would be at risk of Richard producing them and ruining their plans. These two intriguers were therefore reasonably certain as of late 1483 that both boys would not turn up – though it is not proof that their agents had killed the boys or they knew who had done so.

Logical arguments against Richard's innocence

No later pretender appeared claiming to be Edward V even after 1485, so it can be assumed that even the most hardened Yorkist intriguers believed that he was dead. It can be reasonably assumed that once the rumours that the Princes were dead started to circulate at the time of the anti-Richard revolts in southern England in September/October 1483 Richard would have produced them to prove his innocence had he been able to do so. This was Henry VII's response in 1487 as Yorkist plotters appeared in Dublin with a boy who they claimed was Richard's nephew Edward, Earl of Warwick, Clarence's son (born in 1475), who had escaped from the Tower. The real provenance – and name and age – of the mysterious 'Lambert Simnel', supposedly from Oxford, was unclear. But Warwick was still in the Tower, and Henry was able to parade him through the streets of London to a church service where courtiers who had known him in Richard's reign could question him to prove it.[70] The sensible course for Richard to have followed in summer 1483 was to keep the Princes secure in the Tower, ready to produce in case of attempts to impersonate them or claim that they had escaped. Indeed, Richard's replacement of their attendants after his accession would indicate that he intended to follow this course and prevent them being rescued by Woodville partisans. The Ricardians argue that he had no logical reason to alter this policy; but the sudden execution of Hastings (who could have been imprisoned like Stanley and Morton) on 13 June shows that Richard was capable of sudden violent actions that careful thought would have told him would damage his cause.

It would also appear from the French chronicler Philippe de Commignes that his sovereign Louis XI, who died at the end of August 1483, had heard a rumour of the Princes' death before then and reassessed his favourable opinion of Richard. This mass of evidence negates the hopeful Ricardian claim that Edward V or his brother must have been the 'children' referred to in accounts for Richard's household in the North in July 1484 (the Earl of Warwick had not yet been moved there) or the 'Lord Bastard' referred to in Richard's household accounts on 9 March[71] – Richard's own illegitimate son John is a more likely candidate for the latter. There is also a theory that Richard kept the boys alive but made them change their identity. There is no other known case of the latter solution being adopted in the fifteenth-century, and in any case it would have been risky – how could Richard trust the Princes to carry out their part of the bargain once they were out of his power? It is surely bizarre to claim that one of the boys ended up as More's own son-in-law Edward Clements and another as Sir Richard Guildford, a courtier of the 1520s. These men were never rumoured to have suddenly appeared from nowhere in 1483/5 or later; to fit this case they would have had to be adopted as boys by their putative fathers at the ages of twelve and ten and there is no indication that Clements and Guildford were adopted. Clements was apparently studying on the Continent until he received his medical degree at Siena in 1525 and shortly afterwards came/returned to England, where he married More's adopted daughter; he was not in More's orbit when the latter wrote his account of Richard's reign c. 1513 so he was not More's source for the 'killing by Tyrrell' story (or provided More with a reason to write a fake account to protect Clements). Nor is it clear why More would entrust such a secret to the artist, Hans Holbein. The ingenious theory developed by Jack Leslau, involving the hidden iconography of the famous family portrait of More and his relatives c.1525, owes more to twentieth-century mystery enthusiasts' ingenuity than to the practicalities and logic of the situation in 1483–5.[72] It is just not plausible that Richard, in danger of overthrow, would let his potential rivals take on new identities within England; how would he know that they would not reappear later to challenge him? The fact that one document once referred to Guildford's daughter Jane as 'Princess' is more likely to be a slip – muddling her up with her daughter-in-law Jane Grey, who was of royal blood – than a hint at Guildford being royal.

The 'smuggled abroad' theory and Warbeck

Slightly less implausible is the idea that they may have been smuggled out of the country, which would explain their absence from political affairs in 1483–5 without having to assume that they were dead. The likeliest route would have been by ship from London, but then how did they get out of the Tower? This would imply probable permission for their removal by a high-ranking official, whether or not with Richard's approval – and it is possible that Buckingham, Richard's closest ally, could give orders in July-August 1483 that would be obeyed as assuming to come from Richard.

Logically, if Richard – or even Buckingham? – wanted to rid himself of the boys without killing them 'exile' would at least distance them from the risk of the Woodvilles discovering their whereabouts (which would not be the case if they were adopted by the Clements and Guildford families). The man responsible for taking the boys abroad would have had to be loyal and discreet, and to have had access to ships and to foreign 'contacts' to provide a home for the exiles. The likeliest candidate for this may have the international adventurer and Yorkist protégé Sir Edward Brampton (aka the Portuguese merchant Duarte Brandao), a converted Jewish entrepreneur with trading-links across Europe. He had been trusted and honoured by Edward IV. Brampton was clearly in charge of the elusive pretender Perkin Warbeck before 1490, as enquiries made by Henry's agents in Portugal confirmed Brampton's own story that Warbeck had first come to that country as a retainer of Brampton's wife c. 1488 from her previous residence in Tournai, Flanders.[73] Whether or not Warbeck was really the son of a simple boatman, he had first surfaced in Tournai as a teenage protégé of Brampton; therefore if Richard (or anyone else) had sent him abroad it had been to Flanders. The shrewd Richard would hardly have risked sending the boys to France where Louis XI had already used the exiled Lancastrian Queen Margaret and Prince Edward to undermine the Yorkist regime in 1470 and could find and use the Princes too; Richard had fiercely opposed Edward IV's peace with Louis in 1475 and was thus a possible threat to the French government. But the trading-towns of Flanders were a safer haven, being ruled by the stepson (Maximilian of Habsburg) of Richard's sister Duchess Margaret; Richard and Edward IV had taken refuge there on being overthrown in 1470.

The boys – only the younger one if the elder was dead? – could have been exiled on Richard's orders, or by one of his political enemies to protect them from him. At the time of Warbeck's capture and confession, the name of Buckingham was being spoken of as their preserver on the continent.[74] If that was correct, he must have acted while he was still trusted by Richard – July to early September 1483? As Richard's most senior aristocratic supporter (and the husband of the boys' aunt Catherine Woodville), he would have had the authority and the family excuse to gain access to the royal apartments in the Tower and have them spirited out one night. Indeed, it is even possible that he could have included his own men among the Ricardian loyalists placed in charge of them in July with this possibility in mind. But why then did he not reveal the fact or the boys' location to his Woodville allies during the rebellion, enabling the queen's exiled adherents to retrieve the boys when the revolt failed? Was he holding this information as a bargaining counter for use in extorting terms once the alliance had deposed Richard, but his capture and death meant that he could not use it?

It remains to be seen what lay behind his apparent urgent request to speak to Richard face-to-face at Salisbury when he was captured during his revolt and brought there for execution. Richard refused to see him as he was 'the most untrue creature living', and he was swiftly beheaded.[75] He may have just intended to beg for mercy, but it is possible that he had information on the location of the Princes and intended to bargain with Richard to give him details in return for a reprieve. It is possible that if he *had* rescued the boys – as a prelude to his intended revolt? – he would have revealed the fact to his prisoner Bishop Morton at Brecon as he plotted rebellion in August/September, as proof of his goodwill to the Woodville cause (his wife was the queen's sister). If so the bishop would have been able to relay the news to Henry Tudor when he joined him that winter, but in any case neither of the boys was ever located abroad and by Christmas the queen was prepared to arrange her daughter's betrothal to Tudor as the new Woodville ally against Richard. This suggests that if Buckingham had rescued the boys he had not told Morton about it, or else Morton and the Tudor entourage in exile had discounted it. The only argument in favour of Buckingham letting something slip is Henry Tudor's anxiety about Warbeck's Flemish connections in the 1490s. Henry sent his agents to trawl through Flanders for evidence of Warbeck's identity; this might be interpreted as meaning that he had heard back in 1483–4 that the boys had been taken there. And why was Henry so anxious to have Richard's nephew John de la Pole, Earl of Lincoln, taken alive at the battle of Stoke in 1487 to find out the 'root of his danger'?[76] He had shown Lincoln's protégé Lambert Simnel to be a fraud; did he think that Lincoln knew where Richard or Buckingham had sent the real Edward V? The expression 'root of his danger' may only refer to the extent of pro-Yorkist plotting at Henry's court, but the fact that Lincoln was seen as the key to secret information would indicate that he had picked up some extra information Henry needed since he fled abroad.

Logically, this was either details known to Duchess Margaret and/or the real identity of the Yorkist claimant to the throne. Was Simnel a stalking horse for one of the Princes – or at least Henry suspected this?

The possibility of the Princes' successful escape from Richard's clutches raises its own questions. As with the theory of the survival of some or all of the Romanovs after the shooting at Ekaterinburg in July 1918, there is one obvious problem for the proponents of an escape. What then happened to them? If they had been rescued by Woodville partisans – or rescued by Buckingham before he turned on Richard – they would surely have re-appeared on the Continent some time in 1484–5, seeking local rulers' support, as the pretenders Lambert Simnel and Perkin Warbeck later did. Presumably their mother Elizabeth Woodville would have been informed, and in that case she would have backed them, not her daughter Elizabeth's fiancé-to-be Henry Tudor in 1485. Their young age was not a problem to them taking part in a revolt, as Lambert Simnel was of a similar age in 1486–7. That would indicate that if they were smuggled out by enemies of Richard, the latter were not connected to the Woodville cause – this might explain the claim of the later pretender who used the Duke of York's identity, Perkin Warbeck, that he was warned to stay hidden to avoid being murdered.[77] Buckingham might have made this threat to him in order to ensure that he did not approach Woodville agents, or even reveal his identity at all – thus ensuring that he would not appear to complicate Buckingham's own bid for the throne? Or if an alternative candidate for the rescuer, Richard's loyal supporter Sir James Tyrrell, had rescued them (or one of them) without Richard's authority he could have been taking measures to see that the boy did not talk and his story did not find its way back to Richard.

One of Warbeck's stories of his escape had the killer(s) murdering the older boy before taking the younger one abroad, possibly indicating that the lord who had been ordered to kill them feared Woodville retribution as well as that from Richard. Alternatively, one boy had died at sea, possibly in an accident or deliberately thrown overboard.[78] Was this just an excuse to explain the absence of bodies, or did this mean that the killer was hedging his bets – killing the more dangerous boy, the ex-king, as he had been told to do by Richard but saving the other boy so that if Richard's regime was to fall he had a claim on the gratitude of the Woodvilles? Another story featuring an 'accident' was heard by visiting Portuguese nobleman Ruy de Souza, namely that the boys had been hidden away in an unnamed fortress where they had died after a botched 'blood-letting' during an illness by a doctor – but though contemporary medicine was a haphazard business and incompetent doctors were a common hazard it seems unlikely that both boys would suffer from the same mistake. It is conceivable that Richard could then have panicked and hidden the truth as nobody would believe that he had not arranged the 'accident', but why did no gossip from a witness leak out later?

An alternative theory has been put forward recently by David Baldwin, based on the enigmatic master-bricklayer Richard Plantagenet who was claimed – in retrospect in the eighteenth-century – to have presented himself as a son of Richard III. According to the memories of the Finch family, Earls of Winchelsea and living at Eastwell in Kent, their ancestor Sir Thomas Moyle had employed an impressively literate craftsman while building the family residence there in the early decades of the sixteenth-century and asked him how he came to know Latin and read Horace. He had said that he was an illegitimate son of Richard III, brought up in ignorance of his parentage and then taken to visit the king's camp on the eve of Bosworth by an unnamed 'lord' who had been his guardian. Previously he had been in the care of a country parson, and as the journey to Bosworth seemingly took hours not days the location of his home must have been within twenty or thirty miles of the battlefield. (Lutterworth, where the Woodvilles had the right to nominate the resident cleric, has been suggested.) Richard had promised to acknowledge him and make him his heir if he won the battle, but he had been killed and the boy had had to go into hiding. He had trained as a craftsman, working on church building projects until the dissolution of the monasteries, and had never revealed his identity in case he was hunted down by the Tudors. The story was seemingly backed up by the existence of a tombstone to 'Richard Plantagenet' at Eastwell, saying that he had died in 1550 – which if he was aged around twelve to fourteen in 1485 would have meant that he lived to his late seventies.[79]

The man may have been a fantasist, but the story could not be disproved and in fact Henry VII had imprisoned and executed Richard's illegitimate son John in 1490 so a boy in his position had good reason to hide his identity at the time. The legend was duly taken up by the children's novelist Barbara Willard as the centrepiece of her book, *A Sprig of Broom*, which told the story of Richard's visit to his father and life as a craftsman in Kent. The book had 'Plantagenet' having to elude Yorkist plotters as well as Tudor agents, a plausible theory for why a son of Richard III (or Edward IV) who did not want to be used as a front-man for a conspiracy would keep his identity secret. Baldwin claims that the boy may in fact have been the younger of the two Princes, not smuggled abroad but kept in hiding by Richard's trusted lieutenants, and that he pretended to be Richard's illegitimate son not the rightful king to minimise the danger that he would become a political pawn even in the 1530s or 1540s. He cites evidence of a craftsman called 'Richard Grey' who worked for the Abbey of Colchester and its daughter-house, Creake Priory in Norfolk, around 1500 as indicating that that might have been the same man who re-surfaced later at Eastwell. He was then using his mother's family name, Grey, and could have taken refuge at Colchester after Bosworth with the refugee Ricardian loyalist Lord Lovell – the most likely candidate for the anonymous nobleman who looked after 'Richard Plantagenet'. Lovell was Richard's most trusted lieutenant and was involved in attempts to overthrow Henry VII in 1486–7, and he took refuge at Colchester Abbey so Abbot Eastney presumably had Yorkist sympathies and thus could have arranged a safe career and identity for the Prince once Lovell had been killed. It is an intriguing theory, but impossible to prove and if true it would pose its own problems – what happened to Edward V? And if Prince Richard's contact with the king in 1483–5 was Lord Lovell, why was Henry VII so keen on pursuing and forcing a confession of murder out of Sir James Tyrell, another of Richard III's henchmen? Did Sir James Tyrell assist Lovell to hide Prince Richard, and then mislead Henry VII in 1485–6 about the Prince being abroad? And why did Lovell not use the Prince as the figurehead of the 1487 Simnel rebellion, if he knew where to get hold of him? It is more likely that at best the mysterious bricklayer was a son of Richard III, and that the Richard Grey who worked for Colchester Abbey was an ordinary workman with no royal connections.

Tyrrell – the murderer or the Tudor scapegoat?

Alternatively, Richard might have allowed the boys to leave the country after living in seclusion at Sir James Tyrrell's Essex home at Gipping, as a Tyrrell family legend about their residence there cited by Audrey

Williamson implies.[80] The age of this story is unclear, and it cannot be traced back more than a couple of centuries. There is also a claim that the boys were taken under the care of a royal servant of Richard's, James Nesfield – a Yorkshire aide who kept a eye on the Princesses until they and the queen left sanctuary in early 1484.[81] They then left England some time in 1484 – though it is unclear in this case why Richard did not produce them at least once in public in winter 1483–4 to dispel the rumours that he had murdered them. In this scenario, either Tyrrell or Nesfield had charge of them at the time of the autumn 1483 revolt, and once it had failed Richard could produce the boys without fear that Woodville agents would kidnap them. Crucially, the public pledge by Henry Tudor in Brittany to marry their sister Princess Elizabeth assumed that they were dead and she was Edward IV's heiress – which Richard could counter by producing the boys. Richard could seriously embarrass Henry by doing this, but he did not – so by December 1483 the boys were out of his reach.

But if Richard had resorted to exiling the boys, it meant that he was taking a large risk that they would not claim the throne once they were adults – the sort of risk that Richard did not normally take. For him to do this they would still have been in his hands in summer-autumn 1483 during the pro-Edward V rebellion in the home counties – so why did he not produce them briefly to show that they were alive? Logically, it would have taken some weeks to arrange a ship to Flanders and a refuge there, and for the boys' presence at Gipping to have been notable enough to be remembered for generations they would have had to be there for some time, not just a few days. The boys were still in the Tower in early July according to Mancini, and still there at the beginning of September according to the author of the *Croyland Chronicle* continuation (possibly Bishop Russell, now Lord Chancellor?) They were both writing closer to the date of the disappearance than More, who put the date of the murder as mid-August with Tyrrell being sent to London from Warwick. Richard had been looking for a discreet 'hard man' to do the killing and a page obligingly suggested Tyrrell, so More wrote – but in fact Richard knew Tyrrell well already and More did not mention the page's identity. If Tyrrell himself was the key actor in the boys' removal abroad rather than the murderer, his mission to London from Richard's itinerant court early in September was the likeliest time for him to have taken them to a ship (one of Brampton's?). The official reason for his visit seems to have been to collect robes from the royal wardrobe for the investiture of Richard's son as Prince of Wales at York on 8 September,[82] so he had no time to go abroad then – though he might have taken the boys from the Tower to Gipping or handed them over to Sir Edward Brampton. If the boys were sent abroad quickly, not being available to be shown in public at the time of the October rebellion, they might have sailed from the coast near Gipping soon after they left London – Tyrrell would not have had to go to Flanders himself if Brampton was in charge of that part of the plan. If the boys had been taken abroad during September that would explain why Richard could not produce them to confound the rebels in October.

One significant fact is Tyrrell's secret mission to Flanders in 1484 on matters 'greatly touching the king's weal (welfare)'. This seems too much of a coincidence when the Flanders connections of Brampton and Warbeck are considered – if it was so secret a mission that it could not be specified, what else could it have been? There was no political threat to Richard's regime from the area, and the only current pretender – Henry Tudor – was based in Brittany whence Richard was soon to attempt to extradite him. But the secret mission may have been some private diplomatic initiative connected to Richard's sister Duchess Margaret, as opposed to installing or checking up on Prince Richard in some obscure hiding-place. The pretender Warbeck's modern supporters claim that Tyrrell was installing or checking up on the exiled prince in the Warbeck household, or else discussing where to place him with Duchess Margaret. It could be claimed that Warbeck's later 'confession' hinted at the time when he – i.e. Prince Richard – had arrived in Flanders, by stating that he had been seriously ill in 1484. To supporters of Warbeck's authenticity, this could show that the real Peter/Perkin Warbeck had died then and the prince had been substituted for him.[83] It is claimed that the large sum of money paid over early in 1485 to Tyrrell – later accused of the murder by Henry VII and forced to 'confess' in 1502 after being arrested on other charges – by Richard was either 'hush-money' after he killed the boys on Richard's behalf or a fund set up to look after the boys in exile.[84] It is unlikely to have been connected to Richard's major secret overseas plan, bribing the Breton Duke Francis II's chief minister Landois to hand over Henry Tudor, as by this date Tudor had already left Brittany for France.

The truth of the allegations about Tyrrell's role – murderer or preserver? – cannot be ascertained, though his connection with the mystery in Henry Tudor's enquiries in 1486 and his supposed 'confession' in 1502 show that Henry regarded him as a central figure in the case. It is probable that if Tyrrell had been able to show Henry proof that the boys were dead in autumn 1485 by producing the bodies, supposedly hidden in the Tower, the new king would have been keen to expose the fact to prevent the appearance of pretenders. Even if he could not produce the bodies, Tyrrell was clearly under suspicion as a Ricardian loyalist – but was too useful to be executed along with Richard's chief non-noble supporters captured at Bosworth. He was pardoned at the time, but was employed out of England not at court – so that he could not talk about inconvenient facts that Henry wished suppressed? He could be sacrificed as a scapegoat for the killings later, though only once he had proved that he could not be trusted by his dabbling with Richard's refugee nephew Edmund de la Pole.

Tyrrell's (double) pardon in 1486 indicates that Henry preferred to let the matter alone for the moment, showing that if Tyrrell *had* confessed to the killings the king could not construct a strong enough public story about the 'truth' to be sure of satisfying the public. But the fact that he received two separate pardons on 16 June and 16 July that year seem to indicate that during that month he had committed (or more likely that Henry had found out about) some other crime not covered by the first one.[85] It is unlikely that the Ricardians are correct that that crime was the current act of killing the Princes on Henry's orders, as if they had been found in the Tower in August 1485 it is unlikely that some story would not have leaked out. The place was a bustling royal residence not a top-security prison, and even if Richard and then Henry had been holding the boys in a secure set of rooms with limited access some of the other Tower residents would have been able to relay gossip about the mystery into the City. It would then have appeared in the *Great Chronicle*, as did the rumours of spring 1484 that the boys were missing, and if we can accept that More was not a Tudor propagandist but writing a serious historical account he should have heard some story about this too by c.1510.

Significantly, Tyrrell was now required to reside abroad at Calais and sell up his lands in Wales, a possible indicator that Henry's minimal terms for his pardon were that he kept out of Britain. He was regarded as exceptionally dangerous when he came under suspicion over his receiving De la Pole in 1502, not only as commander at the strategically vital fort of Guisnes outside Calais. He had to be superseded as commander to prevent him handing Guisnes over to a local enemy, but in addition Henry saw it as essential to apprehend him and prevent him from fleeing once he knew he was in trouble with the king over his contacts with De la Pole. Henry lured him on board a ship under a safe-conduct, using his captive son as a hostage to induce him to co-operate, and had him kidnapped. Safely lodged in the Tower, Tyrrell was kept incommunicado until he was executed on 6 May[86] – a sign that Henry did not want him talking to anyone.

It is probable that Henry's desire not to revive memories of the scandalous events of 1483 and damage his country's reviving international respectability lie behind the fact that Tyrrell's confession was not widely circulated as closure for the story in 1502. His elder son Arthur had just died leaving him with an 11-year-old heir, there were murmurs among the nobility about future instability, and Richard III's nephew Edmund de la Pole was at large on the continent so it was not politic to remind people that Henry's predecessor was not provably dead. Henry may not have forced Tyrrell to confess and produce an account of the murder in 1485–6 because he had conducted a private enquiry and did not consider the evidence (only verbal?) safe enough to proceed against Tyrrell. If Tyrrell was innocent and had smuggled one or two boys out of England, Henry could have promised not to punish him if he kept quiet about it – and if Tyrrell had not said where the boys were Henry could not then kill them. In 1502, however, Tyrrell had shown his potential disloyalty in his new post at Calais and was under arrest on the charge of admitting Richard's refugee nephew De la Pole on his journey abroad to start claiming the throne. Henry could accordingly have decided to rake up the old accusation as part of discrediting Tyrrell – but he did not name him as the boys' killer at the time, and the execution was cited as due to treason in aiding De la Pole. The same charge was made when Tyrrell was retrospectively attainted in 1504, with no word about regicide.

Henry is supposed to have shown the confession to his senior courtiers, according to Sir Francis Bacon's biography. But the usually well-informed Robert Fabyan, writing in 1504, does not link Tyrrell's execution to the charge of murdering the Princes – or even mention Tyrrell as a possible killer, which surely some courtier would have let out if the king had been showing a confession around.[87] Nor did Polydore Vergil claim to know what had happened to the Princes – which this court insider would have done had any of Henry VII's courtiers told him that Henry had revealed the details of Tyrrell's confession to them. Even More referred to his 'reconstruction' as his own summary of what seemed most likely to him from a mass of conflicting stories[88] – not as a coherent story that he had heard from Henry VII's courtiers. Did Henry avoid circulating it more widely as he feared that much publicity would lead to awkward questions about why the bodies had not been found? Henry VII would rather not remind people that even after seventeen years he had no proof that the 'legitimate' King Edward V was dead.

It is also possible that Sir Thomas More derived some of the details of the killing which he gives from female relatives of Tyrrell and the daughter of Richard's Constable of the Tower, Sir Richard Brackenbury, with whom he had contact in London in the 1500s.[88] They may have been able to relay Tyrrell's and Brackenbury's accounts of what had happened, meaning that More did not only rely on what his detractors maintain was a campaign of Tudor propaganda fed to him by Henry VII's most senior ministers such as Cardinal Morton. In this case, if Tyrrell had smuggled the boys out in September they did not mention it – which is an argument against this happening, though they and More would have known that no account of the murder which exonerated Richard and left the boys' fate uncertain would be publishable under the Tudor dynasty. More did not proceed with publishing his 1510? version of the story – but he chose to write up a coherent story of the murder, not leave it ambivalent. Even if he had not consulted the Tyrrell family or they had not risked telling him the truth as that would lead to confiscation of their remaining estates by Henry VIII, More clearly believed that he had a coherent account of a murder and could name the minor players in it, including the still-alive John Dighton. If he had constructed the entire story, why name the remaining witness to it?

The main doubt in More's account seems to be over the precise date, which is at odds with the better-informed *Croyland Chronicler*; it is also odd that his nephew and publisher Rastell differed from More's account of the killing, which was apparently already written when he published his version. When he came to describe it in a 1529 chronicle he had the boys put in a chest, either being tricked into climbing in alive or else murdered and then hidden there, and thrown in the sea.[89] Did Rastell, presumably with access to all More's then evidence in 1529, hear different stories too and decide that that was more believable than the hiring of Dighton and co. by Tyrrell? And who told him the names of the killers – one of Dighton's friends or family, or a descendant of someone privy to whatever Tyrrell told Henry VII in 1486 or 1502? Other suggestions have been made that More might have heard the names of the killers and other details from the sister of Richard III's deceased Constable of the Tower, Brackenbury (allegedly the man who refused the king's orders to murder them so Richard had to send Tyrrell), who lived in the 1500s at the nunnery of the Minories near the Tower with which More had close connections It seems plausible that Tyrrell was the ultimate source for the details of the killing, whether or not he did the deed on Richard's orders as More said or he had either acted for someone else (presumably Buckingham) or had not been the killer but knew the perpetrators' names. Possibly he denied doing the killing but could not prove it and Henry assumed that this was a lie and charged him anyway in 1502 (but had the trial and execution done in seclusion so the flimsy evidence for Tyrrell's guilt could not be challenged or gossiped about).

If he had told Henry that the boys had been buried within the Tower it should have led to a search for their bodies, but saying that they had been thrown in the sea avoided the risk that anything would be found. Could Tyrrell have made up this story in case Henry carried out a search, as he knew that the king would find nothing? (In one version of events, this was because Tyrell had taken the boys abroad.) Or did Tyrrell say the bodies were at the Tower (which More heard about later), but when Henry VII found nothing he did not know if Tyrrell had lied so he decided to give out that the boys had been thrown into the sea to explain the failure to find them (which Rastell then heard)? The way that Tyrrell firstly had to live abroad out of the way of gossip at the isolated castle of Guisnes implies that at the least Henry did not entirely trust him and wanted him out of the way but had nothing definite to charge him with in 1486 – and his quiet trial and execution in 1502 implies that Henry did not know enough reliable details of the alleged murders in 1483 to be able to release this story to the public. It does not mean that Tyrrell was innocent, merely that the mystery was not solved by his confession so the king continued to shut down the debate in the same way that he had suppressed the contentious Ricardian law *Titulus Regius*.

The question of More's gullibility or his willingness to act as an agent of a Tudor smear campaign has been hotly contested for centuries. But whatever his motives for writing it, he abandoned the text of his biography of the late king around 1510 – at the description of the Buckingham rebellion – and never published it. It has been asserted that his reason was to do with the rehabilitation of Buckingham's son Edward Stafford, by 1510 a major political player and apparently arrogant and foolish enough to boast about his Royal descent from Edward III's youngest son at a time when Henry VIII had no male heir. Buckingham was to be executed in 1521, and might have been a dangerous enemy had More sought to remind his readers that his father had been an attainted rebel and a former Ricardian loyalist in 1483. But this was a well-known fact, so More writing about it could not do much damage – and More could have presented Buckingham's father as Richard's dupe, as Shakespeare was to do later in the century.

The bodies – was there a Tudor search, if not why not, and are the ones found in 1674 genuine?

Henry VII is universally regarded, on contemporary evidence, as being cautious to the point of paranoia. The successful seizures of the crown in the past (apart from 1066) had been by an acknowledged close heir, usually by a claimant with a logical legal case as the rightful occupant or the ex-sovereign's next heir. Stephen had nearly been deposed by his predecessor Henry I's only surviving (female) child, Matilda – to whom Henry had had allegiance sworn as his heir – in 1141. He had then had to acknowledge Matilda's son Henry (II), not his own sons, as heir in 1153. Edward II had been deposed on the name of his eldest son (Edward III) in 1327; Richard II had been deposed in favour of his next-of-kin in the male line, his cousin Henry (IV) in 1399; Henry VI had been deposed in the name of his cousin and the heir of the line of female inheritance to Richard II overlooked in 1399, Edward IV, in 1461; Edward had been deposed in Henry's favour in 1470 and restored in 1471; and Richard III had deposed Edward V as illegitimate (and hinted that Edward IV was too) in 1483. Henry VII had a very weak claim to the throne in his own right, as the senior descendant of the third marriage of Henry IV's father John of Gaunt, Duke of Lancaster. The first generation of this family, the Beauforts, had been born illegitimate and been excluded from the throne by Act of Parliament in 1396 – and Henry was heir through female descent, i.e. his mother Margaret Beaufort, daughter of Lancaster's grandson John Beaufort (d. 1444), who effectively renounced her rights in his favour. Once Henry VI and his son Edward were dead (May 1471) he was the senior male heir to John of Gaunt. But his descent through the House of Lancaster from the latter relied on that female descent which previous Lancastrian monarchs since 1399 had claimed invalidated the claim of the House of York, who were descended from John of Gaunt's elder brother Lionel but through the female line. Henry's strongest legal claim in 1485 lay through marrying the York heiress Elizabeth, though he notably sought to play this down and held up the date of her coronation to 1487 as if marginalising his reliance on her claim.

The great benefit to Henry of the disappearance of the two boys who had a stronger claim to the throne than his wife would be destroyed if either of them turned up alive. As of August 1485, there was no proof that they were dead. Accordingly, he seems to have played down their role rather than present them as martyrs of the tyranny of the man he had deposed. This spin seems to have been continuing as late as the time of Tyrell's arrest in 1502 – when the recent death of his own elder son made his dynasty seem more precarious. The fact that the bodies had never been recovered was probably the chief factor in the relative quietness with which Henry VII dealt with the affair at the time of Tyrrell's confession – he did not want to remind people of the scandal when he could still not prove that the boys were dead.

It is slightly odd that he had not made public efforts to find the bodies in 1485 or at latest in 1502 – after all, they were his wife's brothers and the most notorious victims of his vilified predecessor. The answer may be the simple one that he did so without a 'fanfare' in case he found nothing and that started more rumours that they had escaped after all. The Ricardians hopefully claim the secrecy that Henry observed on the matter was due to a sinister Tudor cover-up of the 'fact' that Henry had hired Tyrell to kill the boys himself after finding them alive in August 1485 (or even that his mother Lady Margaret Beaufort had had them killed in 1483 to aid Henry's immanent invasion by blackening Richard's reputation and causing their maternal relatives to agree to link up with the Tudor cause). This was the argument put forward on Richard's behalf by Sir Clements Markham in 1906. But it is probable that if the boys had been kept hidden in the White Tower in 1483–5 some enterprising official or Royal servant aware of the fact would have told their story or gossip would have leaked out, particularly if Henry had found them alive in 1485 and then had them killed. Any fact that some rooms were cordoned-off to visitors at the time would have leaked out; the Tower was not a top-security prison but a bustling royal residence. The secrecy observed in any search of the Tower may indicate why there was no witness available to tell More a generation later that Henry VII had been looking for the bodies. As suggested above, the 'thrown in the sea' story which Rastell heard may have been put out by Henry after such a search failed to find anything. Indeed, Warbeck's story about being smuggled abroad in 1483 (which he would have told Henry on his capture in 1499) may have suggested this explanation to Henry as a convincing one to put out around court after a failed search in 1502.

There was also clearly confusion over where precisely the alleged murderers had hidden the bodies within the White Tower, assuming that the story More reported of the murder was that which Henry heard either in 1485 or 1502. The story portrayed by More has obvious flaws – not least the timing of events. It is questionable how the alleged killers, Will Slaughter and John Dighton, hired by Tyrrell after Richard suddenly decided on murder during the course of his post-coronation tour, could have dug a hole under some stairs in the White Tower without someone noticing and then telling their story once Richard was safely dead. If they had no advance notice of the murder and had to carry it out during the few hours that Tyrrell had gained them access to the White Tower, how could they excavate a site under some stone stairs and then hide it once they had dumped the bodies there? If the bodies were subsequently dug up by a priest and re-buried in consecrated ground as More said,[90] how was this done without word leaking out among other residents of the royal palace at the Tower? If the bodies had been re-buried by a priest some time after the murder so they were not at the site selected by Dighton and Forrest, as one version had it, why did he not come forward once Richard III was dead and show Henry VII the location? If it was supposed to be consecrated ground, this would probably have been the chapel of St Peter ad Vincula, across a courtyard from the White Tower, or just possibly the Norman chapel within the White Tower – but neither was where the 1674 bodies were found. The site of the latter was that of an annex built onto the side of the White Tower, seen in the 1597 drawing of the Tower by Wyngaerde – a short distance from the windows of the White Tower where the boys were last seen, and from the usual royal apartments around a courtyard to the south-east of that building.

Even if the priest had died by 1485, he clearly told his story to someone for it to leak out – and More believed he had been employed by the Constable of the Tower, Sir Robert Brackenbury. Moreover, in 1494 the English ambassador to emperor Maximilian was so irritated at Perkin Warbeck parading around the Emperor's court claiming to be the Duke of York that he blustered that everyone in London knew the Duke was dead and he could take doubters to the chapel where he was buried.[91] This presumably means one of the Tower chapels – but if this story (ie the priest's) was widely known by 1494 Henry VII had never proclaimed the site of the burial publicly and held a religious service to assure everyone that his potential rivals were dead. How was it that nobody living at the Tower or even Dighton – alive in the 1500s according to More – knew enough to tell Henry where to find the bodies in 1485/6 or 1502, or if Henry knew the probable location by 1494 he had done nothing about it? If Dighton had been questioned post-1485 (as More says) and was the killer, he should have been able to tell Henry where to look and the bodies would have been found then, not in 1674 – so were the bodies not found and Henry let Dighton go? In that case, the priest may have been telling the truth – and the '1674 bodies' were not the Princes after all.

The bodies – apparently of boys the right age, between ten and twelve – which were discovered in 1674 and examined in 1933 were not even the first potentially correct bodies to be found in the Tower, some earlier ones having been found in the early seventeenth century while Sir Walter Raleigh was a captive there according to a note made in 1647 on a copy of More's *History of Richard III*. This discovery was in a 'sealed room' which fits in with the rumour of the place of burial reported around 1500 by the French chronicler Jean de Molinet, though those bodies appeared to be too young.[92] The sealed room was clearly not the chapel mentioned in the 1494 story. The 1674 discoveries seemed to be of boys of the right age, around ten and twelve. The stairs where they were found, in the annex building on the south side of the White Tower, was being demolished in 1674 and could plausibly be described as part of the royal apartments so it was close to the boys' final rooms as mentioned by Mancini. The extent of pathological knowledge available in 1933 was limited and a modern review might produce more precise evidence, as at the time the examiner Dr Wright, Dean of the London Medical College, could not be certain that the bodies were male. The age was approximately correct, with the right difference in age between the two bodies, and Dr George Northcroft's dental examination concurred with Dr Wright's (and suggested that the victims were related). Apparent signs of osteomyelitis in the jaw of the elder boy, as suggested by expert Dr Richard Lyne-Pirkis in 1963, could indicate the illness that made him depressed according to Dr Argentine's testimony to Mancini, and a stain there might indicate suffocation as described by More. But the date of the bodies was not clear and decisive, and it was not certain that they were medieval.[93] Roman remains have been found at the Tower and it was not a restricted royal palace until the late 1060s. Nor was it clear why if More was correct in saying that a priest hd moved the bodies to a more appropriate location the latter should turn up at the foot of the stairs after all, as if not moved. Nowadays DNA comparison with the bodies of Edward IV and Elizabeth Woodville should make the identification more certain, as no other royal children went missing in the Tower.

The most surprising point is that More records that one of the presumed murderers, John Dighton, was still at large and his whereabouts apparently known to him around 1510. He had already been questioned by the authorities in 1502 to confirm Tyrrell's story, so he had been available then to be arrested for regicide as a scapegoat with a confession having been acquired from him. More wrote that Dighton could yet be hanged for his crimes,[94] presumably a reference to him going back to a life of crime as a dubious ruffian in London. Henry VII could easily have forced a public confession that Richard had ordered him to murder the boys in 1502 and then executed him. This would have at least provided one 'witness' that the boys were dead and that Warbeck and his like were all fakes, and Henry could have used him as a scapegoat more easily than Tyrrell. Dighton would seem to have been questioned if More is correct, and the precise details More gives of the murder would have been known to him but not to Tyrrell so More had seen (or been told about) Dighton's testimony. Possibly Dighton mentioned the site that he had used to hide the bodies and Henry had it excavated, but nothing was found so that cast doubt on his testimony and he was allowed to go free. But perhaps Henry was a more scrupulous man than the ruthless Machiavellian that the Ricardians make him out to be, and was unwilling to make an example of Dighton when his guilt was not beyond all doubt or he had only acted on the direct orders of someone higher in authority.

The chances are thus against More's story being accurate as there are so many holes in it, or of the bodies found in the Tower in 1674 being the remains of the Princes – unless a DNA test proves that to be the case. Even if the bodies are genuine, that does not bring us any closer to the question of who did the killing, though it would narrow it down to a probability of Richard, one of his senior henchmen (acting with or without his approval), or as a 'long shot' a Lancastrian/ Tudor/ Beaufort partisan. Nor should the possibility of an accidental death for at least one boy, by the rumoured bloodletting or by a drowning during an escape, be ruled out – though that would still be convenient for Richard. Given the other evidence of Richard's cold-blooded or hot-blooded executions, his greed, his use of terror as a political weapon, his obsession with 'sin', and his treatment of his wife, the least that can be said after all the modern investigations is that the notion of a 'saintly' Richard as a traduced man of honour and justice is probably wide of the mark.

Chapter 5

Edward IV's Marriage(s) – Was He a Bigamist?

The unexpected marriage in 1464: why was it secret?

Edward IV may have been lacking in shrewdness or foresight in building up Richard's vast power in the north, given that Somerset (1464) and Warwick (1468 and 1470) had already betrayed him, and he was taken by surprise by the 1468 rebellion and by Montague's defection to Warwick in 1470. But his mistakes are more visibly obvious with his marriage. Alone among post-Conquest sovereigns, he was married in secret and not in a well-known church or cathedral, at the manor of Grafton Regis (probably at a chapel there where his heraldic arms have been found on tiles) in a remote area of Northamptonshire around May Day 1464.[1] His choice of wife was also unusual, in that he did not marry a foreign princess – something which was even more than usual politically desirable in his precarious position. He had come to the throne unexpectedly by usurpation in March 1461, as the heir to his father Richard, Duke of York whose own claim to be Henry VI's heir depended on the supposed illegitimacy of the latter's son Prince Edward. Duke Richard had been his cousin Henry's heir until the prince's birth in 1453. Given the mental instability and well-known religiosity of the prudish and pious king and the ruthlessness of the anti-York faction at court, the idea that a 'stud' could have been used to make up for the king's inability to conceive an heir was plausible.But when the intense and increasingly violent struggle for power at court finally led to the exiled York faction returning to take power by force in summer 1460, Richard's decision to claim the throne at once (not just rule as the feeble Henry's heir and regent, as in 1454) aroused dismay among much of the nobility. By male descent, he was the heir of the line of Edward III's fourth surviving son (Edmund, Duke of York) and Henry was the heir of his third surviving son (John of Gaunt, Duke of Lancaster). In the female line Richard was heir, via his mother, of Edward III's second surviving son (Lionel, Duke of Clarence); but did this count against the Lancastrian incumbent, whose grandfather Henry IV had been recognised as King by Parliament in 1399?

Another round of violent struggle followed, and once York had been killed by Queen Margaret's men that December it became clear that the only way his heir Edward could preserve his safety was to gamble for the throne itself. He had defeated the local royal partisans in the Welsh Marches at Mortimer's Cross, marched on London to claim the throne, and then routed the Queen's party in a bloody battle at Towton Moor – but he had failed to capture Henry VI, who remained at large until he was found hiding in Lancashire in 1465. As of 1464, Henry himself was still at large, his wife Margaret was organising invasions of the North from Scotland, and Louis XI of France still recognised their claim to the throne. He desperately needed a foreign ally against Margaret, the regency in Scotland, and Louis XI, and there were currently negotiations with France's southern neighbour across the Pyrenees, Castile, that involved the possibility of Edward marrying the young king Henry III's half-sister Isabella (born 1451, and nine years Edward's junior).[2] Had these succeeded, Isabella – not yet Henry's potential heiress as her brother Alfonso was still alive – would not have been in Castile in 1469 to be placed at the head of a noble faction who opposed Henry's decision to proclaim his 'daughter' Juana (presumed by many to be a bastard due to his wife's alleged promiscuity) as his successor. Isabella would not have been Queen of Castile from 1469–1504, or united Spain by marrying Ferdinand of Aragon; she would have been Queen of England instead. Alternatively, Edward could have married some French nominee of Louis XI's as his cousin Warwick wanted – and back in the late 1440s when England still held some French lands in Normandy and Maine his father Duke Richard of York had been involved in an abortive move to marry the infant Edward off to an equally young daughter of King Charles VII of France, Madelaine, as part of an Anglo-French peace treaty. In October 1461 Warwick's ally Lord Wenlock had been sent on a diplomatic mission to the new regime's Burgundian ally, Duke Philip (more reliable than Henry VI's wife's uncle and backer Charles VII of France) to seek the hand of Philip's son and heir Charles' sister-in-law

Mademoiselle de Bourbon. Philip proved unwilling, but the match was considered again in early 1464 according to rumour and was more diplomatically useful to England than the distant Castile marriage. But Edward now chose to throw away the valuable card in his hand in marriage to a foreign princess and marry a minor English Lancastrian peer's half-Luxembourgois widow. Why?

Edward's choice did not have any political value in England either, as the daughter of a major peer would have done. She was Elizabeth, Lady Grey (née Woodville), widow of a minor Lancastrian noble (Sir John Grey, son of the Midlands peer Lord Grey of Groby) who had been killed fighting Edward at the bloody battle of Towton in Yorkshire in a blizzard in spring 1461. She had two sons, so at least she was known to be fertile. Around five years his senior, she was the daughter of Jacquetta of St Pol, Luxembourg-born widow of Henry VI's uncle the Duke of Bedford (died 1435), by her husband's ex-steward Sir Richard Woodville, Lord Rivers. Sir Richard was from the widespread 'middle-ranking' English rural gentry on whom the king's local administraton in the counties relied, and was the son of a younger son (though his uncle died without sons so his prospects improved as he grew older and he inherited the latter's Grafton estate); he had made his way as a loyal vassal and household administrator of the Duke of Bedford as the latter served as Henry VI's regent in and governor of the English dominions in France in 1422–35. By her Luxembourg maternal kin, Elizabeth was descended from the minor ducal houses of the Low Countries and distantly from Charlemagne; her parents' marriage probably owed most to Bedford's links as regent in France to the branch of the French Valois dynasty that ruled Burgundy and its Low Countries co-dependencies (eg Luxembourg) and who had 'defected' from France to England as of 1420. The Bedford regency thus relied on Duke Philip of Burgundy, who had recognised Henry V and his son (Henry VI) rather than the French King's bastard son (Charles VII) as the rightful heirs to France in the Treaty of Troyes in 1420, and the Luxembourg dynasty was thus an important prop to Bedford's regime – bringing Bedford's aide Sir Richard Woodville into contact with them. Elizabeth was probably born back in England after Sir Richard and his bride returned there, in 1437.[3]

King Edward's choice of her as a bride had no political advantages, a rarity for a royal marriage as even the marriages of a king's brothers and cousins within the English aristocracy almost always involved a substantial inheritance of estates and/or a title. Indeed the ceremony removed him from the usual continental royal marriage-market, in which a major foreign marital ally was vital to a new ruler who had deposed his predecessor (still at large at the time) and had a dubious title to the throne. Henry VI might be simple-minded and had spectacularly mismanaged his political role until mental illness made him a cipher in the 1450s, but his energetic and formidable wife Margaret of Anjou and their son were in exile in Scotland – later in France – and the Scots had aided the Lancastrians in keeping control of isolated border castles in Northumberland. The ex-king's half-brother Jasper Tudor was still holding out in Wales where rebel-held Harlech Castle was practically impregnable, and as Edward was secretly courting Elizabeth his main lieutenant in the North, Henry Beaufort, Earl of Somerset, had turned rebel and joined his family's traditional Lancastrian allies. Edward's marriage took place as the campaign unfolded to defeat the new Lancastrian revolt, with victory at Hexham coming a few weeks later.

Edward's subsequent shock announcement of his marriage confounded the diplomatic efforts of his powerful cousin and senior adviser Richard Neville, Earl of Warwick (born 1428), aka 'The Kingmaker'. He was Edward's principal diplomat and in contemporary terms had the noble (semi-royal) blood and 'showiness' as a courtly figure with large resources necessary to impress international rulers and statesman. The shaky new regime needed to prove its stability and right to rule to sceptical overseas observers who might well prefer the legitimate but deposed King Henry VI, and Warwick was in 1464 currently negotiating for a foreign queen and hoping for an alliance with Louis XI of France (who had previously been sending military aid to his cousin Queen Margaret, Henry VI's wife). The son of Richard Neville, Earl of Salisbury (killed by Margaret's men along with Edward's father the Duke of York and brother the Earl of Rutland in December 1460) and the brother of Edward's mother Cecily Neville, the so-called 'Kingmaker' was fourteen years older than Edward and in a sense his politico-military mentor, having been at his side during the Yorkist campaign for the throne in 1459–60. The most powerful landed magnate in the realm with a concentration of estates in the north and in South Wales, Warwick – who held his title and much of his land by marriage to the heiress of the Beauchamp Earl of Warwick – was invaluable to a king crowned at nineteen though his military skills have been exaggerated (he lost the battle of Northampton and possession of Henry VI in 1460). He was also one of the two people who had been most noticeable for killing captured lords in cold blood in or after battles recently and so exacerbating the element of blood feud that embittered the civil wars, the other being Edward's father Richard of York. (To be fair, they may merely have had more opportunity of winning more battles; they and Edward had a narrow escape from Queen Margaret at Ludlow in 1459.) Having just faced revolt by one principal ally set up in the North to replace the pro-Lancastrian Percys, the young Duke Henry of Somerset, Edward would have been wiser not to antagonise Warwick too. Luckily, Warwick was very unlikely to join up with ex-Queen Margaret who had supported the killing of his father as well as of Edward's father and brother, carried out in and after the battle of Wakefield in December 1460. Margaret had put Salisbury's and York's heads up on Micklegate at York, and this made their reconciliation almost impossible – though not, as events turned out, totally so.

Edward is agreed by the early sources to have been a notorious womaniser, Sir Thomas More claiming that he was in his youth 'greatly given to fleshly wantonness'.[4] As early as the time of his marriage, 1464, it was reported that people were surprised that someone so sexually adventurous was unmarried and it was believed that he was unchaste. The French chronicler Commignes claimed that his loss of his throne in 1470 was due to his love of luxury.[5] Whether the modern sense of the word was meant or not, the concept encompassed over-indulgence and laziness – and this arguably accounted for his not acting against the threat of Warwick earlier. Taken by surprise by Warwick as the latter revolted in 1469, he was captured by the earl's men after his own army was defeated but Warwick apparently changed his mind about deposing him and installing his younger brother Duke George of Clarence (just married to Warwick's elder daughter Isabel despite Edward's ban on this) and eventually had to release him. Their 'reconciliation' did not last and Warwick was soon exiled and fled to France where Louis XI used him as a pawn to attack and destabilise England, but then Edward was again caught off-guard by Warwick landing – or at least by the desertion of Warwick's brother John Neville, Marquis of Montague to the invaders – in 1470. He was also known to favour mistresses from the mercantile class as well as the aristocracy, though arguably from More's comments (made fifty or so years later so within living memory of his exploits) this improved his popularity in London as a man of the people.[6]

His most well-known mistress, 'Jane', actually Elizabeth Shore, was the wife of a City of London merchant and was the only woman he was connected with from a non-aristocratic background. She was to take part in the plot to stop Richard of Gloucester seizing the throne in June 1483 – for which he had her paraded through the streets as a harlot. After that 'lesson' Richard did not stop her marrying respectably, to the king's solicitor Thomas Lynom. She may have been alive when More wrote his book, which refers to her comely charms in glowing terms[7] – so was she a source for him? In 1483 the Italian visitor Dominic Mancini heard that Edward 'was licentious in the extreme... He pursued with no discrimination the married and the unmarried, the noble and the lowly.'[8] *The Croyland Chronicle 'Continuation'* refers to his subjects' surprise that he could conduct business adequately as well as his 'debauchery, extravagance and sensual enjoyments'.[9] Even though much of this is said with reference to his reputation by 1483, in 1462–3 Edward had already had at least one mistress, Elizabeth Lucy née Wayte[10] – a young widow like Elizabeth Woodville. The length of his relationship with her is uncertain, but the facts that their son Arthur was a vigorous and sport-loving companion to the young Henry VIII (born 1491) after 1509 and was made Viscount Lisle in 1523 (via his marriage to the Lisle title's heiress, a relative of Elizabeth Woodville's first husband) and Arthur was still active as governor of Calais in 1540 suggest that he is more likely to have been born in the 1470s than the early 1460s. Sir Thomas More was confused over who Edward had married before he met Elizabeth Woodville, and says that it was Elizabeth Lucy and that the 22 June 1483 official revelation by Friar Shaa at St Pauls Cross, London of Edward IV's alleged pre-contract to a woman named Elizabeth Lucy before he married Elizabeth Woodville. Most of Edward's mistresses, an indeterminate number, were reasonably well-born; as well as Arthur he had one daughter who married into the Lumley family and another, Grace, who was ranked as a household attendant of Elizabeth Woodville when she appeared at the latter's funeral in 1492. The unadvantageous and initially secret Woodville marriage was clearly a love-match, whatever the truth of the unprovable stories of its illegal nature written about it later. Traditionally

Elizabeth lay in wait for the king with her children while he was hunting in Whittlewood Forest, under a tree which was later pointed out, in order to beg his support in her poverty after her first husband's death in battle against him at Towton at Easter 1461.[11] Edward had confiscated her late husband's estates as he was a Lancastrian; and coincidentally or not he had done similarly to some of Eleanor Butler/Talbot's late Lancastrian husband's estates. Did both women initially seek him out on a business matter, and Edward then seduced them?

In fact, the Woodvilles were already rising – though not prominent – courtiers by 1464. The marriage was not that socially inferior, given Jacquetta's high birth and dynastic descent from Charlemagne, and was probably played up as such by the hostile Warwick who had berated Elizabeth's father in person at Calais in 1460 for his presumption in marrying 'above' him – and who then murdered Elizabeth's father, by now Lord Rivers and Treasurer of England, and younger brother Sir John Woodville at the earliest opportunity in 1469. Edward had arguably made matters worse for the proud and 'touchy' Warwick by bending the acceptable practice of arranged marriages conducted for financial and political advantage by marrying the 'twenty-something' John off in January 1465 to Warwick's aunt, the very wealthy Dowager Countess of Norfolk (Katherine Neville), who was over sixty and had survived three husbands already – despite the resultant scandal at the age-difference[12] Warwick's violent reaction was extreme even for this era, and possibly if the new Queen's family had been an established noble dynasty (or closely related to one) he would have been more cautious out of self-preservation. He was similarly angry about another 'arriviste' at Edward's court who seemed to threaten his leading role, ie the rising South Wales Yorkist 'strongman' Sir William Herbert who was 'middling gentry' like Elizabeth and was based at Raglan Castle near his own Glamorgan lands and his Brecon wardship. Having been granted a mass of South Wales offices and lands by Edward plus a peerage as Earl of Pembroke, Herbert (who was also the guardian of the young Lancastrian noble Henry Tudor) was clearly Edward's choice to run the region in the early-mid 1460s – until Warwick seized and executed him during the 1469 rebellion.

Herbert, executed at the same time as Elizabeth's kin in the aftermath of Warwick's defeat of the king's army at Edgecot, was another example of Warwick getting rid of potential rivals by extreme violence – a tactic which he had been employing as early as the 1460 Yorkist revolt against Henry VI when the Duke of Buckingham was his target. Thus the Woodvilles were not a unique example of Warwick's malice. The political hostility which the Woodville alliance aroused to insiders like Warwick, particularly concerning the quick rise to prominence via marriages and grants of land and office to Elizabeth's siblings, was more important than her social rank. It presumably caused most of the subsequent 'Woodville myth' of their insatiable greed and pretensions. The hostile remarks about the Sir John Woodville/Duchess Katherine of Norfolk marriage show that antipathy to the arrangements – or at least their intensity – did not only follow the family's purge by Warwick in 1469 or Richard III's barrage of propaganda about them in 1483, in which case it could be written off as political spin by their enemies, not honest contemporary opinion. The fact that she had four brothers in search of patronage and numerous sisters in search of rich husbands added to the problem, given that most English queens had been foreign princesses with no relatives in England to assist. However the last foreign-born Queen with a large number of ambitious male relatives at Court to promote, Henry III's wife Eleanor of Provence in the mid-thirteenth-century, had aroused equal indignation at her alleged acquisitiveness and the family had been abused as foreigners.

The principal royally-connected dynasty amassing titles and bishoprics for their males and noble husbands for their females in mid-fifteenth-century England was the Nevilles, so the Woodvilles were likely to be regarded by them as competition and a similar reaction could have been expected if any family not allied to them married into the King's immediate kin and acquired rank and 'loot' from this. Warwick and his father the Earl of Salisbury – the latter being a younger son of the Earl of Westmorland by his second marriage, who owed his Salisbury lands and title to his own wife – had helped to secure well-connected husbands for their female relatives as (for Salisbury's sisters) the Dukes of York, Northumberland, and Norfolk; and (for Salisbury's daughters) Lords Hastings, Stanley, Maltravers (Earl of Arundel), Oxford, and Tiptoft. Warwick's clerical uncle Robert (d. 1457) was Bishop of Durham; his clerical brother George was Archbishop of York. The large and ambitious Woodville family thus presented the Nevilles with unwelcome competition – which a smaller family would not have done, particularly if they had been an established noble dynasty already secure in their long-held honours and with powerful kin able to protect them from Warwick's wrath. Had the Woodvilles' rise to prominence and threat to his control of patronage not infuriated Warwick, the marriage may well have faded from controversy. But did Warwick's efforts to destroy the Woodvilles in 1469 lead to the invention of the claim that the ceremony was illegal? Can the story be traced to Warwick's malice and thus an unreliable political campaign, or to solid evidence?

The king's movements at the time of the marriage are known well enough to plausibly reconstruct the sequence of events. He probably took advantage of his staying at the nearby royal manor of Stony Stratford to slip away to Elizabeth's nearby estate at Grafton, traditionally on the morning of May Day 1464 while on his way North for the campaign against Somerset (but possibly on the way south a few weeks later). The only witness of note appears to have been her mother (her father may not have known of the romance), with no courtiers present or even aware of it, and the 1484 *Titulus Regius* Act which declared the marriage illegal maintained that it had not even been carried out in a church, contrary to law. That may have been a Ricardian smear, but commemorative 'White Rose of York' tiles and the Woodville heraldic arms were discovered at the Hermitage Chapel (not at the parish church) in Grafton in 1965 so this may have been the site of the wedding. Edward then consummated the relationship before returning to his entourage claiming that he had been hunting, and paid some furtive night-time visits to Elizabeth's manor-house before leaving the district. Jacquetta rather than her husband was responsible for arrangements on these occasions. When the Woodvilles were in disgrace and Warwick had seized power in 1469 and 1470–1 allegations were made that Jacquetta had resorted to witchcraft to ensnare the king. Thomas Blake of Blisworth in Northamptonshire, a Neville ally, submitted a claim that Jacquetta had used witchcraft to ensnare the king into the marriage and cited John Dauger, parish clerk of nearby Stoke Bruerne, to back up as witness his claim that Jacquetta had made wax models of her daughter and the King to use in an occult ceremony, but luckily (or due to Warwick changing his mind or being distracted by other priorities?) the case did not come to court quickly. By the time that Dauger was called to give evidence Edward IV was back in full power, and this key witness accordingly denied the story;

the case was dropped.[13] The story was then revived in the '*Titulus Reguis*' Act declaring the marriage invalid and its resultant children (including Edward V) bastards in 1483/4, which cited that the Woodville marriage had been due to witchcraft by Elizabeth and Jacquetta as known by 'common report' and as allegedly would be proved by witnesses when the time was right.[14] This threat to prove it was not carried out – possibly as there were really no reliable witnesses and it was bluff (or a complete fabrication) by Richard III to excuse his usurpation of Edward V's throne, as his detractors claim.

The claim in *Titulus Regius* can also be linked to Polydore Vergil's account of the crucial 13 June 1483 Council meeting in the Tower of London where Richard suddenly had Hastings seized and executed and his 'fellow-plotters' arrested, as just before the arrests Richard allegedly claimed that he could not sleep or eat properly due to the queen employing black magic against him and showed his famous 'withered arm' (which recent investigation of his skeleton shows was perfectly normal) which he alleged was also her fault.[15] The scene on 13 June 1483 was also recorded by Sir Thomas More in his 'Life of Richard III' with a comment that most of the Council knew the Queen was too cautious to indulge in witchcraft,[16] and presumably Bishop Morton was his past employee More's source. Given his physical problems and his repeated instances of paranoia about his enemies, it is possible that Richard genuinely believed the queen to be capable of such activities (and he had also been brought up in her enemy Warwick's household in the mid-1460s, so he could have heard gossip there). All this is evidence that the story about Jacquetta and/or her daughter was current in 1469 and 1483, but not that it was more than a calculated smear by their enemies – the secret nature of the marriage was an added reason for prurient speculation about what had really happened. In political terms, a charge of witchcraft (however unlikely or if it was invented) was one legal way to nullify the marriage and free the king to make a more suitable alliance, and was presumably the idea of Elizabeth's enemy, Warwick. The second wife of Henry VI's uncle, Duke Humphrey of Gloucester, Eleanor Cobham – also of 'low' birth – had fallen victim to a similar politically-inspired charge of witchcraft in the 1440s. This had possibly also been due to an attempt to break up her marriage and prevent her having any children who might become the childless Henry VI's heirs and she was divorced and deported to life imprisonment on the Isle of Man, but her 'crimes' involved planning to using black magic against the king's life which was a more usual charge.[17] Similar charges, vaguer as to witnesses and accomplices, had been made by cash-strapped Henry V against his stepmother Joan of Navarre in 1421 and her property had been seized; clearly politics as much as superstition were behind most such charges in the fifteenth century – with the seriousness of the charge guaranteed to scandalise the public and hopefully shut down debate. It is also arguable if a marriage was legal in the mid-fifteenth century if it was carried out in private rather than in front of a church congregation, even if it was physically in a church. Certainly all previous post-Conquest royal marriages had been in public – and had been approved by their Councils too. So would challenging the match on these grounds have been safer for Warwick in 1469 and Richard in 1483?

The way in which the marriage was kept secret may be due to its haste – Edward was supposed in one romancer's interpretation to have been desperate for Elizabeth and Lady Grey to have insisted on a legal ceremony before she would have sex with him. The story mentioned by Mancini about his putting a dagger to her throat in order to force her to have sex with him but being resisted, circulating on the continent by 1468, is unprovable. Another early – and Italian – version has been found which has Elizabeth producing the dagger; in any event, the secrecy and the disparate social status (and ages) of the participants encouraged melodramatic speculation.[18] According to the 'official' version of the story of the supposed pre-contract (a phrase which would technically cover a formal marriage ceremony, not just a betrothal, according to legal expert H A Kelly)[19] to Eleanor Butler which was released in June 1483, this was not the first time that Edward had resorted to going through some sort of secret ceremony as the prelude to a seduction to satisfy his partner's scruples.[20] The expected shock and opposition of the Council to such a misalliance would indicate why Edward did not take any senior advisers into his confidence or invite them to attend to prove that the ceremony had taken place. As mentioned, Warwick had berated Elizabeth's captured father Lord Rivers – in Edward's presence – about his insolence and presumption in marrying a duke's widow at Calais in 1460. He may have been seen by Edward and/or Elizabeth as ruthless enough to physically prevent the ceremony if he found out. The only councillor who had any known – and sympathetic – connection to Elizabeth was Lord Hastings, Edward's Chamberlain and close confidante, who as the new king's lieutenant of the eastern Midlands (his own home region) was the man to whom she appealed for help in 1463 regarding a family inheritance dispute with her late first husband's mother, Lady Ferrers of Groby.

Following a dispute over Lady Ferrers trying to regain lands assigned to her late son, to pass on to his and Elizabeth's elder son, Lady Ferrers had attempted to entail some of her own estates to remain with her much younger second husband for his lifetime, not to pass on to her late son's and Elizabeth's sons as originally planned. Elizabeth sought Hasting's help to have this blocked in court, and in return arranged (or was pressured by him to arrange?) a marriage between her elder son and Hastings' unborn daughter – or if Hastings had no daughter and the arrangement had to be cancelled to pay him 250 marks.[21] The future queen and the chamberlain thus knew each other and dealt on normal inter-elite family business matters; but that is not to say that Hastings knew about her subsequent secret affair with Edward. Indeed, the steepness of Hastings' demands for financial compensation if their children's marriage had to be called off might imply that Elizabeth would resent this as extortionate.

But it is surprising that the announcement of the marriage was delayed so long, as it could not be hidden indefinitely – unless the delay was due to Edward having second thoughts. Did he consider denying it if the political fallout from admitting it was too great and use the lack of witnesses as an argument that he could do that, and Elizabeth forced him to admit it by threatening to do so herself? At best, his delay in announcing it shows his concern over the potential problems involved; at worst he had originally planned to deny it – as he had never admitted any legal link to Eleanor Butler – but Elizabeth was more resolute over her 'rights'. The possibility thus arises that the successful secrecy of any arrangement, be it verbal pre-contract or a formal legal ceremony, with Eleanor Butler (see below) and Eleanor's lack of objection to his behaviour gave him the idea of doing the same again – but Elizabeth was more worldly and more determined. Once the Somerset revolt was over, Edward was in no danger of angry councillors linking up with the rebels. Was this delay entirely due to Edward's fecklessness or fear of Warwick – or did he have second thoughts about the marriage afterwards? For that matter, who insisted on there being so few witnesses – Edward (as a potential double-crosser or out of fear of Warwick?) or Elizabeth? Logically, even if Elizabeth's demands for some sort of ceremony before she would yield to his advances meant a hurried ceremony he could have trusted a few close court companions to attend. Could he have trusted Hastings to be 'in the know' and help – or had Elizabeth warned him off doing that?

The aftermath and Warwick's revenge

The long delay in announcing the ceremony may not be entirely due to the king's pressure of business in the north Midlands, where he remained into July while Warwick's brother Lord Montagu put down the Lancastrian revolt and retook the Northumbrian castles. In the meantime, the Anglo-French peace-conference at St Omer which Warwick was supposed to attend in June was delayed while the earl was dealing with Lancastrian outbreaks in northern England, though Warwick's ally Lord Wenlock turned up for the preliminary talks with Louis and his ministers; the full conference itself (which was to discuss Edward's marriage to Louis' sister-in-law Bona of Savoy) was postponed until October. It is unknown if Edward was behind the delay, and doing this to give himself time to announce to the Council that the proposed marital cornerstone of the Anglo-French peace was now impossible – or to consider denying that he had married in order to save the plan? Meanwhile, whether or not his undoubted embarrassment ever led to thoughts of denying the marriage, he failed to reveal it for months. The marriage was only revealed at a Council meeting at Reading in September 1464, when Warwick was still promoting his plan to marry Edward to Louis XI's sister-in-law Bona of Savoy to secure a French alliance and end the threat of Louis sending troops and ships to aid rebels in Northumberland as he had done in 1461–3. The area was now quiet, but could easily break out into rebellion again as the Lancastrian hard-liners (led by King Henry and Queen Margaret) had been given refuge in Scotland by the regency for young King James III – whose late grandmother had been sister to the Duke of Somerset, killed by Edward's father in 1455. Margaret was Louis XI's cousin and was now in exile in France with her son; Henry was on the run in northern England but was too simple-minded to be much of a threat on his own. Edward admitted that he could not agree to marry Bona as he was already married. The Council met on either 14 or 28 September, and Polydore Vergil described the councillors' reaction as dismay that Edward had let himself be ruled by his passions, not reason.[22] Elizabeth's formal presentation to his court took place on the 29th, and on 3 October Wenlock wrote to one of Louis' ministers to announce the marriage.[23] Whatever Warwick or others had feared, Louis was too hard-headed to let the marriage cause him to break off talks – his need of English help against his foe Duke Philip of Burgundy was too great, as Edward may have reckoned. At this point there was no attempt by angry councillors to get the church to invalidate the marriage and thus enable the French match to proceed, although the Burgundian chronicle of Jean de Wavrin indicates that there was discontent among the Council on account of its secrecy and the disparity in social status between the two parties.[24] Recent analysts, principally J. R. Lander in an article in *Bulletin of the Institute of Historical Research* in 1963, have argued that most of the evidence for hostility in 1464 is late and is 'back-dated' from the events of 1483 when the marriage was legally invalidated.[25]

This time its critic was Edward's younger brother Richard, Duke of Gloucester, who had just taken over the regency for his son Edward V from the Woodvilles – and was in the process of taking over the throne as well. If the marriage was illegal, Edward V was a bastard and could legally be deposed and his next brother Richard, Duke of York, was disqualified from the throne too. The intervening heir between the two Richards, the son of the late Duke of Clarence (ie Edward, as of 1475 the new Earl of Warwick), was only eight and could be disqualified too as the son of a man attainted for treason. Back in 1464 the king's secret marriage to a commoner while public plans were underway for a foreign marital alliance must have been controversial, and Warwick 'the Kingmaker' – in charge of those negotiations – had every reason to be the principal objector. Warwick had showed hostility to the bride's father even in 1460 so his haste to execute him and her brother in 1469 cannot be put down to development of hostility after 1464 due to the Woodvilles' acquisitiveness.

Given that the attempt to invalidate the marriage in 1483 was to make a supposed pre-contract by Edward to another party the principal evidence, it is surprising that even the powerful and unscrupulous Warwick could not find this sort of evidence in 1464–5. The other party cited in 1483 – Elizabeth Lucy or Eleanor Butler? and the priest who had carried out the ceremony – possibly the man said to have made the revelation, Robert Stillington who in 1464 as in charge of the king's private household administration as Keeper of the Great Seal – did not reveal anything that Warwick could use in 1469, and anyway he was the king's client not Warwick's. Possibly he kept his head down and the earl was not aware that he was a key witness. Eleanor was Warwick's own niece though not apparently having much dealings with him (the Nevilles were a large family), and there had been rumours in the early 1460s about Edward having an affair with a niece of Warwick's which probably refer to this relationship.[26] She was the daughter of the great Lancastrian military commander John Talbot, Earl of Shrewsbury, companion-in-arms of Henry V and the last English commander in France in the early 1450s. He was killed at the battle of Castillon in 1453, the final military disaster preceding the fall of Bordeaux, and was in his late sixties; an article in the *Ricardian* in 1997 suggested that Eleanor was his daughter by his second marriage (1424) to Margaret Beauchamp. She was slightly older than Edward – as was Elizabeth Woodville – and was born around 1436. She married Sir Thomas Butler, eldest son of Ralph, Lord Sudeley, and was a widow by 1462 so available for Edward to promise with marriage. Her husband probably died in 1460, so he may have sustained injuries fighting for Henry VI in the anti-Yorkist campaign of 1459; Elizabeth Woodville's first husband was to be killed in the same cause at Towton in March 1461. Like Elizabeth, she may have sought out Edward to have confiscated estates returned; her husband had been granted a manor by his father without royal permission in 1460 so this was confiscated by Edward on his accession. Her first cousin Joan Barre was married to the Leicestershire lawyer Sir William Catesby, a client of Edward's friend Lord Hastings, so she may have approached Edward through Hastings (as Elizabeth did?).

A suggestion has been made by Peter Hancock of friendly connections between the young Butlers, as resident in the later 1450s at their estate of Burton Dassett in Warwickshire, and Eleanor's cousin Joan's husband Sir William Catesby (and Joan's stepson William, Richard III's later minister?). This would be implied by similar wall-paintings on the walls of the churches in Burton Dassett and the Catesbys' home parish; could they have commissioned the same artist? This is possible, but too much may be read into this; the similar style may be coincidental.[27] Even more tentative is the suggestion by Graham Hancock that the existence of a former Templar preceptory (suppressed 1308 with the Order) at Burton Dassett and Eleanor's religious interests might indicate that she was sympathetic to an alleged secret cult of Templar devotion and/or protecting rumoured Templar treasure. Templar devotion is less likely in that Eleanor, interested in the religious life, had no desire to be Queen. On firmer ground, it might be possible to see Edward's relationships in the early 1460s following a pattern, with him exploiting the two slightly older and financially needy ex-Lancastrian widows for his own pleasure but Elizabeth being less easy to keep quiet than the spiritually-minded Eleanor.

Eleanor lived in semi-religious retirement in Norfolk in the mid-1460s, according to her recent biographer John Ashdown-Hill, probably at her sister Elizabeth (Talbot) Mowbray's marital home at East Hall, Kenninghall. The latter was married to the heir of the Duke of Norfolk, who succeeded to the title in 1461, and in 1619 Richard III's biographer Sir George Buck was to claim that Elizabeth had been privy to Edward and Eleanor's marriage. She also endowed a fellowship at Corpus Christi College, Cambridge, whose Master (Dr. Cosin) was recorded in a college history as commending her piety.[28] It may or may not be significant that a cousin and neighbour of the Mowbray Dukes of Norfolk (who died out in the direct male line in 1476) was John Howard, later to be a confidante of Richard III who awarded him the Dukedom in 1483. Could he have heard rumours of Eleanor's relationship and passed them on to Richard? Ironically, the infant heiress Anne Mowbray and the Dukedom had been passed to Richard, the barely older Duke of York – one of the Princes in the Tower – by Edward IV in 1478. Anne died in 1481 but Edward illegally kept the Dukedom and its lands for his son, thus probably alienating the rival claimant John Howard who had as much reason as Richard or Buckingham to turn on the Woodvilles.

Eleanor died in or near Norwich on 30 June 1468. She was buried at the church of the Carmelite convent of the Minories in Norwich, of which she had been a patroness for some years. Her seal bore a Carmelite motif, suggesting personal identification with the Order – a strict reformist organization of nuns originating in the Holy Land (on Mount Carmel) during the crusades, well-known for its austere anchoresses. Her choice of protégés would suggest enthusiasm for their fervour, in backing an Order that took their vows very seriously rather than a more lax conventional one. She appears to have resided in the convent in the mid-1460s, possibly having taken postulant's vows. Their church was abandoned and partly demolished at the Reformation, so no tomb or marker-slab is extant for current historians to check. It was however recorded in a work on monuments in 1631.[29] Family genealogies were the only clue to her existence. Given Eleanor's enthusiasm for the religious life in her final years (shown by her life as a residential associate of the convent), she may well have kept quiet about the ceremony out of embarrassment. Her monastic sponsorship was a fairly conventional sign of upper-class piety for the fifteenth century, and the church constantly sought generous noble patrons – Richard himself and his wife Anne Neville were to be members of a confraternity of the Holy Trinity in York and to found a religious college of canons at their castle of Middleham. So was endowing a college fellowship. But taking up residence, as Eleanor did, was an unusual step and would indicate a hankering after the religious life. Possibly she was the person referred to in Edward IV's reported comment that he had the 'holiest harlot' in England as a mistress, as well as the 'jolliest' (Mistress Shore?) and the 'most cunning'.

Stillington, who either carried out the betrothal or knew the priest who had done so, was keeper of the Privy Seal in 1464, Stillington was the person who dealt with the king's most confidential legal business and so was a natural choice to be involved in the marriage. He was distantly related to the Talbot family via Eleanor's aunt Lady Lisle, so he may also have been chosen as a useful go-between or already been the devout Eleanor's spiritual adviser or 'confessor'. Both were alive in 1464–8, but did not challenge Edward's marriage. A pre-contract ceremony, a formal act of betrothal in a church in front of a priest, counted as a legal marriage as far as medieval canon law was concerned. There had been a previous royal imbroglio over the legality of Richard II's mother Joan of Kent contracting such a ceremony – in similar secrecy – with Sir Thomas Holland as a teenager living in Queen Philippa's household. She had subsequently married William Montague, Earl of Salisbury, in 1347 during Holland's absence at the siege of Calais, and on his return he had launched a legal case to get her back and invalidate her marriage to Salisbury. The latter had more influence as a senior noble and close friend of the king, but the papal legal machinery had found in Holland's favour in

1349 and Joan had returned to him; their subsequent children, Richard II's half-siblings, were all regarded as legitimate. The legal precedents were thus in Eleanor's favour, had she launched a legal challenge to Edward's marriage in 1464 – provided that Stillington would give evidence in her favour. But Edward clearly showed by marrying Elizabeth that he would deny that the ceremony with Eleanor had occurred, so revealing it could lay her open to the charge of fornication. The marriage does not seem to have been known by her own family, the Talbots (Earls of Shrewsbury), or if it was they did not see fit to complain to Warwick about Eleanor's treatment when her 'seducer' Edward had been deposed. Her father, the Earl of Shrewsbury, heroic commander against the French, was dead and her late husband Thomas Butler's family were Lancastrians so out of favour at Court. Thomas' father, Ralph Butler, Lord Sudeley, was a former court official of Henry VI. He was to be forced to hand over his lordship and castle to Richard of Gloucester in 1469 and to return his late son's manor of Burton Dassett to the king (and then re-purchase it at an extortionate sum). This was possibly a risky act for Edward to do if he knew Ralph could cause trouble about his treatment of Eleanor, and indicates confidence that Ralph would not stand up to him. Possibly Ralph's failure to retaliate by telling Warwick of Edward's behaviour in 1469–70 indicates that he did not know the secret.

It is probable that Warwick made enquiries in the hope of finding some obstacle, and found nothing. Stillington was logically paid off by Edward IV with the bishopric (Bath and Wells) which he acquired in October 1465; his appointment to the first vacant bishopric after Edward's marriage to Elizabeth may or may not be coincidental. He had received no office during the relationship with Eleanor. He later acquired the Lord Chancellorship in 1467 – replacing Warwick's brother the archbishop of York. This may have earned him Warwick's enmity – and when Warwick seized power in 1469 he was quick to remove Stillington and restore the archbishop, which might make them foes. Nor could Warwick acquire any information when he had the King in his power in 1469, had just executed the queen's father and brother, and would have been pleased to find a legal excuse to force Edward to divorce Elizabeth and marry a princess of his own choice (or to invalidate the marriage so if he deposed Edward the latter's children were neutralised). Edward's next surviving brother George of Clarence would also have benefited from having

Edward's marriage invalidated, which would keep their two daughters from the throne in his favour. But on this occasion Stillington did not seek to ingratiate himself with the all-powerful Earl by showing that the king's marriage was a fraud. The reason may have been personal loyalty to Edward; Stillington was clearly trusted by him as he twice became chancellor, and the earl may have regarded the bishop as an enemy of his family after he replaced the archbishop as chancellor.

The humiliation of having his foreign policy undermined in secret this way probably accelerated the earl's antagonism towards the Woodville family, to which their 'low' birth and their relentless acquisition of lands and advantageous marriages added during the mid-1460s. The new queen, who was crowned in May 1465,[30] was apparently a noted beauty, and her ability to overcome handicaps of age and background to secure the young king is evident though the extent of her political ambition is more uncertain. The circumstances of her marriage would have made certain political figures such as Warwick antagonistic in any case, but the existence of a large number of brothers (who would want titles and lands) and sisters (who could be married off to influential husbands) meant that the Woodville family would be a rival source of political influence to the Nevilles at court. The spectacle of a senior English family able to exploit their influence as the king's in-laws was rare at the medieval court, where the sovereign usually married a foreign princess and her relations did not frequent his court. The previous queen to have a large family seeking influence in England had been Henry III's wife Eleanor of Provence; Henry had also had a brood of acquisitive Poitevin half-brothers. Both had aroused the same sort of antagonism as the Woodvilles were to do. The nearest equivalent had been the Holland children and marital connections of Richard II's mother Joan of Kent in the later fourteenth century, also subject to revenge from jealous rivals at the king's downfall. Richard's nephew the Duke of Surrey, one of his favourites in 1397–9 after the exclusion from power of the great nobles who had humiliated Richard in 1387–8, was accused of over-reaching his social station, forced to hand his title back, and soon executed for a plot. Did this give Warwick a useful precedent for what to do with the 'low-born' Earl Rivers?

The 'low birth' of the Woodvilles was also made a subject for criticism in 1469, though in fact Jacquetta was of the highest continental nobility (the ducal family of Luxembourg) and descended from Charlemagne.

The advantageous marriages of some of the queen's brothers and all of her numerous sisters were not that outrageous given the current intense marriage market among the ultra-competitive nobility, and the bias of some marriage contracts' terms in favour of the Woodville participants was no more extortionate than could be expected from hard bargainers in a strong position. The way that Anthony Woodville, Elizabeth's next brother, acquired the heiress and title of the Scales lordship was perfectly usual for an upwardly-mobile courtier. However, the very numbers of Woodville brothers and sisters meant that the number of royal in-laws to be satisfied was bound to have an impact and arouse jealousy. The marriage of Elizabeth's younger brother Sir John to the ageing Dowager Duchess of Norfolk, Warwick's aunt (about forty years his senior) was both unusual and blatantly opportunistic. The age-difference between the two mattered more if the woman was the elder partner than if the man was, and Henry VIII's niece Frances Brandon was to be attacked in the 1550s for marrying the much younger (and socially inferior) Adrian Stokes.

The Woodville marriages were not concentrated in the 1460s, not least as Elizabeth's younger siblings were probably not yet of age. (Jacquetta and Woodville had probably married in 1436.) Some of the marriages did not take place until the 1470s, after Warwick's removal, though four sisters had acquired rich aristocratic husbands (the Stafford/Buckingham, Bourchier/Essex, Grey/Kent, and Herbert heirs) in 1466-7.[31] Only two of the brothers – Anthony, the eldest, already married to the heiress to the Scales peerage by 1465, and John – were old enough to feature as political players by 1469. John's marriage to his elderly Mowbray bride was scandalous, even for the blatant marital alliances forged at the time, and in general terms. According to Mancini, the young Duke Henry (Stafford) of Buckingham, a descendant in the female line of Edward III's youngest son Duke Thomas of Gloucester and himself later to play for high stakes as Richard III's co-conspirator in the 1483 coup (and end up betraying him too and being executed), was furious at having to marry the new queen's sister Catherine Woodville as she was so far his social inferior.[32] Possibly Warwick was annoyed at this too, as his ex-ward Buckingham (born 1455?) could have been a good catch for his own elder daughter Isabel (born 1451) and that would add to his family affinity by linking him closer to the semi-royal Staffords and Bourchiers, close kin of the current Archbishop of Canterbury. Edward IV, who had to agree even if his queen and her parents pressed for good catches for her siblings, must bear a lot of the responsibility. Other legal arrangements of his not involving the Woodvilles were even more blatant. He declared Warwick's widow legally dead in 1473 so her estates would go to her sons-in-law, his brothers, and he married off his own baby son Richard to the ultimate Mowbray heiress and when she died he illegally kept her lands and titles. Edward was clearly as much to blame for dubiously legal or blatant marital arrangements as his wife, given that arrangements that did not involve Woodvilles were just as provocative.

The political influence of the queen's siblings was small, apart from that of Anthony as a patron of the arts (including Sir Thomas Malory), leading jouster, and in the 1470s guardian of his nephew Prince Edward of Wales. Elizabeth's father Lord Rivers was made an Earl and acquired the Treasurership (March 1466) and later the Constableship of England, and Anthony acquired the lordship of the Isle of Wight and the castles of Carisbrooke and Portchester. All the other brothers were too young to be promoted in the 1460s, but even when they were older only seem to have been minor courtiers of no political weight apart from Lionel, made Dean of Exeter in 1478 and Bishop of Salisbury in 1482.[33] The most that can be said is that the queen and her family were genuinely acquisitive as well as being perceived as such, and had built up a poor reputation for exploiting their position even in the four years to 1469. The pointed joke by the royal jester around this time that he had difficulty getting to court because the 'rivers' were so high in the realm – Elizabeth's father Richard Woodville was Earl Rivers – may have been an isolated one, but surely indicates a general mood in which this reference was welcome.

The *Great Chronicle of London* presents clear evidence of the Woodvilles trying to influence the treason-trial of their enemy, former Lord Mayor Thomas Cook of London, in 1468 – he had been in dispute over the price of some furnishings with Elizabeth's mother Jacquetta. The family looted his house while he was in gaol, seem to have pressurised the jury and when he was only found guilty of a lesser offence had the judge dismissed, and ensured that Cook received a crippling fine out of proportion to his offence. (The author, Robert Fabyan, was Cook's apprentice so he knew the facts even if he no doubt bore a grudge against the queen).[34] There was also a long-running story that Elizabeth arranged the dismissal of Thomas Fitzgerald, Earl of Desmond, as Deputy Lord Lieutenant (and effective full governor for his titular senior, Clarence) of Ireland in 1467 in revenge for his advising Edward to annul their marriage in 1464 and then arranged for the new deputy, the ruthless Earl of Worcester (John Tiptoft), to execute him at the Drogheda Parliament in February 1468. This was cited as part of the myth of Woodville greed and vengefulness for centuries and apparently Richard III said in 1483 when allowing Desmond's son legal backing to investigate his father's unjust death that the Woodvilles had been involved in that (and in Clarence's death). But the story first emerged in a paper written by Desmond's grandson in the reign of Henry VIII, and Charles Ross does not believe that the story stands up; Desmond had made a mess of a recent (1466) government campaign in County Offaly and was expendable and the harsh and execution-prone Worcester had enough reason by his usual standards to execute Desmond without being persuaded to do it by the queen.[35]

The antagonism supposedly aroused by the Woodvilles was no doubt exaggerated by their triumphant foes at the time of their political eclipses – by Warwick in 1469 and 1470–1 and by Richard of Gloucester in 1483–5. Warwick was probably behind the allegations that Jacquetta had used witchcraft to bring about the marriage, as well as killing Elizabeth's father and one brother, and after the coups of May-June 1483 Richard of Gloucester's official propaganda waxed lyrical about the immorality and corruption of the family and how they had lured Edward IV into riotous living that caused his death.[36] The extent of resentment among the higher nobility may not have been that extensive outside the Neville-Gloucester affinity, though there was a feud between Elizabeth's eldest son the Marquis of Dorset and Edward IV's chamberlain Lord Hastings by 1483. Back in 1464, at the time of the marriage Elizabeth and Hastings had been political allies with the latter as the more powerful – as shown by the arrangement that her elder son by the late Lord Grey should marry his daughter. Indeed, if the traditional story of the first meeting of Edward and Elizabeth is correct, Elizabeth sought out the king in Charnwood Forest in spring 1464 to appeal for his aid in having the confiscated inheritance of her late Lancastrian husband restored. This would indicate that she could not rely on support from powerful allies at Court, like Hastings, to have justice done and at this date her brother Anthony lacked influence there.

There is no evidence of rejoicing in London at the news that Richard had arrested Anthony Woodville and his nephew and halted the alleged Woodville plot to take over the regency in May 1483; rather there was fear and panic. It is only surmise that the queen caused Edward IV to put Clarence to death in 1478, presumably so he could not spread stories about her dubious marital status – though the story was known to Mancini in summer 1483, at least as current gossip.[37] Richard is supposed, as mentioned earlier, to have alleged that the Woodvilles were behind the execution in a 1483 letter to the executed Earl of Desmond's son. The logic behind the charge that Elizabeth had got rid of Clarence was that Stillington, arrested for alleged slander at the time of the Clarence trial, had told the foolish duke that the marriage was illegal and so encouraged his boasts about being the king's heir – which led the queen to have Clarence killed. It has been alleged that if Edward had really been punishing Clarence for finding out and making threats about his illegal marriage Stillington would have been arrested before, not after, Clarence's arrest and trial in winter 1477–8.

Clarence was apparently publicly alleging that Edward was illegitimate and had no right to rule, as stated in the Act of Parliament that attainted him in 1478 – a presumed reference to the story about Duchess Cecily and the archer Blaybourne (see next chapter). Richard's ally Buckingham was to bring this up again in June 1483. The fact that Clarence was also claiming that an astrologer had prophesied that Edward's successor would be 'G' – that is, himself, George of Clarence – not Edward's son Edward, implied that he suspected that the latter was legally illegitimate. By this reckoning, Clarence had justice on his side even if he could not prove it, and in recent years controversy has raged over Clarence's motives for his behaviour.[38] Was he dropping hints to the king that he knew the truth and Edward should disinherit his sons and make Clarence his heir, as he had been until Elizabeth Woodville had children? Stillington's evidence would surely have been valuable at the Clarence trial – or, if that was too embarrassing to Edward, the king would have questioned him in private. Instead, Stillington was only placed in custody for 'issuing words prejudicial to the King' at the time of Clarence's secret execution, in February 1478. Possibly, however, Edward only found out Stillington's part in the duke's erratic behaviour at a late stage in the proceedings. Some mainstream modern historians such as Charles Ross prefer to argue that the lack of clear evidence for Stillington's involvement with or tip-off to Clarence in 1477–8 argues that the whole pre-contract/marriage story was an invention of 1483 by a power-crazed Richard.

Edward IV's deposition by the exiled Earl of Warwick, in autumn 1470 was opportunistically carried out in Henry VI's name but owed nothing to Lancastrian sympathies. The king's marriage had begun their estrangement. Warwick had already seized the king by surprise in a coup in August 1469, apparently taking advantage of local discontent in the north to stage-manage a rebellion by the mysterious 'Robin of Redesdale' (probably his client Sir John Conyers) and luring the king north to deal with it. On that occasion he joined up with Edward's treacherous brother George, Duke of Clarence, who had just agreed to marry his elder daughter Isabel, and after the wedding (at Calais, away from royal interference) marched on London to seize power in July 1469. He then attacked and defeated the – conveniently quarrelling – royal forces, heading from Wales and the west country to deal with 'Robin' at Edgecote, with the King still seemingly unaware that he had turned rebel. Evidently Edward did not reckon Warwick's hatred of the Woodvilles as being strong enough to lead to revolt, but this is not an argument against the idea that there was major noble discontent with the queen's family. Surprisingly, Edward was a poor judge of those close to him – Somerset betrayed him in 1464, Warwick did so in 1469, Montagu did so in 1470, and in 1483 he left his surviving brother Richard, his brother-in-law Rivers, and his stepson Dorset all murderously at odds with each other.

While the victorious Warwick was executing Edward's father-in-law Earl Rivers, brother-in-law Sir John Woodville, and principal lieutenant in Wales, the Earl of Pembroke, his brother Archbishop George Neville of York led a party to intercept the king at Olney. The so-called 'Kingmaker' now had two kings – Edward IV, shunted around the Neville castles of Warwick, Middleham, and Pontefract, and his predecessor Henry VI in the Tower of London – under his control. But he refrained from deposing Edward, contenting himself with removing his own main rivals as the King's principal advisers. (One source, the Milanese ambassador to France, says that he did intend to enthrone Clarence).[39] The likeliest excuse for removing Edward was that which was to surface in 1483, namely his own illegitimacy due to his mother Cecily Neville's alleged affair in 1441–2 with an archer called Blaybourne. Warwick is more likely to have known of this story (which was circulating on the continent in the 1470s) than about the Eleanor Butler relationship, but if so he did not make it public. Possibly he had scruples about exposing his aunt Cecily as an adulteress – which her son Richard did not stop happening in 1483. While he was dithering, another Lancastrian rising broke out in the north, and Edward was able to summon his youngest brother Richard and other loyal magnates to bring troops to Pontefract to deal with them while Warwick was in London. The loyalists outnumbered whatever Neville guards were at the castle, and the latter gave way enabling the king to leave and return to his capital with his new army.

An uneasy truce followed, but the king's humiliation made a clash between them inevitable if Edward was to reassert his authority. Unwilling to continue under open threat of Warwick repeating this action and deposing him next time, Edward dissimulated until a new uprising in Lincolnshire by Warwick's partisan Lord Welles, 'captain of the commons', in March 1470 enabled him to act. Whether or not the rebels' apparent use of Warwick's and Clarence's names was with those magnates' permission as part of a new attempt to overthrow Edward, the king was able to defeat the rebels easily at the evocatively-nicknamed 'Lose-cote Field'. He then proclaimed the two suspects traitors and drove them into fleeing into exile in France.[40]

Warwick returned to south-west England in autumn 1470, having been induced by Louis XI of France to form an uneasy alliance with Henry VI's exiled Queen Margaret who had executed Warwick's own father in December 1460. Her son Edward was now to be married to Warwick's younger daughter Anne.[41] Warwick was joined by Clarence, who evidently expected to be named as Henry VI's heir in return for deserting his brother (thus confirming the argument of the Yorkists in the 1450s that Henry's son was illegitimate). The agreement was not carried out despite the fact that Warwick undoubtedly preferred Clarence, his own son-in-law, to the son of Queen Margaret; did Louis or Margaret force it on Warwick by insisting on this as a *sine qua non* of an alliance? The uneasy rapprochement that Louis XI of France had forced between Warwick and Margaret held. Edward was caught by surprise for a second time in the east midlands as he confronted local disturbances as Warwick's brother John, Marquis of Montague, principal lieutenant of the North, joined the rebellion. Montagu had been given the hand of

Princess Elizabeth, Edward's eldest daughter, for his son George and thus the prospect of his grandson on the throne as a consolation for having to hand back the Earldom of Northumberland to the reinstated ex-Lancastrian Percy heir, but backed his brother Warwick instead of the king. Significantly, Warwick is said to have had civilian recruits (up to 30,000 according to the official Coventry records) flocking to his standard as he advanced – an indication that citizens were disgruntled that Edward's rule had not brought peace?[42] At best Edward may have had around 3,000 of Lord Hastings' east midlanders,[43] and he clearly lost his nerve or else feared treachery as in 1470. He had not taken the effort to have a larger army with him on this interrupted northern campaign, though despite rumours that Warwick would land in the east to join it there was every possibility, given his cunning, that he would attack further south (and so give himself time to raise volunteers safe from the king's intervention). Philippe de Commignes in France blamed the sudden collapse of Edward's cause on his sloth;[44] over-confidence is more likely. But Edward and his brother Richard managed to escape via King's Lynn to the Netherlands with a small escort, and Warwick entered London to release Henry VI from the Tower and parade him though the apathetic city as the restored sovereign. Elizabeth Woodville, forced to flee to sanctuary at Westminster Abbey while heavily pregnant, gave birth to Edward's eldest son and heir there on 1 or 2 November.

The fact that Clarence deserted Edward to back his father-in-law Warwick's rebellion in spring 1470 and then invaded England with him in the autumn might be linked to anger at the illegal Woodville marriage and its 'bastard' offspring disinheriting him. But at this point Edward and Elizabeth had only daughters, not sons, until November 1470 and it is not clear that Edward definitely intended his eldest daughter Elizabeth rather than Clarence to succeed him in 1466–70. Even if Clarence or Warwick had some idea that Edward's marriage was illegal in 1469–70, the point is that neither was able to prove it and order the marriage dissolved after they seized power and deposed Edward in Henry VI's favour in October 1470. That would argue that Stillington had not told either of them about the ceremony. The most serious political 'block' to them declaring Edward a bastard and so advancing Clarence's claim, Henry's Queen Margaret – who was insisting that her son by Henry, Edward of Westminster (born 1453), be recognised as Henry's heir not Clarence – was still in

France as of winter 1470–1 so she could not stop a legal enquiry. The only other political actors who might have acted as a brake on Warwick and Clarence were her allies, the Beaufort family – descendants of Henry V's grandfather John of Gaunt by his third marriage, born illegitimate but later legitimated and barred from the throne. The current Beaufort Duke of Somerset, Edmund (son of the Duke killed by York and Salisbury at St Albans in 1455 and brother of the Duke executed by Warwick's brother John in 1464 so 'at feud' with Warwick), was a possible heir to the throne himself – or a next heir behind Prince Edward – if Clarence was kept out of the running so he might have been unwilling to see Edward IV bastardised.

Edward IV returned to Yorkshire with a small force in March 1471, initially claiming only to be seeking his rightful Duchy of York, not the crown (as Henry IV had started his invasion in 1399 only claiming the Duchy of Lancaster). This helped him as the locals were mostly hostile due to the large numbers of Yorkshiremen who had been killed by his troops at Towton in 1461, and the Earl of Northumberland, head of the Percy dynasty, stood aside and let him proceed unmolested.[45] Edward's restoring the Earldom to Percy in 1470 thus acted to his benefit in the long term. His troops were allowed to proceed into the Midlands by Montague whose loyalties appear to have been equivocal, and at Coventry Clarence returned to his side[46] – possibly after giving up hope that his double-dealing father-in-law Warwick would ever force Margaret and Henry VI to give in to his demands on land and the succession. Warwick did not challenge him immediately, and Edward reached London ahead of him to reclaim his crown while Warwick's brother-in-law Lord Stanley, principal landed power in Lancashire, failed to join him either due to a private local confrontation with the Harringtons or due to deliberate calculation that he did not want to be caught on the losing side. (Later Stanley notoriously abandoned Richard III at Bosworth.) The joint armies of Warwick and Montague were then defeated and their leaders killed in a close-fought and muddled battle in the fog at Barnet Heath just North of London, as the pro-Warwick Earl of Oxford's troops returned from chasing Edward's left wing off the battlefield to be fired on by Neville soldiers and fled. (The heraldic devices of Edward of York, the 'Sun in Splendour', and of Oxford, a star wth rays, were very similar – especially if seen in poor visibility.) Montague's body was found to be wearing

Edward's heraldic emblems under his surcoat, possibly indicating that he intended to change sides again during the battle.[47]

Margaret landed at Weymouth with French aid to link up with local Lancastrians and found her Neville allies dead. Heading for Wales to join Henry VI's half-brother Jasper Tudor, she was intercepted and defeated at Tewkesbury on 4 May and her principal commanders either killed in the battle or dragged out of sanctuary in Tewkesbury Abbey afterwards for execution. Margaret was captured, and her son Prince Edward was cut down in the aftermath of the battle at Tewkesbury, allegedly calling out in vain to his brother-in-law Clarence for help as Edward's men cornered and killed him.[48] The powerless Henry VI, back in Edward's hands in the Tower of London and still a rallying-point for rebels, died conveniently just after Edward had returned to London. He was supposed to have died naturally of 'pure displeasure and melancholy' according to the pro-Yorkist author of the *Arrivall of Edward IV...*,[49] probably one of Edward's lieutenants in the campaign, but was more plausibly rumoured to have been stabbed.[50] Within a few years writers were calling this the first killing by the future Richard III,[51] but if he did do the deed – he was Contable of the Tower so the person authorised to carry out executions – it would have been on Edward's orders.

Clarence's fall and Elizabeth Woodville: did he know the truth?

However Clarence continued to cause trouble for Edward, apparently threatening to claim to be his heir in place of Edward's own sons. This was probably on account of the illegality of Edward's (secret) marriage to Elizabeth Woodville, though it is also possible that the Blaybourne story was known to Clarence and he was using this. As part of his presumed terms for pardon in 1471 he was no longer able to claim that he was the rightful king rather than his elder brother, so he was resorting to blocking the succession of Edward's children. Clarence's desertion to his father-in-law Warwick's cause in 1469–70 had been followed by attempts to obtain the promise of the succession from Henry VI. Commonsense should have dictated that he abandon this claim after 1471 as he was lucky not to have been executed for treason. So why should he have risked his life, or at least his liberty, to challenge his brother so blatantly? Was it merely greed and arrogance, or did he think he had a legal case? And what was his legal ground for his claim – Edward IV's illegitimacy or the future Edward V's illegitimacy?

The death of Clarence's wife Isabel Neville in 1476 may have unbalanced his reason, though his failed attempt to secure Royal support for his planned marriage to the heiress of Burgundy gave him a political grudge too. The surprise death of Duke Charles while attacking the Swiss in January 1477 had left his extensive lands leaderless and his daughter in need of a husband to protect them from being swallowed up by Louis XI. Back in the 1460s there had been talk of one of Edward's brothers moving to lands within Burgundy as their ruler, possibly Holland and Clarence's name had been mentioned. Clarence, his hopes of a crown in England fading with Edward having a second son in 1473, clearly saw himself in this role – and his and Edward's sister Margaret, Charles' widow, would logically support her brother's candidature. Edward might have been glad to have Clarence removed from England, but instead he refused to countenance the match – probably due to fear that if successful Clarence would use Burgundian resources to invade England. Duchess Mary of Burgundy duly married a rival candidate, Maximilian of Habsburg, and her lands (apart from those which Louis seized) were swallowed up into the Habsburg Holy Roman Empire. Clarence was enraged, and proceeded to openly challenge the king. Some bizarre and provocative behaviour followed that questioned his sanity, including consulting an astrologer (who Edward had executed), arriving uninvited at a Council meeting to make his spokesman read out a statement of the innocence of one of his servants who the King had executed for treason, and abducting, trying, and executing his late wife's maid Ankarette Twynho for allegedly murdering her. The jury who had found her guilty assured the subsequent enquiry that they had only condemned her out of fear of Clarence's wrath if they refused.

Who was supposed to have been behind the 'murder' of Isabel – Queen Elizabeth in revenge for Isabel's father killing her father and brother? The execution of Clarence's astrologer Stacy and his fellow-plotter Burdett in 1477 for planning the king's death was presumably intended as a warning to Clarence by the King,[52] but his public defiance continued and led to his own trial, condemnation to death, and execution early in 1478.[53] The threat of another civil war and the apparent impossibility of threatening the duke into political nullity made his eventual execution inevitable, with Dominic Mancini hearing in 1483 that Richard had been angered at it though the later 'Tudor legend' made him the king's chief encourager in it. It is only a plausible theory that Clarence had evidence that Edward's marriage was illegal because of a pre-contract to another party and threatened to use it, as the question of the pre-contract to another party only surfaced in 1483. But it would explain why this vain and treacherous character, already forgiven for abandoning his brother in 1470–1 and lucky not to be in prison or executed, launched another extremely unwise claim on the succession in 1477.

Richard III and the revelation of the pre-contract in 1483: did he invent it?

The argument about Edward's marriage came into the open when Richard III used it – or invented it, according to sceptics such as Alison Weir (*The Princes in the Tower*, 1992) – in June 1483 to justify setting aside Edward's sons and taking the throne for himself. The crucial point was a pro-Richard sermon by Ralph Shaa/Shaw (brother of the current Lord Mayor) at St Paul's Cross on 22 June, concerning the text that 'Bastard slips shall not take root' (*Wisdom*, chap. 4. verse 3). Sir Thomas More's account of the event says that Shaa argued that the pre-contract invalidated Edward IV's marriage (though he has the wrong notion that Elizabeth Lucy not Eleanor Butler was involved) as well as Edward himself being a bastard; Polydore Vergil only mentions the latter. The *Croyland Chronicle* refers to a pre-contract to marry Eleanor Butler, though possibly quoting from the *Titulus Regius* Act not from the sermon – and technically a pre-contract meant a fully legal marriage not a betrothal ceremony which is the usual modern interpretation of the word.[54] Richard's ally Henry, Duke of Buckingham (Eleanor Butler/ Talbot's first cousin so possibly aware of her involvement with Edward IV earlier), then addressed the principal citizens of London on 24 June on Richard's claim, concentrating on the Blaybourne story of Edward IV's illegitimacy and asserting that it could be seen that Richard resembled his undersized, dark-haired father but the six-foot Edward IV did not. Richard then appeared at a window to remind the audience of this fact.[55] According to More, Buckingham spoke more openly about the issue of Edward IV's bastardy than Shaa/

Shaw had done; the latter had only dropped hints, for fear of annoying Richard by openly saying that his mother was an adulteresss.

Modern historians disgree fiercely whether the pre-contract and the witness to it (Bishop Stillington, according to Philippe de Commines[56] who was not in England at the time unlike Mancini) were a new invention of June 1483, Richard's biographers Paul Murray Kendall and James Gairdner (*History of the Life and Reign of Richard III*, 1969) being in favour of its essential truth. Alison Weir regards it as an invention hastily cobbled together ahead of 22 June and Mortimer Levine thinks that the lack of agreement as to what was said on 22 June and other evidence implies that the pre-contract claim was only set out in Parliament in 1484 for the *Titulus Regius* Act.[57] Charles Ross also thinks the claim a nakedly political invention by the unscrupulous Richard.[58] As mentioned earlier, there is also the question of the apparent reference to Stillington as the author (of the claim or just of the *Titulus Regius?*) in the 1486 legal records, for which see P.W. Hammond's article in 'The Ricardian' in 1976. But Bertram Fields (*Royal Blood: Richard III and the Mystery of the Princes*, 1998) points out that the mysterious meeting of leaders of the 'estates' with the Council in Richard's chamber at Westminster Palace on 9 June on some important matter could refer to the story being discussed at an emergency meeting of the political elite. The reference by well-connected Londoner Simon Stallworth (an employee of Bishop John Russell) to 'great business against the coronation' in his letter to a Stonor on 10 June may refer to the meeting and its threat to abort the coronation if Edward V was illegitimate – but the term 'against' may only mean 'connected to'.[59] Stallworth does not refer to any major new political developments, though, which could mean that the meeting did not discuss the pre-contract/marriage revelation. An argument was made by Sir Clements Markham in his favourable 1906 biography of Richard that a version of the *Grafton Chronicle* said specifically that it was Stillington who revealed the pre-contract to the Council. However a recent investigation by Peter Hancock shows that the 'he' in question in the account refers to Richard, not the bishop. But this is a side issue; whether or not Richard revealed the details to the Council, he would have needed an ecclesiastical expert's legal support to tell the councillors that the Woodville marriage was illegal. Stillington was the means to provide this, and was duly the – only – ecclesiastic rounded up immediately on

Henry VII's accession. The only implausible part of Commignes' story of the pre-contract was a piece of gossip he cited, that Stillington had a grudge against the Yorkist Royal Family because he had been promised one of Edward IV's daughters for his illegitimate son and this 'deal' had been broken.

Markham's research also revealed details of a 1486 debate by the Barons of the Exchequer at the time of the repeal (and unprecedented total removal from the record) of the Act of *Titulus Regius*, by which Richard confirmed that the pre-contract had been legal so all Edward IV's children were illegitimate. This debate apparently referred to Stillington as the author of the document – but Hancock argues that this means that Stillington was the author of the Act and not necessarily of the revelation of the pre-contract. He argues that Stillington only confirmed a story that Richard had already heard before questioning him, and prefers to believe that it was Richard's henchman Sir William Catesby who discovered the pre-contract through his family connections with Eleanor's family. Catesby's father had been the Talbot family lawyer, and had married Eleanor's cousin.[60] But this does not deny that the ceremony was accepted by Stillington (a witness or the celebrant) as legal, which he then told the Council in early June 1483 – even if this fitted in with Richard's plans to depose Edward V. Nor does this mean that Richard had revealed the Stillington story to some or all the Council in early June and this panicked Hastings into thinking that Richard intended to depose Edward V so he got in touch with Elizabeth Woodville to plan to stop this – and his messages were betrayed to Richard who decided to kill him. This is one solution to the drastic action which Richard took on 13 June, but is unprovable. Richard's letters to his supporters in Yorkshire on 10 and 11 June to send troops urgently to London to protect him from a Woodville plot to depose him need not imply that he suddenly needed the men to stage his immanent Council coup and eliminate Hastings, an action which took place on the 13th – far too soon for any of these men to arrive from York.

The coronation of Edward V was due to take place at the end of the month, along with the meeting of Parliament, and these are likely to have been Richard's target-dates when summoning his men. The suddenness of the 13 June coup – before his men arrived and he could be sure of controlling London – would suggest that he acted in haste on the 13th and had not foreseen this possibility two or three days earlier. It is logical that it was news of the pre-contract – or at least the fact that Lord Hastings would not back him in using it to depose Edward V – which caused his sudden arrest of Hastings' faction on 13 June.

The mistaken naming of Elizabeth Lucy may be due to the fact that More – writing around 1510 – had no reliable witness available around twenty-five years later who could remember which woman had been named in the sermon, which took place unexpectedly so nobody except a pre-warned Council member would have been likely to be ready to write the contents down. (More's old employer Bishop Morton, probable source of most of his details about Richard III, was by this date under arrest for resisting the usurper's takeover.) Elizabeth Lucy was the mother of Edward's bastard Arthur Plantagenet, Lord Lisle, who by 1510 was a Household knight at his nephew Henry VIII's court. Arthur may have been born before the king's marriage in 1464 – a matter which is unclear – and it is possible that the affair continued for years afterwards, given Arthur's participation in the young Henry VIII's close court circle of roistering young Household nobles in the 1510s. Among the other participants in this group only Henry's best friend Charles Brandon, born at the latest in 1485/6 (his father was killed at Bosworth), was significantly older than Henry – so what would an Arthur born in 1462/4 be doing as an intimate of people so much younger? He was not noticeably aged and incapable in his role as Captain of Calais in the 1530s, though he is said to have died of relief at his release from captivity in the Tower in 1542 which suggests fragile health. It would seem more logical that Arthur was born after the early 1460s, than that he was already in his forties when he was a member of Henry's inner circle of young nobles of the next generation. But no evidence exists for the continuation of the relationship between his parents, and the fact that he was neglected regarding patronage before 1509 may mean that he was anxious thereafter to make up for lost opportunities.

Edward and Elizabeth Lucy had been involved with each other in 1462–3, and so the latter was a logical candidate for an uncertain More to name as the other party to the pre-contract. He was clearly wrong, as if this had been the case the paranoid Henry VIII would surely not have trusted Arthur – possibly the rightful king? – to govern the crucial overseas base of Calais in the 1530s. When Arthur was eventually arrested during the 'Plantagenet conspiracy' of Yorkist relatives – including Clarence's grandson Lord Montague – of the late 1530s there was no hint that he could be accused of claiming the throne. Instead the proposed claimant was Montague as Clarence's heir. It seesm unlikely that Henry's efficient chief minister Thomas Cromwell would have passed up the opportunity to accuse Arthur of slanderous claims that the current king's mother was illegitimate in order to make sure he was executed, had there been a case for saying Arthur's parents had been legally married.The pre-contract story was definitely still an issue in England in the 1530s, as Emperor Charles V's ambassador Eustace de Chapuys reported that people said that Charles had more right to the throne than Henry VIII due to Elizabeth of York, Henry's mother, being illegitimate on that account. (Charles was descended from John of Gaunt, ancestor of the Lancastrian and Beaufort families, through his daughter Catherine's marriage to the King of Castile.)

It did not help accurate recollection that Richard III's *Titulus Regius* Act, legalising the bastardisation had been cancelled and all copies destroyed by Henry VII in order to protect the legitimacy of his own wife, Edward IV's eldest daughter Elizabeth of York. If the story had been revealed to the political leadership on 9 June, it would be scepticism about it or Richard's motives in publicising it that led to Lord Hastings' sudden execution and others' arrests on 13 June. It would seem probable that the detailed account of the pre-contract and its legal implications presented to and duly approved by the meeting of the 'estates' on 25 June (which transferred the crown to Richard) must have taken time to draw up. It is unlikely all to have been done after the Shaa/Shaw sermon on the 22nd, though it could have been done after the Council coup on the 13th. There may have been legal proofs of the marriage too, if we can believe the account by More that Buckingham told Morton that he had been shown these documents by Richard. More wrote that the duke said he had realised that they were fakes – but the Tudor throne rested partly on the legitimacy of Edward IV's children so More had to take that line. The drastic action Henry VII took to ban all mention and record of *Titulus Regius* might also suggest that he recognised that it had some truth in it; if the pre-contract story could be easily disproved, it would not have been so dangerous. Notably, Henry had Stillington taken into custody after Bosworth but the latter never appeared in public to confess that he had made up the story at the behest of the usurping tyrant Richard – a logical course for Henry to take. Henry also secured a papal legal ruling that his right to the throne rested solely on his claim as heir of the House of Lancaster, rather than on his marriage to Edward IV's heiress. This protected him from being seen as no more than 'King Consort' to the legal queen – but did it also safeguard him in case legal proof should turn up that Edward IV's children were illegitimate after all?

Legally Richard could have accepted the story but deferred his claim in favour of Clarence's son Edward, Earl of Warwick, who was technically debarred by Clarence's attainder and practically so by being only eight (and possibly feeble-minded). Attainders were frequently reversed by compliant Parliaments if that was what the political leaders of the nation wanted, but – as on previous occasions – an ambitious adult was preferred to a minor. The pro- and anti-Richard III arguments on this issue continue to this day, centring on whether Edward IV was pre-contracted to Eleanor Butler before he married Elizabeth Woodville and thus his marriage was illegal under fifteenth-century canon law. This is the identification made in the text of *Titulus Regius* preserved in the *Croyland Chronicle* – the Act based on Richard's claim of June 1483. Unfortunately her burial-site at the convent of the Minories in Norwich cannot be identified due to its demolition at the Reformation, though a recent biographer has presented evidence of her connection with the establishment and her residence at her Butler husband's estates nearby. She died in 1468 according to the evidence – and so could not be questioned about the truth of the allegations even by Warwick in 1469. Of course if she did die at that date Edward V, born in 1470, could be legitimate if Edward IV had subsequently 're-married' his wife; the best modern legal investigation of this complex question is by Mortimer Levine (in *Speculum*, vol. XXXIV, July 1959) who says that it would have had to be a public re-marriage to be fully legal.[61] This certainly did not take place. But in any case Henry VIII's mother Elizabeth of York (born 1465) would still be illegitimate so no Tudor writer could allow themselves to accept that Edward and Eleanor had been legitimately engaged. The Early Stuart writer Sir George Buck even claimed that Edward and Eleanor had had a child, but this is not supported by any other account.

It is possible that the story was invented by Richard to justify his coup, presumably before 13 June 1483, but more likely that its 'revealer' Bishop

Stillington was speaking the truth. He did not receive any reward from Richard, as might be expected for fabricating the claim that gave him the throne. Nor did he denounce the story as a fabrication once Richard was safely dead in 1485–6, which would have secured him the gratitude of Henry VII. Stillington may have been the priest who carried out the ceremony, or merely have heard the story from the actual celebrant – one of his subordinates in his diocese? The amorous Edward IV was a womaniser even by 1462, though our earliest written evidence for his habits is from 1464 when it is said that men marvelled that he was still unmarried and feared that he was unchaste. He was devious enough from his other actions to have made a form of promise to Eleanor – probably in order to achieve her acquiescence for a secret seduction. He would have gone through a secret ceremony before a priest with her, much as he did with Elizabeth Woodville – but on this earlier occasion the other participant did not keep up the relationship and see that the ceremony was revealed. Did the worldlier Elizabeth make sure that her marriage could not be disavowed later by forcing Edward's hand – even though it took around four months from May to September 1464 to do so? Once the incident leaked out to powerful enemies of the Woodvilles – evidently after 1470–1, or Warwick would have used it then – it could be used as an argument for the marriage's illegality by Edward's sons' rivals for the throne.

Clarence possibly knew of the 'pre-contract' in the 1470s and regarded it as justifying his claim to be Edward's heir; Stillington's mysterious arrest after Clarence's disgrace for words prejudicial to the king was presumably connected to Edward IV believing that he had tipped off the duke. The prejudicial words about the king that Stilllington had to swear to cease using in 1478 were thus connected to the legality of the royal marriage. This is not to say that the king definitely was a bigamist and that Clarence had justice on his side, and even if Clarence was the rightful heir to the throne rather than any of Edward's children in 1466– 78 he went about promoting his claim in a haphazard and politically disastrous way. Legally, cancelling Richard III's *Titulus Regius* Act in 1485–6 made Edward's eldest daughter Elizabeth the rightful heir to the throne on her brothers' (presumed) deaths and so identified the legitimate line of succession as her and her children, though Henry VII had not claimed the throne in his capacity as her fiancée/husband in

August 1485 but by his own Beaufort descent from the legitimised eldest son of the third marriage of Edward III's son John of Gaunt. But at the least the mass of allegations swirling around Edward IV's private life and sexual relationships show that he, like his brother Richard, was a controversial and ruthless character of dubious honesty. As with Richard, the controversies cannot all be written off as spin by the enemies of the House of York.

Note

Was Edward IV a Bastard?

It is also possible that there was some truth behind another story about Edward IV that was circulated at the time of his deposition in 1470 to excuse its legality and was revived in June 1483 – according to Dominic Mancini's contemporary account of the usurpation as well as More's version of c.1513. This was that he was not entitled to the throne either, as he was not the son of Richard, Duke of York, but of his mother Cecily Neville's affair with the archer Blaybourne. The 'Edward IV was illegitimate' allegation appeared as a reason for Richard claiming the throne over the rights of Edward's son Edward V in the *Titulus Regius* Parliamentary Act (as quoted in the *Croyland Chronicle*), without naming Blaybourne, and this presumably came from the formal petition to Parliament in late June 1483 invalidating Edward V's rights. As mentioned earlier, it is not certain that the precise naming of Blaybourne as the culprit (as opposed to a vague assertion of Edward IV being a bastard) was 'active' in England in June 1483, let alone that use of it was more than a blatantly political claim without viable evidence. Edward's enemy Louis XI of France however referred to him under this name to annoy him in the 1470s, showing that the naming of Blaybourne was not just a story thought up in 1483. Mancini also refers to Duchess Cecily being so furious at Edward's proposal to execute his brother Clarence in 1478 that she fell into a frenzy and said that she would testify on oath to a public legal enquiry that Edward was not the son of her late husband Richard of York and so was not entitled to be King of England.[63] This, however, might be a frantic attempt by her to save Clarence's life by challenging Edward's legal right to try and sentence him, and it is not clear how Mancini (not in England in 1478) knew about this or how accurate the story (gossip he heard in London in 1483?) was. Polydore Vergil also heard that she had complained bitterly after the alleged revelation of the Blaybourne affair – by the Duke of Buckingham in his address to the peers on 24 June 1483, not directly by Richard or by Friar Shaa – of the injustice and insult that Richard had thus done to her.[64] However, the two remained on friendly terms in real life so Vergil's story that they were estranged over it was at least exaggerated – possibly Buckingham went too far in slandering Cecily, out of dislike of her or else a ruthless determination to add new 'evidence' to the reasons why Edward V could not be king.

At the time of Cecily's pregnancy her husband was Henry VI's lieutenant in Normandy, which was under attack from the French, and they were based at the Duchy's capital of Rouen where Edward was born on 28 April 1442. The location shows that it is possible that local residents, at the time English subjects, knew the story and that Louis and his courtiers duly acquired it from them. Alternatively, it may have been mere gossip at York's residence which French agents used to undermine his reputation or to annoy Edward at the time of his invasion of France in 1475. Recent investigations of the itinerary of the Duke of York at the time that Edward must have been conceived in mid-late July or early August 1441 (depending on whether he was a full-term baby or born early), based on the records of the cathedral church at Rouen, were publicised in a Channel Four documentary presented by Dr Michael Jones that first went out on 3 January 2004. They showed that the clergy were ordered to pray for the Duke of York while he was absent at the siege of French-seized Pontoise on 14 July – 21 August; thus he was not in Rouen in the crucial weeks. Also, Edward IV's baptism was in a minor side-chapel of the cathedral, not the main nave as with his next brother Edmund (born in 1443) – so was it a low-key affair and if so why? The records have been taken as indicating that York was away on campaign, not with Cecily (shown by records to have been at Rouen) at the time in question. The quiet nature of Edward's baptism, unusual for the eldest son of a senior royal duke, has also been cited as suspicious.[65] However, the ducal household may have been preoccupied on other matters or the duke was not bothered to celebrate the baptism in case the baby did not survive, and as an earlier baby son of the couple's had died as an infant they may have feared that this would happen again.

For that matter, as Pontoise was only sixty miles away from Rouen on a good road there was nothing to stop York riding back to Rouen for a day or two to see his wife (and conceive Edward) when the siege was safely underway and all was quiet. It would not be publicised so the besieged and their potential French royal army rescuers did not feel emboldened to attack the leaderless besiegers. The only 'political' use made of the incident later was by Richard III in 1483 when his petition for assuming the throne to Parliament reminded the public that he, unlike Edward, had been born in England (and hence was more 'English'). At the time people made more of the fact that the six-foot Edward did not physically resemble his under-sized father (whereas Richard III did). Mancini quotes this 'proof' of Edward's illegitimacy as being cited in the Duke of Buckingham's speech to the principal citizens of London on 24 June.

As early as August 1469, when Edward had been seized by his cousin Warwick and was being held captive, the Milanese ambassador reported a rumour that the earl intended to depose Edward as a bastard and give his crown to his son-in-law, Clarence. The interpretation of this evidence is however all highly speculative; it is possible that York had other reasons for holding a quiet baptism apart from doubting his son's parentage, and Edward IV did resemble earlier Plantagenet kings and princes such as Edward III's second son Lionel (though Cecily was also of royal descent so he could have inherited the looks through her). Warwick did not need a genuine story of Edward's irregular birth to get rid of him in 1469 had he wanted to do so, and was capable of inventing one. It is apparent that the subject of Edward's parentage was not pressed forward by Richard III's partisans in June 1483 with the same ardour as the claims about Edward's marriage, presumably because the unpopular Elizabeth Woodville could be more safely vilified and Richard's supporters were more wary of labelling his mother a slut. It may have been Buckingham, an ambitious man who was soon to show that he had his own agenda in the coup of 1483, that raised the matter rather than Richard. This would partly account for Shaa's reluctance to mention it in detail, and for the fact that there is no evidence that Cecily Neville turned against Richard. The matter was not referred to in the legal Act justifying and explaining the usurpation. In any case, Henry VII was so keen to have both claims wiped from the public consciousness when he took the throne and re-legitimated his bride, Edward IV's eldest daughter, that he went to the unprecedented steps of having every copy of the Ricardian legislation on Edward IV's marriage (the *Titulus Regius*) recalled and destroyed.

Evidently sensitive about any claims that Elizabeth might be illegitimate after all, Henry had *Titulus Regius* cancelled and destroyed all copies that he could find. Bishop Stillington was brought in urgently for questioning – no doubt about the truth of the story – but later released. Notably, Henry did not force Stillington to assert that the pre-contract story was fabrication – which may suggest that Stillington refused to co-operate (as he was telling the truth?). Henry did not marry Elizabeth with any haste, though as a distant cousin he had to wait until a papal dispensation for the marriage arrived in London and the ceremony swiftly followed this event. He did not allow Elizabeth to be crowned on their marriage, and delayed her coronation for over a year as if to stress that he held the throne in his own right. His own dynastic right as heir of Lancaster through the Beaufort line was dubious, given that his ancestress Katherine Swynford – John of Gaunt's third wife – had not been married to John at the time that her children were born. They had been excluded from the succession by Act of Parliament when the marriage occurred and they were legitimised in 1396. In any case it was his mother Margaret, only daughter of John and Katherine's eldest grandson, who was technically the Beaufort heiress though her waiving her rights could be excused as no woman had ruled in England since the disastrous Empress Matilda briefly held power in 1141. Henry's assertion of his dynastic right to the throne at the expense of that of the Yorkist line cannot be interpreted as implying concern about the legal status of the latter. Nor can it be taken as a hint that although he had to marry Elizabeth, as promised at Christmas 1483, to secure Yorkist lordly support (and deny Elizabeth to a rival) he believed her claim to be weak – either on account of her father's bastardy or her parents' marriage. Fear of seeming too politically dependent on his wife – and her mother – is more likely.

If Edward IV or His Daughter Had No Right To the Throne…?

If Edward IV is ruled out as legitimate King of England on account of his bastardy or his eldest daughter Elizabeth (Henry VIII's mother) is ruled out on account of her parents' bigamous marriage, George of Clarence transmitted the legitimate claim to the throne. Thus the correct line of succession would run:

Edward, Earl of Warwick (son), ex. 1499

Lady Margaret Pole (sister), ex. 1541

(Henry Pole, Lord Montague, son, executed 1538)

Ursula Pole, daughter, d. 1576 (married: Francis Hastings, second Earl of Huntingdon)

Henry Hastings, third Earl of Huntingdon, son, d. 1595. He was actively considered as a potential king when Elizabeth I was seriously ill with smallpox and had no clear heir in October 1562, as adult, male, and safely Protestant. The queen is said to have mistrusted him and his ambitious wife after this and kept them away from court.

George, fourth Earl of Huntingdon, brother, d. 1604

Henry, fifth Earl, grandson, d. 1643

Ferdinando, sixth Earl, d. 1656

Theophilus, seventh Earl, d. 1701

George, eighth Earl, son by first wife, d. 1705

Theophilus, ninth Earl, half-brother, d. 1747.

Francis, tenth Earl d. 1789

Elizabeth, Lady Botreaux, sister (d. 1808), m. first Earl of Moira.

Francis Rawdon-Hastings, marquis of Hastings, son (d. 1826)

George, second Marquis of Hastings (d. 1844) – brother of Lady Flora Hastings, famously slandered by Queen Victoria's circle for a falsely assumed pregnancy in the Royal Bedchamber Scandal of 1839.

Paulyn, third Marquis, son (d. 1851).

Henry, fourth Marquis, brother – rake, gambler, stud-owner, and friend of Edward VII; went bankrupt (d. 1868).

Edith, Countess of Loudoun, sister – from whom the direct Clarence line of descent proceeded to the Earl of Loudoun who died in Australia in 2012.

Conclusion

As shown above, the medieval era in England was as prone to 'fake news' and deliberate political chicanery as modern times – and these cases are merely the most important and best-documented ones. Similarly, even if the surprise death of a powerful leader was 'above board' if the circumstances were unusual or there were few witnesses – and they were all from one faction with an interest in his removal – the public and later writers might not believe the official version of events. One controversial and unconventional king died suddenly in a hunting-accident, in the company of his ruthless younger brother whose main rival was abroad and who duly seized the throne. Another, alleged to be homosexual and to be lavishing power and property on his lovers, was overthrown by his neglected wife and then died in custody, with rumours of a plot by his wife and her lover, was buried in a low-key event with few people having seen the body, and was later widely said to be alive after all. This was seemingly a fraudulent attempt to trap his supporters into a plot and have them executed, but centuries later an independent overseas source emerged that seemed to confirm that he had escaped to Italy or been freed. Another controversial and deposed 'tyrant' died suddenly in custody as well, was supposed to have been starved to death by his ruthless cousin but could have killed himself, and despite this death being more certain assorted pretenders then appeared claiming to be him and were widely believed. The under-age ex-king Edward V and his younger brother vanished from the Tower of London while in the custody of their uncle and replacement king, and their remains were supposedly dug up centuries later – not at the exact location specified in the most detailed story, but officially accepted and reburied as genuine (and still not given a DNA test). Their ambitious and ruthless uncle's reputation is still a matter of major controversy and he is fiercely defended by his partisans over 500 years later – and his body disappeared and has recently been dug up too.

Were they ever killed, and are other suspects more plausible villains than the official culprit Richard III? There may be more written evidence for these cases than for earlier British royal mysteries, but much of this is dubious in the light of the agendas of those who recorded – or distorted – it. Discovering which sources are unreliable and why provides an extra layer to these stories, though it makes some even murkier and more complex than before. It is also useful to examine why certain potential mysteries attracted increasingly wild and unlikely rumours and a host of 'suspects' for apparent crimes, but others did not. The love of a good detective story and a charismatic villain like Richard III – or, for those with a wider knowledge, a bizarrely unconventional king like Edward II – is one explanation, and amateur detectives with a urge to suggest new solutions (some serious historians, some complete 'outsiders') have sprung up over the centuries. Even modern analytical science can only go so far where vital evidence is missing and 'reliable' sources turn out to have their own agendas. But science has already helped to find Richard III and provide some answers and intriguing new possibilities, though it is no nearer to answering the question of motive for his alleged crimes – and now the hunt for the remains of William II's supposed killer, Henry I, is on at his monastic foundation of Reading Abbey. One thing that is clear is that the bids to provide definitive answers will continue.

Notes

Chapter 1

1. *Orderic Vitalis*, trans Marjorie Chibnall (6 vols, Oxford UP 1968–80) book 4, chapter 94.
2. Ibid, book 3, chapters 114–15; William of Malmesbury, Gesta Regum, book 1 chapters 202–5.
3. *Orderic*, trans Chibnall, book 2, chapters 356–60.
4. Ibid, book 4, chapters 236–7; *Anglo-Saxon Chronicle*, p. 226.
5. *Orderic*, book 5, chapter 298; *Eadmer*, ed Martin Rule (London Rolls Society 1884) pp. 121–6; Warren Hollister, *Henry I* (Yale UP 2001), pp. 126–7.
6. Hollister, pp. 128–9.
7. Frank Barlow, *William Rufus*, pp. 110, 225.
8. *Orderic*, book 4, chapter 148; Hollister, pp. 39–40.
9. *Orderic*, book 4, chapters 150–8.
10. Ibid, book 6, chapters 20–32; *Anglo-Saxon Chronicle*, pp. 237–8.
11. *Orderic*, book 4, chapter 250; Hollister, pp. 79–82.
12. *Orderic*, book 4, chapters 222–6; *William of Malmesbury*, book 2 chapter 649.
13. Henry's reported comment was confirmed by Robert of Torigny: see *The Gesta Normannorum Ducorum of William of Jumieges and Robert of Torigny*, ed Elisabeth van Houts (3 vols, Oxford UP 1992–5) vol 2 p. 222.
14. Edmund King, *King Stephen* (Yale UP 2012) pp. 42–7.
15. Frank Barlow, *William Rufus*, pp. 420–5.
16. Duncan Grinnell-Milne, *The Killing of William Rufus* (1968); Hugh Williamson, *The Arrow and the Sword: An Essay* in *Detection* (1955).
17. *William of Malmesbury*, book 2, chapter 377.
18. *Orderic*, vol 5, chapter 284.
19. *William of Malmesbury*, book 2, chapters 377–9.
20. Article in the *Gentleman's Magazine* in 1789 by J. Milner.
21. See *A Survey of Southampton and Its Region* (British Academy for the Advancement of Science, 1964) pp. 66–70, 140–7.
22. As n. 19.

23. Emma Mason, 'William Rufus: Myth and Reality' in *Journal of Medieval History*, vol 3 (1977) p. 18 n.7.
24. *Orderic*, book 5 chapter 282; *William of Malmesbury*, book ii p. 373.
25. *William of Jumieges*, vol 2 pp. 124–5.
26. *Anglo-Saxon Chronicle*, p. 221.
27. *William of Malmesbury*, as n. 19; *Orderic*, book 5, chapters 284–8.
28. Abbot Suger, *Vie de Louis VI le Gros*, ed H Waquet (Paris 1929) p. 12.
29. *Orderic*, book 5 chapters 289–92; *William of Malmesbury*, book 2, chapter 279.
30. John of Salisbury, *Vita Sancti Anselmi, in Complete Works*, ed Migne, vol CXCIX p. 103.
31. *William of Malmesbury*, book 2, chapters 377–8.
32. *Anglo-Saxon Chronicle*, p. 235.
33. Eadmer, *Vita Anselmi* (ed R.W. Southern, 1962), p. 28.
34. *Orderic*, book 5, chapter 284 ff.
35. *Orderic* and *Eadmer*, as nn. 34 and 35; *William of Malmesbury* (trans R.A.B. Mynors, R.H.C. Davis, and M. Chibnall, 1998), book 2 pp. 470–1.
36. Williamson, op cit, pp. 105–19.
37. As n. 30.
38. Horace Hutchinson, *The New Forest* (Methuen 1905) p. 95, account of Charles having the oak off which Tyrrell's arrow glanced identified and fenced off.
39. *Florence of Worcester*, vol 2 p. 45.
40. *A Survey of Southampton and its Region*, ed F.J. Monkhouse (British Associaiton for the Advancement of Science, 1964) : Chapter 6, 'The Place-Names of Hampshire' by A.T. Lloyd, p. 191.
41. *Eadmer*, pp. 116–17; *William of Malmesbury*, book 2 chapter 373.
42. *William of Malmesbury*, book 5 chapter 271; *Orderic*, book 2 chapter 314.

Chapter 2
1. H. Johnstone, *Edward of Carnarvon 1284–1327* (Manchester 1946) pp. 122–4.
2. Alison Weir, *Isabella: She-Wolf of France, Queen of England*, pp. 19–20.
3. Ibid, pp. 66–7.
4. See the character assessment of Edward II in article by J.R.S. Phillips for the *New DNB*: vol 17, p. 836.
5. Ian Mortimer, *The Greatest Traitor: The Life of Sir Roger Mortimer, Ruler of England 1327–1330* (Pimlico 2004) pp. 130–1.
6. Henry Knighton, *Chronici Henrici Knighton, monachi Leycestrensis* (2 vols, ed J. Lumby, Rolls Series, London 1889–1893) and Thomas Walsingham, *Historia Anglicana* 1272–1422 (2 vols, ed H.T. Riley, Rolls Series, 1863–4).
7. See Weir, pp. 119–20 and 126–7.
8. Mortimer, pp. 212–13; Weir, pp. 315–22.

9. As described in T.F. Tout, 'The captivity and death of Edward of Carnarvon', in *Bulletin of the John Rylands Library, 1921*: based on the accounts in the *Annales Paulini* and in *Geoffrey le Baker*.

10. Weir, p. 267.

11. Ibid, pp. 273–4.

12. *Vita Edwardi Secunda Monachi Cuiusdem Malmesburensis: The Life of Edward II by the So-Called Monk of Malmesbury*, trans and ed N. Denholm-Young (Nelson's Medieval Texts, 1957).

13. R. Haines, 'The afterlife of Edward of Carnarvon', in *Transactions of the Bristol and Gloucestershire Archaeological Society*, vol 114 (1996), pp. 69–70; Weir, pp. 272–3.

14. Mortimer, pp. 173, 176.

15. Weir, p. 273.

16. Mortimer, pp. 276–7.

17. D.A. Harding, 'The Regime of Isabella and Mortimer, 1326–1330', M A Phil. Thesis, Durham 1985, p. 145; Haines, p. 85, n. 98.

18. S.A. Moore, 'Documents relating to the Death and Burial of King Edward II' in *Archaeologia*, vol 50 (1887) p. 226.

19. Mortimer, p. 186.

20. Adam Murrimuth, pp. 63–4.

21. Ibid, p. 255. On Pecche: Ian Mortimer, *The Perfect King: The Life of Edward III, Father of the English Nation*, p. 409.

22. Roy Haines, 'Sumptuous Apparel for a Royal prisoner – Archbishop Melton's Letter, 14 January 1330' in *English Historical Review*, vol 124 (2009) pp. 893–4; Warwickshire County Record Office: CR 136/ C 202–7.

23. T.F. Tout (see n. 25) was the main proponent of this theory, which assumed that more politically experienced people like Archbishop Melton were equally naive .

24. Mortimer, *Greatest Traitor*, p. 249.

25. T.F. Tout, 'The Captivity and Death of Edward of Carnarvon' in *Bulletin of the John Rylands Library*, vol 6 (1921) pp. 109–10.

26. Murrimuth, pp. 52–3.

27. For the 'Brut' versions: (i) Short: The Anonimalle Chronicle 1307–1344, ed W.R. Childs and J. Taylor, in *Yorkshire Archaeological Society*, vol 147 (1993), p. 135. (ii) Long: *The French Chronicle of London*, ed C.J. Aungier (Camden Society, Old Series, vol 28, 1844) p. 58. For the *Annales Paulini: Chronicles Illustrative of the Reigns of Edward I and Edward II*, ed W. Stubbs (Rolls Series, vol 76, 1882–3) vol 1 pp. 337–8.

28. *Polychronicon Ranulfi Higdeni*, ed J.R. Lumby (1882), vol 3 p. 324.

29. For the Prior of Bridlington's account: see *Chronicles Illustrative...*, ed Stubbs, vol 2 p. 97. Also H.C. Hamilton, ed, Chronicon Domini Walteri de Hemingburh (*English Historicla Society*, 1849) vol 2 p. 297; for Geoffrey le Baker, see *Chronicon Galfredi le Baker de Swynbroke*, ed E. Maunde Thompson (Oxford 1889) p. 33.

30. An inspiration from the assassination of King Edmund 'Ironside' on the privy in 1016 has also been suggested; in any case, Le Baker does not make it clear where his extensive circumstantial detail of the murder came from.
31. See Kathryn Warner, *Edward II: The Unconventional King* (Amberley 2014) pp. 239–40 on whether or not Edward is likely to have escaped with the Dunheved raiders.
32. See account in Tout, op. cit.
33. Weir, p. 275.
34. Cuttins and Lynam, 'Where is Edward II?', pp. 526–7; Mortimer, *Greatest Traitor*, pp. 251–2.
35. Mortimer, *Greatest Traitor*, pp. 187, 196–7.
36. R. Haines, 'The afterlife of Edward of Carnarvon', pp. 69–70.
37. Transcribed in Mortimer, *Greatest Traitor*, pp. 251–4.
38. Tout, op. cit.
39. Roy Haines, 'The afterlife of Edward of Carnarvon' in *Bulletin of the Bristol and Gloucestershire Archaeological Society*, vol 114.
40. Cuttins and Lynam, pp. 536–7.
41. Weir, pp 352–3.
42. Mortimer, p. 259.
43. Mortimer, pp. 259–60.
44. Cuttins and Lynam, p. 530.
45. Lyon et al, *The Wardrobe Book of William Nowall*, pp. 212, 214.
46. Mortimer, pp. 259–60.
47. As implied by the timing of the Wardrobe grants to 'William le Waleys'.
48. Mortimer, *The Perfect King*, p. 408.
49. Ibid, p. 410.
50. On Ockley's role see Kathryn Warner, op. cit., pp. 241, 2442, 244, 254.
51. Mortimer, p. 414.
52. Weir, p. 334.
53. Mortimer, pp. 416–18.

Chapter 3

1. *The Peasants' Revolt of 1381*, ed R.B. Dobson (London 1983 edition) pp. 163, 171–4, 177, 185–6, 194–6.,
2. *The Westminster Chronicle 1381–94*, ed L.C. Hector and B.F. Hervey (Oxford 1982) pp. 112–14.
3. *Chronicle of Adam of Usk*, ed E.M. Thompson (London 1904) p. 90; *Kirkwall Abbey Chronicles*, ed J. Taylor (*Thoresby Society*, vol xii, 1952) p. 83; *Chronicles of the Revolution 1397–1400*, ed Chris Given-Wilson (Manchester 1993) p.242.
4. See Ian Mortimer, *The Fears of Henry IV*, pp. 364–5; C. Given-Wilson, *Henry IV* (Yale UP 2016) p. 11.
5. British Library Harleian Mss. 3600.

6. Nigel Saul, *Richard II*, p. 380; *Knighton's Chronicle 1327–1396*, ed G Martin (Oxford UP 1995) pp. 424–6; Thomas Walsingham, *Chronicon Angliae ab anno domini 1328 usque ad 1388*, ed H.T. Riley vol 2 (Rolls Series 1863–4) p. 172.

7. *Chronicles of the Revolution*, pp. 14–15, 79–83, 211–12, 219–23; *Sir John Froissart, Chronicles*, ed T Johnes vol ii, p. 665. On the murder of Gloucester, see A.E. Stamp, 'Richard II and the murder of the Duke of Gloucester' in *EHR* vol 37 (1923) pp. 249–51, and J Tait, 'Did Richard II murder the Duke of Gloucester?' in *Historical Essays by Members of the Owens College Manchester*, ed J. Tout and J. Tait (Manchester 1902) pp. 193–216.

8. *Chronicles of the Revolution*, pp. 192–7 for different versions.

9. Saul, p. 396.

10. A. Tuck, *Richard II and the Nobility* (London 1973) p. 214.

11. *Rotuli Parliamentorum*, vol iii p. 355.

12. Saul, pp. 384–6.

13. Ibid pp. 385–7; *English Historical Documents*, ed A.N. Myres (1969) pp. 374–5.

14. Saul, pp. 389–90.

15. Ibid p. 274.

16. *Historiae Vitae et Regno Ricardi Secundi*, ed G.B. Stow (Philadelphia 1977) p. 134.

17. E. Curtis, *Richard II in Ireland* 1394–5 (Oxford 1927) p. 80–5.

18. *Chronicles of the Revolution*, p. 40, 192–7.

19. Adam of Usk, pp. 182–4; Ian Mortimer, *The Fears of Henry IV*, pp. 183–4. For the legal position, see G. Caspary, 'The deposition of Richard II and the Canon Law' in *Proceedings of the Second International Congress of Medieval Law* (Boston 1965) pp. 189–201.

20. *Chronicles of the Revolution* p. 122.

21. Ibid pp. 122, 154.

22. Ibid pp. 106, 12102, 131–2, 139–40, 154, 222.

23. Ibid pp.146–51; also on Richard's death, *Froissart*, vol 2 p. 178; *Historiae Vitae et Regno Ricardi Secundi*, in *Chronicles of the Revolution* p. 141; *The Brut*, vol ii p. 360; Jean de Creton's version in *Chronicles of the Revolution* p. 244; J H Wylie, *The History of England under Henry IV* (4 vols, 1884) vol I p. 229.

24. *Chronicles of the Revolution*, pp. 146–51, 155, 159.

25. Saul, p. 415.

26. Ibid.

27. Mortimer, pp. 295–6.

28. Peter MacNiven, 'The problem of Henry IV's health, 1405–1413' in *EHR* vol 100 (1985) pp. 397, 765–6.

29. J.H. Wylie, vol 2, pp. 246–52.

30. *Annales Ricardi Secundi et Henrici Quarti*, in J. Trokelowe et *Anonymi, Chronicon et Annales*, ed H.T. Riley (Rolls Series 1886) pp. 311, 313; *Rotuli Parliamentorum* vol 3 p. 326.

31. *Traison et Mort de Richard II*, p. 228.
32. *Kirkstall Abbey Chronicles*, ed Taylor, p. 82.
33. Mortimer, pp. 199–201; *Chronicles of the Revolution*, pp. 202–12.
34. J. Kirby, *Henry IV of England* (London 1970) pp. 87–90.
35. Mortimer, pp. 211–12; J.J.N. Palmer, 'The authorship and date of the French chronicles of the Lancastrian Revolution' in *Bulletin of the John Rylands Library*, vol 61 (1978–9) pp. 145–81.
36. Jed Burden,' How do you bury a deposed King?' in G. Dodds and H. Biggs, eds, *Henry IV: The Establishment of the Regime* (Boydell 2003) pp. 35–54.
37. Mortimer pp. 210–12.
38. Ibid p. 216.
39. *Chronicles of the Revolution* pp. 229, 241.
40. Wylie p. 229.
41. *Chronicles of the Revolution* p. 51; *Chronicle of John Hardyng*, ed H Ellis (London 1812) p. 357.
42. *Chronicles of the Revolution* pp. 241, 243.
43. Ibid pp. 194–5.
44. Ibid p. 357.
45. J.H. Wylie and W.T. Waugh, *The Reign of Henry IV* (3 vols, Cambridge 1914–20) vol I pp. 207–11.
46. Mortimer p. 250.
47. J.D. Grifffiths, ed, .An English Chronicle of the Reigns of Richard I, Henry IV, Henry V and Henry VI. (*Camden Society*, Old Series, 1856, vol 64) pp. 24–5.
48. Walter Bower, *Scotichronicon*, ed D.E.R. Watt (Aberdeen 1987) vol 8 p. 29.
49. J.J.N. Palmer, op. cit., pp. 151–4.

Chapter 4

1. Bertram Wolffe, *Henry VI*, pp. 30–2.
2. C.L. Scofield, *The Life and Reign of Edward IV* (2 vols, 1923), vol ii pp. 135–6, 140. *Commignes, Memoires*, ed J. Calmette and G. Durville (3 vols, Paris 1924–5), vol ii p. 67.
3. *Croyland Chronicle*, in *Rerum Anglicarum Ascriptores Veterum*, ed W Fulmar (Oxford 1684) pp. 564–5; Dominic Mancini, *The Usurpation of Richard III*, ed and trans C.A.J. Armstrong (Oxford 1969) pp. 73–5.
4. Mancini, ibid.
5. *Croyland Chronicle*, p. 565.
6. Mancini, pp. 76–9.
7. Ibid, pp. 78–81; Michael Hicks, *Richard III and His Rivals* (Hambledon Press 1991).
8. Mancini, p. 121; Sir Thomas More, *The Usurpation of Richard III*, edited R S. Sylvester, in *Complete Works* (Yale UP 1973) vol ii, p. 22.
9. Mancini, pp. 78–83.
10. Ibid, pp. 78–80.

11. John Rous, *Historia Regum Angliae*, ed T. Hearne (Oxford 1745) p. 216: More, op. cit. pp. 49–52; *The Great Chronicle of London*, ed A.H. Thomas and I.D. Thornely (1938) p. 231; Polydore Vergil, *Anglica Historia*, ed and trans D. Hay (*Camden Society* vol LXXIV, 1950) p. 179; Mancini, pp. 90–1.

12. See also Peter Hancock, *Richard III and the Murder in the Tower* (especially pp. 139–41) on the events of 13 June 1483 and what lay behind it, and passim for the career and role of Catesby.

13. Mancini, pp. 88–9.

13. Ibid, pp. 94–7; *Great Chronicle*, pp. 231–2; *Croyland Chronicle*, p. 567; Charles Ross, *Richard III*, p. 8.

14. More, pp. 54–7; Paul Murray Kendall, *Richard III* (1955) p. 471; Ross, *Richard III*, pp. 137–8; Nicholas Barker and Robert Birley, 'Jane Shore' in *Etoniana*, no. 125 (June 1972) pp. 383–414. Also M.M. Scott, *Re-Presenting Jane Shore: Harlot and History* (Ashgate Press 2005).

15. For Edward V's attendance or not at the coronation, see Bertram Fields, *Royal Blood*, pp. 125–6; for the Princes seen in the Tower gardens, see *Great Chronicle*, p. 234.

16. Mancini, pp. 92–3.

17. Fields, pp. 132, 135.

18. Michael Hicks, 'Unweaving the Web; the Plot of July 1483 against Richard III and its Wider Significance'.

19. Mancini, as n.16.

20. Rous, op. cit; quoted in Alison Weir, *Richard III and the Princes in the Tower*, p. 171.

21. Mancini, in introduction to edition by C.A.J. Armstrong, pp. 22–3.

22. Quoted in P.A. Hammond and W. White, 'The sons of Edward IV: a re-examination of the evidence of their deaths and the bones in Westminster Abbey' in *Richard III: Loyalty, Lordship and Law* (1986) p. 109.

23. *Great Chronicle*, pp. 234, 236.

24. More, p. 98; Vergil, p. 193.

25. Vergil, pp. 201–4.

26. BL Harleian Mss. 433, f. 308.

27. Vergil, pp. 210, 214.

28. *Croyland Chronicle*, p. 572.

29. More, pp. 8–9; Mancini, p. 63; Ross, *Richard III*, pp. 32–3; for the letter to the Earl of Desmond's son, see BL Harleian Mss. 433, f. 265.

30. P. Murray Kendall, pp. 217–18.

31. C. Ross, *Edward IV*, pp. 156–7. But the Yorkist destruction of all the records of the 'Readeption' makes it impossible to know Clarence's position in the succession for definite.

32. *Great Chronicle*, pp. 231–2.

33. More, op. cit.

34. As n. 13.

35. Ross, p. 81.

36. Fields, pp. 87, 93.
37. Ibid, pp. 85–6.
38 Alison Hanham, 'Richard III, Lord Hastings and the Historians' in *English Historical Review*, vol 87 (1972); J.A.F. Thomson, 'Richard III and Lord Hastings – a Problematical Case Reviewed' in *Bulletin of the Institute of Historical Research* vol 48 (1975) pp. 22–30; Alison Hanham, 'Hastings Redivivus' in *EHR* vol 90 (1971) pp. 821–7; B. Wolffe, 'Hastings Reinterred' in *EHR* vol 91 (1976) pp. 813–24; C.H.D. Coleman, 'The execution of Hastings – a neglected source' in *BIHR* vol 53 (1980) pp. 244–7.
39. For P.W. Hammond on Stillington's role and the 1486 records, see his article 'Stillington and the Pre-Contract' in *The Ricardian*, vol 54, 1976, p. 31, citing reference in the Chancery Records, 1 Henry VII (1485–6), Hilary Term 1486, appendix, no. 75.
40. *Great Chronicle*, p. 231; Mancini, pp. 290–1.
41. Fields, p. 193.
42. A speech of Henry VII at Bosworth recounted by James Gairdner in his Richard III (1898).
43. Ross, *Richard III*, p. 226.
44. Fields, p. 8.
45. Kendall, pp. 368–9.
45. See Terry Bretherton, *Richard III: The King in the Car-Park* (Amberley 2013).
46. See quotations from these Welsh poems in Terry Bretherton, op. cit., pp. 142–7.
47. Fields, pp. 14–15.
48. Alison Hanham, *Richard III and the Early Historians 1483–1535* (Oxford UP 1975).
49. See Sir W. Cornwallis, *Encomium of Richard III* (London 1617). On Buck and the claim about Morton, see his *The History of King Richard The Third*, ed A.N. Kincaid (Gloucester 1979) p. cxii.
50. Horace Walpole, *Historic Doubts on the Reign of Richard III* (1767, reprinted 1965).
51. Sir Clements Markham, *Richard III: His Life and Character* (1906).
52. Sharon Penman, *The Sunne in Splendour: A Novel of Richard III* (Holt, Rinehart and Winston, 1982).
53. Paul Murray Kendall, *Richard III* (1955).
54. Fields, pp. 290–2.
55. Mancini, pp. 92–3.
56. L.E. Tanner and W. Wright, 'Recent Investigations concerning the Fate of the Princes in the Tower' in *Archaeologia*, vol 84 (1934) pp. 1–26. Tanner's report reprinted in J. Ashdown-Hill, *The Mythology of the Princes in the Tower* (Amberley 2018), pp. 223–57.
57. K. Dockray, *Richard III: A Source-Book* (Amberley 1997) pp. 276–9.
58. Fields pp. 146–7.

59. Melvin J. Tucker, *The Life of Thomas Howard 1443–1524* (The Hague 1964); refuted by Anne Crawford, 'John Howard, Duke of Norfolk: a Possible Murderer of the Princes' in *The Ricardian*, vol 5 (1980) pp. 230–4.
60. Michael Hicks, *Anne Neville: Queen to Richard III* (History Press, 2006) supports the theory that he may have poisoned Anne. The opposite view is taken by Amy License in her *Anne Neville: Richard III's Tragic Queen* (Amberley 2013).
61. Charles Ross., *Edward IV* pp. 187–93; *Croyland Chronicle* p. 557 for the origin of the 'Anne Neville hidden in cookshop' story. *Croyland Chronicle*, p. 299 claims that there were rumours of poison at the time.
62. For the question of the papal dispensation for the marriage and if it was 'watertight', see Michael Hicks, *Anne Neville: Queen to Richard III* (Amberley 2006) pp. 131–49 and M. Barnfield, 'Richard and Anne's Dispensation' in *Ricardian Bulletin*, spring 2006, pp. 30–2. .
63. *Croyland Chronicle* p. 556; Paul Murray Kendall, pp. 451–2.
64. See David Baldwin, *Richard III* (Amberley, 2015 edition) pp. 229–38.
65. Fields, p. 137.
66. Richard F Green, 'Historical Notes of a London Citizen, 1483–88' in *EHR* vol 96, pp. 585–90.
67. See *The Stonor Letters and Papers 1290–1483*, ed C L Kingsford (2 vols, Camden Society 3rd series, vols 19–20, 1919–20) vol 2 p. 161.
68. Fields, p. 150.
69. Gairdner, pp. 68–9.
70. C. Jenkins, 'Cardinal Morton's Register' in R W Seton-Watson, *Tudor Studies* (1924) p. 74.
71. Fields, p. 140.
72. Jack Leslau, 'Did the sons of Edward IV outlive Henry VIII?' in *The Ricardian*, vol 4, no. 62 (September 1978).
73. 'Setubal Testimonies' transcribed in Ann Wroe, *Perkin: A tale of Deception* (Vintage 2003) pp. 525–7.
74. Ibid p. 71–2, 108.
75. Gairdner, pp. 138–40.
76. Polydore Vergil, *Anglica Historia*, ed D. Hay (Camden Society, New Series, vol 74, 1950) p. 24.
77. Accounts of the Lord Treasurer of Scotland, ed Thomas Dickinson (3 vols, *Scottish Record Series*, Edinburgh 1877) vol 1 p. 199.
78. Fields, p. 143.
79. For the 'accident during bloodletting' story, see Ian Arthurson, 'Perkin Warbeck and the Princes in the Tower' in H.M. Aston and R. Horrox, eds, *Much Heaving and Shouting: Essays for Colin Richmond* (2005) pp. 158–66. For 'Richard Plantagenet of Eastwell', see the original 'revelation' of this by F. Peck in *Desiderata Curiosa*, vol 2 (1779) pp. 249–51. For the 'RP was Prince Richard' claim, see David Baldwin, *The Lost Prince: The Survival of Richard of York* (History Press 2008).

80. Audrey Williamson, *The Mystery of the Princes* (Alan Sutton 1981).
81. Ross, Richard III, p. 121.
82. Fields, p. 147.
83. Quoted in Wroe, p. 380.
84. Fields, p. 218.
85. Ibid, pp. 197–8.
86. Ibid, pp. 231–2.
87. Ibid, p. 232.
88. Ibid.
89. As n. 78.
90. Fields, p. 241.
91. Wroe, pp. 155, 203.
92. Fields, p. 247.
93. Ibid, pp. 249–50, 252.
94. Ibid, p. 236.

Chapter 5
1. R. Fabyan, *New Chronicles of England and France*, p. 654.
2. Scofield, *Edward IV*, vol I p. 320.
3. David Baldwin, *Elizabeth Woodville: Mother of the Princes in the Tower* (Sutton 2004) pp. 1–2.
4. Sir Thomas More, *Life and Reign of King Richard the Third*, ed R.S. Sylvester, in *Complete Works*, vol 2 (Yales UP 1963) p. 4.
5. *Commignes, Memoires*, ed A Scobie (1856) vol I p. 203.
6. As n. 4.
7. Ibid, pp. 55–6.
8. Mancini, *Usurpation of Richard III*, ed Armstrong, p. 67.
9. *Croyland Chronicle*, p. 567.
10. Muriel de St Clare Byrne, ed, *The Lisle Letters* (6 vols, 1981), vol 1 introduction.
11. Baldwin, *Elizabeth Woodville*, p. 10.
12. *Letters and Papers Illustrative of the Wars of the English in France*, ed J. Stevenson (2 vols, Rolls Series, 1864) vol 2 part 2, p. 783.
13. Baldwin, pp. 151–3; H.A. Kelly, 'The case against Edward IV's marriage and offspring – secrecy; witchcraft; secrecy; precontract' in *The Ricardian*, vol 10 (1998) p. 326–35.
14. A.F. Sutton, *Richard III – the Road to Bosworth Field* (1985) pp. 155–6.
15. *Three Books of Polydore Vergil's English History*, ed Sir H. Ellis (Camden Society 1844) p. 180.
16. More, p. 47.
17. Bertram Wolffe, *Henry VI*, pp. 127–8.
18. C. Fahy, 'The marriage of Edward IV and Elizabeth Woodville: a new Italian Source' in *EHR*, vol 76 (1961) pp. 660–7.
19. H.A. Kelly, as n. 13.

21. *Croyland Chronicle*, in Rerum Anglicanum Veteres Scriptorum, ed W. Fulman, p. 567.
22. HMC Reports, no. 78: Report on the Manuscripts of R.R. Hastings (4 vols, 1928–47), vol 1 pp. 301–2; J.R. Lander, *Government and Community* (1980) pp. 237–8 and n. 4.
23. Polydore Vergil, p. 117.
24. De Wauvrin, *Anchiennes Chroniques d'Angleterre*, ed E. Dupont (3 vols, paris 1858–63) vol ii pp. 326–7.
25. Ibid, pp. 327–8.
25 J.R. Lander, 'Marriage and Politics in the Fifteenth Century: Nevills and Wydvills' in *BIHR* (1963).
26. Mancini and Vergil, quoted in John Ashdown-Hill, *Eleanor: The Secret Queen* (History Press 2009) pp. 105, 111.
27. Peter Hancock, *Richard III and the Murder in the Tower* (History Press, 2009).
28. See Ashdown – Hill, *The Secret Queen*; and for the Norwich endowmen, see Corpus Christi College Cambridge: Parke Library Mss. XXX!, f. 121.
29. Ashdown-Hill, ibid; and Ashdown-Hill, 'Further Reflections on Lady Eleanor Talbot' in *The Ricardian*, vol 11, no. 14 (march 1999), p. 465.
30. G. Smith, *The Coronation of Elizabeth Woodville* (1935).
31. J.R. Lander, *'Marriage and Politics…'* pp. 135–49; Charles Ross, *Edward IV*, p. 93.
32. Mancini, p. 75.
33. Ross, pp. 95–6.
34. Ibid pp. 99–101; *Great Chronicle*, pp. 204–8.
35. Ross, pp. 101, 203–4.
36. Mancini, pp. 63, 69.
37. *Croyland Chronicle*, pp. 78–9.
38. For the controversy over Clarence's motivation and whether he believed (correctly or not) that Edward V was illegitimate: M. Smith, 'Edward, George and Richard' in The Ricardian, vol 77, 1982, p. 49; Michael Hicks, 'The middle brother: False, Fleeting, Perjur'd Clarence' in *The Ricardian*, vol 72, 1981, pp. 302–10; I. Wigram, 'Clarence still perjur'd' in ibid, vol 73, 1981, pp. 352–5; Hicks, 'Clarence's calumniator corrected' in ibid, vol 74, 1981, pp. 399–401; Wigram, 'False, Fleeting, Perjur'd Clarence: A further exchange, Clarence and Richard' in ibid, vol 76, 1982, pp. 17–20. 9 39. Rotuli Parliamentorum vol 6 p. 194; also see Calendar of Close Rolls Edward IV pp. 85–7; J. Calmette and G. Perinelle, *Louis XI et Angleterre* (Paris 1930) p. 108.
39. Calendar of Close Rolls 1468–76 (HMSO 1953), pp. 85–7.
40. Ross, pp. 138–43.
41. Ibid, p. 417.
42. Coventry Leet Book, ed M.D. Harris (*Early English Text Society*, Original Series 1907–13) vol ii pp. 358–9.

43. *Commignes*, vol I p. 202.
44. Ibid, vol I p. 204.
45. J. Warkworth, *A Chronicle of the First Thirteen Years of King Edward the Fourth*, ed J. Halliwell (Camden Society 1839) p. 14; *The Arrivall of King Edward the Fourth*, pp. 3–7.
46. *Arrivall*, pp. 7–12.
47. Ibid, pp. 18–21; *Great Chronicle* pp. 216–17; Polydore Vergil, pp. 144–7; Paul Murray Kendall, *Warwick the Kingmaker* (1957) pp. 317–22.
48. *Arrivall*, pp. 30–1; Polydore Vergil, p. 152; Warkworth, p. 18; C. Kingsford, *English Historical Literature in the Fifteenth Century* (Oxford 1913) pp. 374 ('Yorkist Notes, 1471')and pp. 377 (9) '*Tweksbury Abbey Chronicle*').
49. *Arrivall*, p. 38.
50. Calendar of State Papers Milan vol I p. 157.
51. Kendall, Richard III, pp. 451–2; Gairdner, Richard III, pp. 16–19; Calendar of Patent Rolls 1476–85, pp. 172–3.
52. Scofield, Edward IV, vol 2 pp. 190–1.
53. Ross, Edward IV, pp. 241–2.
54. Mancini, pp. 94–7; *Croyland Chronicle* p. 567.
55. Mancini, ibid.
56. *Commignes*, ed Calmette, pp. 64–5.
57. Mortimer Levine, 'Richard III: Usurper or Lawful King?' in *Speculum*, vol 34 (1959) pp. 391–401.
58. Charles Ross, *Richard III*, pp. 88–9.
59. Fields, *Royal Blood*, pp. 106–7.
60. Peter Hancock, op. cit.
61. As n. 57.
62. As stated by his memorialist *Commignes*.
63. Mancini, pp. 61–2.
64. Polydore Vergil pp. 186–7.
65. In a Channel Four documentary first broadcast on 3 January 2004.

Bibliography

Chapter 1

The Anglo-Saxon Chronicle, ed M. Swanson (Dent 1996).

Frank Barlow, *William Rufus* (New Haven and London, 2000 edition)

David Bates, *William I* (Yale UP 2018).

Eadmer, as edited by Martin Rule (London Rolls Society 1884).

——, *Vita Anselmi* (ed R.W. Southern, 1962).

Barbara English, 'William the Conqueror and the Anglo-Norman Succession' in *Historical Research*, vol 64 (1991) pp. 221–36.

E.A. Freeman, *The Reign of William Rufus and the Accession of Henry The First*, 2 vols (Oxford 1882).

Duncan Grinnell-Milne, *The Killing of William Rufus* (Newton Abbot, 1968).

Warren Hollister, 'The Strange Death of William Rufus' in *Speculum*, vol 48 (1973) pp. 637–53.

—— *Henry I* (Yale UP 2001)

Horace Hutchinson, *The New Forest* (Methuen 1905).

John of Salisbury, *Vita Sancti Anselmi*, in Complete Works, ed Migne, vol CXCIX

Edmund King, *King Stephen* (Yale UP 2012) .

Norman Le Patourel, The Norman Succession 996 – 1135' in *EHR* vol 86 (1971) pp. 225–50.

Emma Mason, 'William Rufus: Myth and Reality' in *Journal of Medieval History*, vol 3 (1977) p. 18 n.7.

——, 'William Rufus and the Historians' in *Medieval History*, vol 1 (1991) pp. 6–22.

John of Worcester, *Chronicle*, ed J. Weaver (Oxford UP 1908).

Orderic Vitalis, Historia Ecclesiastica, trans Marjorie Chibnall (6 vols, Oxford 1969–80).

Robert of Torigny: see *The Gesta Normannorum Ducorum of William of Jumieges and Robert of Torigny*, ed Elisabeth van Houts (3 vols, Oxford UP 1992–5) vol 2.

Abbot Suger, *Vie de Louis VI le Gros*, ed H. Waquet (Paris 1929).

A Survey of Southampton and its Region (Southampton University, 1964): Chapter 6, *'The Place-Names of Hampshire'* by A.T. Lloyd.

William of Malmesbury, *Gesta Regum*, ed and trans R.M. Thompson and M. Winterbottom, 2 vols (Oxford UP 1998).

Hugh Williamson, *The Arrow and the Sword: An Essay in Detection* (1955).

Chapter 2

The Anonimalle Chronicle 1307–1344, ed W.R. Childs and J. Taylor, in *Yorkshire Archaeological Society*, vol 147 (1993), p. 135.

J.M. Aungier, ed, *French Chronicle of London* (Camden Society, Old Series, vol 28, 1844).

Chronicon Galfredi le Baker de Swynbroke, ed E. Maunde Thompson (Oxford 1889)

J.S. Bothwell, ed, *The Age of Edward III* (York 2001).

Pierre Chaplais, *Piers Gaveston: Edward II's Adopted Brother* (Oxford 1994)

Chronicon de Domini Walteri de Hemingburgh, vol 2 (*English Historical Society* 1849).

J. Conway Davies, *The Baronial Opposition to Edward II* (Cambridge 1918).

Kathryn Warner, *Edward II: The Unconventional King* (Amberley 2014)

G. Cuttino and T. Lynam, 'Where is Edward II?' in *Speculum*, vol 53, no. 3 (July 1978).

Froissart, John, *Chronicles of England, France and Spain and the adjoining countries*, 2 vols, ed T. Johnes (London 1839).

Nathalie Fryde, *The Tyranny and Fall of Edward II 1321–26* (Cambridge 1979).

R. Haines, 'The afterlife of Edward of Carnarvon', in *Transactions of the Bristol and Gloucestershire Archaeological Society*, vol 114 (1996)

——, 'Sumptuous Apparel for a Royal prisoner – Archbishop Melton's Letter, 14 January 1330' in *English Historical Review*, vol 124 (2009) pp. 893–4.

J.S. Hamilton, *Piers Gaveston, Earl of Cornwall 1307–1312* (1988).

H.C. Hamilton, ed, Chronicon Domini Walteri de Hemingburh (*English Historical Society*, 1849) vol 2.

D.A. Harding, 'The Regime of Isabella and Mortimer, 1326–1330', M A Phil. Thesis, Durham 1985.

H.J.A. Holmes, 'The rebellion of the Earl of Lancaster, 1328–29' in *Bulletin of the Institute of Historical Resaerch*, vol 28 (1955).

Hilda Johnston, 'The eccentricities of Edward II' in *EHR*, vol 47 (1933).

——, *Edward of Carnarvon 1284–1327* (Manchester 1946)

Henry Knighton, *Chronici Henrici Knighton, monachi Leycestrensis* (2 vols, ed J. Lumby, Rolls Series, London 1889–1893).

The Chronicle of Lanercost, ed J. Stevenson (Edinburgh 1839).

Lyon et al, *The Wardrobe Book of William Nowall*, pp. 212, 214.

Sophia Menache, 'Isabella of France, Queen of England: A Reconsideration' in *Journal of Medieval History*, vol 10 (1984).

S.A. Moore, 'Documents relating to the Death and Burial of King Edward II' in *Archaeoligia*, vol 50 (1887) p. 226.

Ian Mortimer, *The Greatest Traitor: The Life of Sir Roger Mortimer, Ruler of England 1327–1330* (Pimlico 2004).

——, *The Perfect King: The Life of Edward III, Father of the English Nation.*

Adam Murrimuth: *Adae Murimuth, Continuatio Chronicarum*, ed E. Maunde Thompson (Rolls Series, vol 93, 1889).

W. Mark Ormrod, *Edward III* (Stroud, 1990).

Annales Paulini: Chronicles Illustrative of the Reignsof Edward I and Edward II, ed W. Stubbs (Rolls Series, vol 76, 1882–3) vol 1 pp. 337–8.

Polychronicon Ranulfi Higdeni, ed J.R. Lumby (1882), vol 3 p. 324.

Michael Prestwich, *Edward I* (Yale UP 1988).

C. Robinson, 'Was King Edward the Second a Degenerate?' in *American Journal of Insanity*, vol 66 (1910).

Giles St Aubyn, *Edward II* (London 1979).

Chronicles of the Reigns of Edward I and Edward II, ed W. Stubbs, 2 vols (London, Rolls Series 18823–3), vol 2.

F.J. Tanquerery, 'The conspiracy of Thomas Dunheved, 1327' in *EHR* vol 31 (1916).

T.F. Tout, 'The captivity and death of Edward of Carnarvon', in *Bulletin of the John Rylands Library*, 1921

C. Valente, 'The Deposition and Abdication of Edward II' in *EHR* vol 113 (1998).

Vita Edwardi Secunda Monachi Cuiusdem Malmesburensis: The Life of Edward II by the So-Called Monk of Malmesbury, trans and ed N. Denholm-Young (Nelson's Medieval Texts, 1957).

Thomas Walsingham, *Historia Anglicana* 1272–1422 (2 vols, ed H.T. Riley, Rolls Series, 1863–4).

The Chronicle of Walter of Guisborough, ed Harry Rothwell (Camden Society, 3rd series, vol 89, 1957).

Warwickshire County Record Office: CR 136/ C 202–7.

Alison Weir, *Isabella: She-Wolf of France, Queen of England* (Pimlico, 2006).

Chapter 3

New Dictionary Of Nat. Biography article: vol 46 pp. 724–46 (N. Tuck).

The Chronicle of Adam of Usk, ed E.M. Thompson (London 1904)

Chronicle Anonimalle, ibid.

M. Aston, *Thomas Arundel* (London 1967)

R.L. Atkinson, 'Richard II and the Death of the Duke of Gloucester', *EHR* xxxviii (1923).

C.M. Barron, 'Richard II: Image and Reality', in *Making and Remaking: the Wilton Diptych* (London 1993).

—— , ' The Tyranny of Richard II', *BIHR* xli (1968).

Michael Bennett, *Richard II and the Revolution of 1399* (Sutton 1999).

D.R. Briggs, 'A Wrong whom Conscience and Kindred bid me to right: a Reassessment of Edmund of Langley, Duke of York, and the Usurpation of Henry IV', *Albion* vol xxvi (1994).

Calendar of the Patent Rolls, 1401–5.

Capgrave, Liber de Illustribus Henricis, ed F. Hingston, Rolls Series vol 7 (1858).

J.E. Caspary, 'The Deposition of Richard II and the Canon Law' in *Proceedings of the Second International Congress of Medieval Law* (Boston 1965).

M. Clark and V. Galbraith, 'The deposition of Richard II' in *Bulletin of the John Rylands Library*, vol xiv (1930).

E. Curtis, *Richard II in Ireland 1394–5 and the Submission of the Irish Chiefs* (Oxford 1927).

G. Dodd and D. Bigg, *Henry IV; the Establishment of the Regime, 1399–1405* (Boydell 2003).

Chronicles of the Revolution, ed Chris Given-Wilson (Manchester 1992).

C. Given-Wilson, 'Richard II and his Grandfather's Will' in *EHR* vol xciii (1978).

——, 'The Manner of Richard II's Renunciation: a Lancastrian "Narrative"', *EHR* vol cviii (1993) pp. 65–70.

—— 'Richard II, Edward II and the Lancastrian Inheritance' in *EHR* vol cix (1994).

D. Gorden, *The Court of Richard II and the Artistic World of the Wilton Diptych* (London 1996).

J. Griffiths Davies (ed), *An English Chronicle of the Reigns of Richard II, Henry IV, Henry V and Henry VI*, Camden Society, Old Series vol 64 (1856).

J.H. Harvey, 'The Wilton Diptych' in Fourteenth Century Studies.

——, 'The Wilton Diptych: a Re-Examination' in *Archaeologia* vol xcviii (1961).

The History of Parliament: House of Commons vol I, 1386–1421, ed J. Roskell, I. Clark, C. Rawcliffe.

D.B. Johnston, 'Richard II and the Submission of Gaelic Ireland' in *Irish Historical Studies*, vol xii (1980).

—— , 'The Departure of Richard II from Ireland in July 1399' in *EHR* vol xcviii (1983).

R.H. Jones, *The Royal Policy of Richard II: Absolutism in the Later Middle Ages* (Oxford 1968).

Chronicles of London, ed H. Kingsford (Oxford 1905).

Kirkstall Abbey Chronicles, ed J. Taylor (Thoresby Society, vol xii, 1952).

Knighton's Chronicle, 1327–1396, ed. G. Martin (Oxford 1995).

K.B. MacFarlane, *Lancastrian Kings and Lollard Knights* (Oxford 1972).

Peter MacNiven, 'The Problem of Henry IV's Health 1405–13' in *EHR* vol c (1985) pp.747–59.

G. Mathew, *The Court of Richard II* (London 1968).

Philip Morgan, 'Henry IV and the Shadow of Richard II', in R. Archer (ed), *Crown, Government and People in the Fifteenth Century* (Sutton 1995

Ian Mortimer, *The Fears of Henry IV: the Life of England's Self-Made King* (Vintage 2008).

A.J. Otway-Ruthven, *Medieval Ireland* (London 1968).

J.J.N. Palmer, 'The Anglo-French Peace Negotiations, 1390–6' in *TRHS* series 5, vol xvi (1986).

——, 'The Background to Richard II's marriage to Isabel of France (1396)', in *BRHS* vol xliv (1971).

Alexander Rose, *Kings in the North: The House of Percy in British History* (Phoenix 2005).

G. Sayles, 'Richard II in 1381 and 1399', *EHR* vol xciv (1979).

——, 'The deposition of Richard II: Three Lancastrian Narratives' in *BIHR* vol liv (1981) pp. 257–70.

T.A. Sandquist, 'The Holy Oil of St Thomas of Canterbury' in *Essays in Medieval History Presented to Bertie Wilkinson*, ed T. Sandquist and M. Powicke.

Three Prose Versions of the Secreta Secretorum, ed R. Steele (*EETS*, extra series, vol lxxiv, 1898).

J. Sherborne, 'Perjury and the Lancastrian Revolution of 1399' in *Welsh History Review* vol xiv (1988).

A.E. Stamp, 'Richard II and the Murder of the Duke of Gloucester', *EHR* vol xxxvii (1923) pp. 249–51.

C.B. Stowe, 'Richard II in Walsingham's Chronicles' in *Speculum* vol lix (1984).

J. Tait, 'Did Richard II Murder the Duke of Gloucester?' in *Historical Essays by Members of Owens College Manchester*, ed J. Tout and J. Tait (Manchester 1902).

J. Taylor, 'Richard II's Views on Kingship', *Proceedings of the Leeds Philosophical and Historical Society*, vol xiv (1971).

Nicolae Triveti, *Annales*, ed T Hog (1845).

Johannis de Trokelowe et Henrici de Blaneford, chronici et annals, ed H.T. Riley (Rolls Series, vol 28, 1861).

Historiae Vitae et Regni Ricardi Secundi, ed G.B. Stow (Philadelphia 1977).

Walsingham, ibid: 1863–4 edition, ed H.T. Riley.

——, *The St Albans Chronicle: the Chronica Majora of Thomas Walsingham, 1376–94*, ed J Taylor, Wendy Childs, Leslie Watkiss (Oxford 2003).

The Westminster Chronicle, 1381–94, ed L.C. Hector and B.F. Harvey (Clarendon Press 1982).

H.G. Wright, 'The Protestation of Richard II in the Tower in September 1399' in *BJRL* vol xxxii (1939).

J.H. Wylie, *The History of England under Henry IV*, 4 vols (London 1884).

Chapters 4 and 5

Accounts of the Lord Treasurer of Scotland, ed Thomas Dickinson (3 vols, *Scottish Record Series*, Edinburgh 1877) vol 1 p. 199.

Bernard Andre, *Historia Regum Henrici Septimi*, ed J. Gairdner (Rolls Series, vol 10, 1858)

W.A.J. Archbold, 'Sir William Stanley and Perkin Warbeck' in *EHR* vol 19 (1899) pp. 530–3;

Ian Arthurson, 'Perkin Warbeck and the Princes in the Tower' in H.M. Aston and R. Horrox, eds, *Much Heaving and Shouting: Essays for Colin Richmond* (2005) pp. 158–66.

John Ashdown-Hill, 'Further Reflections on Lady Eleanor Talbot' in *The Ricardian*, vol 11, no. 14 (March 1999), p. 465.

—— , Eleanor: *The Secret Queen* (History Press 2009).

—— , *The Mythology of the Princes in the Tower* (Amberley 2018).

Sir Francis Bacon, *The History of the Reign of King Henry The Seventh* (Folio Society reprint 1971).

David Baldwin, *Elizabeth Woodville: Mother of the Princes in the Tower* (Sutton 2004).

—— *The Lost Prince: The Survival of Richard of York* (History Press 2009).

—— *Richard III* (Amberley, 2015 edition)

Nicholas Barker and Robert Birley, 'Jane Shore' in *Etoniana*, no. 125 (June 1972)

M. Barnfield, 'Richard and Anne's Dispensation' in *Ricardian Bulletin*, spring 2006, pp. 30–2. .

BL Egerton Mss. 616/ 3.

BL Harleian Mss. 433, f. 308.

Michael Bongiorno, 'Did Louis XI Have Edward IV Assassinated? '*The Ricardian Register*, vol 22 no. 3 (1997) pp. 23–4.

Terry Bretherton, *Richard III: The King in the Car-Park* (Amberley 2013).

Sir George Buck, *The History of King Richard The Third*, ed A N Kincaid (Gloucester 1979).

Calendar of State Papers and Manuscripts in the Archives of Milan, ed Allen B Hinds (1912) vol I.

J. Calmette and G. Perinelle, *Louis XI et Angleterre* (Paris 1930).

S.R. Chrimes, *Henry VII* (Methuen 1972).

Chronicles of the White Rose of York, ed J A Giles (1845).

H.D. Coleman, 'The execution of Hastings – a neglected source' in *BIHR* vol 53 (1980) pp. 244–7.

Philippe de Commignes, Memoires, ed J. Calmette and G. Durville (3 vols, Paris 1924–5).

Corpus Christi College Cambridge: Parke Library Mss. XXX!, f. 121.

Sir W. Cornwallis, *Encomium of Richard III* (London 1617)

Courtrai Codex, 8840, f. 581; 8841, f. 50v; 8842, f. 53v; 8843, ff. 62v – 63r; 8844, ff. 54v – 55r; 8845, f. 59v; 8846, f. 53v.; f. 69; f. 111, ff. 188v – 189r.

Coventry Leet Book, ed M.D. Harris (*Early English Text Society*, Original Series 1907–13) vol ii.

Croyland Chronicle, in *Rerum Anglicarum Ascriptores Veterum*, ed W Fulmar (Oxford 1684).

The Great Chronicle of London, ed A.H. Thomas and I.D. Thornely (1938).

Anne Crawford, 'John Howard, Duke of Norfolk: a Possible Murderer of the Princes' in *The Ricardian*, vol 5 (1980) pp. 230–4.

C.S.L. Davies and Mark Ballard, 'Etienne Frion: Burgundian Agent, English Royal Secretary and "Principal Counsellor to Perkin Warbeck"' in *BIHR*, vol 62 (1989).

K. Dockray, *Richard III: A Source-Book* (Amberley 1997).

David Dunlop, 'The masked comedian: Perkin Warbeck's adventures in Scotland and England from 1495 to 1497' in *Scottish Historical Review*, vol 70 no. 190 (October 1991) pp. 100–01.

J. Edwards, 'The second continuation of the Crowland Chronicle: Was It Written In Ten Days?' in *Bulletin of the Institute of historical Research*, vol 39 (1966).

R. Fabyan, *The New Chronicles of England and France, in Two Parts*, ed Henry Elllis (London 1811).

C. Fahy, 'The marriage of Edward IV and Elizabeth Woodville: a new Italian Source' in *EHR*, vol 76 (1961) pp. 660–7.

Bertram Fields, *Royal Blood: The Mystery of Richard III and the Princes* (Sutton 1998).

Sir James Gairdner, *The History of the Life and Reign of Richard III* (Cambridge, 1898).

Richard F. Green, 'Historical Notes of a London Citizen, 1483–88' in *EHR* vol 96, pp. 585–90.

P. Hammond and Maaike Lulofs, 'Richard III: Dutch Sources' in *The Ricardian*, vol 3 no. 46 (1974) pp. 11–13.

P. Hammond and W. White, 'The sons of Edward IV: a re-examination of the evidence of their deaths and the bones in Westminster Abbey' in *Richard III: Loyalty, Lordship and Law* (1986).

W.E. Hampden, 'The White Rose under the First Tudors' in *The Ricardian*, vol 7. No. 97 (June 1987) pp. 414–17.

Peter Hancock, *Richard III and the Murder in the Tower* (History Press, 2009).

Alison Hanham, 'Richard III, Lord Hastings and the Historians' in *English Historical Review*, vol 87 (1972)

——, 'Hastings Redivivus' in *EHR* vol 90 (1971) pp. 821–7

——, *Richard III and the Early Historians 1483–1535* (Oxford UP 1975).

——, 'Sir George Buck and Princess Elizabeth's Letter: A Problem in Detection' in *The Ricardian*, vol 7, no. 97 (1987) pp. 398–400.

Michael Hicks, 'The middle brother: False, Fleeting, Perjur'd Clarence' in *The Ricardian*, vol 72, 1981, pp. 302–10

—— , 'Clarence's calumniator corrected' in ibid, vol 74, 1981, pp. 399– 401.

——, *Richard III and His Rivals* (Hambledon Press 1991).

——, 'Unweaving the Web; the Plot of July 1483 against Richard III and its Wider Significance' in *The Ricardian*, volume 9, no. 114 (September 1991), pp. 106–9.

——, Anne Neville: *Queen to Richard III* (History Press, 2006)

C. Jenkins, 'Cardinal Morton's Register' in R.W. Seton-Watson, *Tudor Studies* (1924) p. 74.

H.A. Kelly, 'The case against Edward IV's marriage and offspring – secrecy; witchcraft; secrecy; precontract' in *The Ricardian*, vol 10 (1998) p. 326–35.

Paul Murray Kendall, *Richard III* (1955).

——, *Warwick the Kingmaker* (1957).

C. Kingsford, *English Historical Literature in the Fifteenth Century* (Oxford 1913) pp. 374 ('Yorkist Notes, 1471')and 377–9 *'Tewksbury Abbey Chronicle'*).

J.R. Lander, 'Marriage and Politics in the Fifteenth Century: Nevills and Wydvills' in *BIHR* (1963).

——, 'The Treason and Death of the Duke of Clarence: A Re-Interpretation' in *Canadian Journal of History*, vol 2 (1967).

——, Government and Community (1980)

John Leland, Collectanea, ed T. Hearne (6 vols, London 1770) vol iv.

Jack Leslau, 'Did the sons of Edward IV outlive Henry VIII?' in *The Ricardian*, vol 4, no. 62 (September 1978).

Letters and Papers Illustrative of the Wars of the English in France, ed J. Stevenson (2 vols, Rolls Series, 1864) vol 2 part 2.

Mortimer Levine, 'Richard III: Usurper or Lawful King?' in *Speculum*, vol 34 (1959) pp. 391–401.

Amy License, *Anne Neville: Richard III's Tragic Queen* (Amberley 2013).

Norman Macdougall, *James IV* (Edinburgh 1989)

Frederick Madden, 'Documents relating to Perkin Warbeck, with Remarks on his History' in *Archaeologia*, vol 27 (1838) app. 2, pp. 198–200.

Dominic Mancini, *The Usurpation of Richard III*, ed and trans C.A.J. Armstrong (Oxford 1969) pp. 73–5.

Sir Clement Markham, *Richard III: His Life and Character* (1906).

Wendy Moorhen, 'Four Weddings and a Conspiracy: the Life, Times and Loves of Lady Katherine Gordon, part 1' in *The Ricardian*, vol 12, no. 156 (March 2002) pp. 202–3.

Sir Thomas More, *The Usurpation of Richard III*, edited R.S. Sylvester, in *Complete Works* (Yale UP 1973).

A. Morel-Faro, 'Marguerite d'Yorke et Perkin Warbeck' in *Melanges d'histoire offerts a Charles Bemat* (Paris 1993) p. 414.

A.F. Pollard, *The Reign of Henry VIII from Contemporry Sources*, Vol 1: Narrative Extracts (1913).

Charles Ross, *Edward IV* (Methuen 1974)

——, *Richard III* (Methuen 1981).

Rotuli Scotiae, ed D. Macpherson et al, (2 vols, Edinburgh 1814–19) vol ii.

John Rous, *Historia Regum Angliae*, ed T Hearne (Oxford 1745).

C.L. Scofield, *The Life and Reign of Edward IV* (2 vols, 1923).

M.M. Scott, *Re-Presenting Jane Shore: Harlot and History* (Ashgate Press 2005).

Gordon Smith, 'Lambert Simnel and the King from Dublin' in The Ricardian, vol x, no. 135 (December 1996) pp. 498–506.

M. Smith, 'Edward, George and Richard' in *The Ricardian*, vol 77, 1982, p. 49.

The Stonor Letters and Papers 1290–1483, ed C.L. Kingsford (2 vols, Camden Society 3rd series, vols 19–20, 1919–20) vol 2 p. 161.

A.F. Sutton, *Richard III – the Road to Bosworth Field* (1985).

L.E. Tanner and W. Wright, 'Recent Investigations concerning the Fate of the Princes in the Tower' in *Archaeologia*, vol 84 (1934) pp. 1–26.

J.A.F Thomson, 'Richard III and Lord Hastings – a Problematical Case Reviewed' in *Bulletin of the Institute of Historical Research* vol 48 (1975) pp. 22–30.

Melvin J. Tucker, *The Life of Thomas Howard 1443–1524* (The Hague 1964).

Livia Visset-Fuchs, 'The Divisie Chronicle' in *The Ricardian*, vol 9 no. 118 (September 1992) pp. 119–22.

Horace Walpole, *Historic Doubts on the Reign of Richard III* (1767, reprinted 1965).

J. Warkworth, *A Chronicle of the First Thirteen Years of King Edward the Fourth*, ed J. Halliwell (Camden Society 1839).

De Wauvrin, Jean, *Anchiennes Chroniques d'Angleterre*, ed E Dupont (3 vols, Paris 1858–63) vol ii.

Christine Weightman, *Margaret of York, Duchess of Burgundy* (Leicester UP 1989).

Alison Weir, *Richard III and the Princes in the Tower* (Vintage, 2014).

I. Wigram, 'Clarence still perjur'd' in *The Ricardian*, vol 73, 1981, pp. 352–5;
—— 'False, Fleeting, Perjur'd Clarence: A further exchange, Clarence and
—— Richard' in ibid, vol 76, 1982, pp. 17–20.

Audrey Williamson, *The Mystery of the Princes* (Alan Sutton 1981).

Bertram Wolffe, 'When and why did Hastings lose his head?' in *EHR*, vol 89 (1974).

—— , 'Hastings Reinterred' in *EHR* vol 91 (1976) pp. 813–24.

—— , *Henry VI* (Methuen 1981).

Charles Wood, 'The Deposition of Edward V' in *Traditio*, vol 31 (1975).

Ann Wroe, Perkin: *A Tale Of Deception* (Vintage 2003).

Polydore Vergil, *Anglica Historia*, ed and trans D. Hay (Camden Society vol XXIV, 1950).

—— *Three Books of Polydore Vergil's English History*, ed Sir H. Ellis (Camden Society 1844).

Index